OLDER PERSONS IN INDIA

DR. ARVIND K. JOSHI
Reader Department of Sociology
Banaras Hindu University
Varanasi - 5

SERIALS PUBLICATIONS
NEW DELHI

First Published - 2006

ISBN: 81-8387-000-7

Published by

SERIALS PUBLICATIONS
4830/24, Prahlad Street, Ansari Road
Darya Ganj, New Delhi-110002 (India)
Phone : 23245225
Fax : 91-11-23272135
E-mail: serials@satyam.net.in

DEDICATED TO
MY FATHER
AN EMBODIMENT OF
ACTIVE AGEING

CONTENTS

PREFACE

I

All over the world the population of aged is increasing relative to the level of development. There is no doubt that population ageing will affect every single individual of the society in many ways. India too, faces many demographic problems in the shape of the rising profile of the aged population. The population of the aged, that is, those of the age of 60 years and above is on the increase. In 1971, they were 28 million and in 1981, 42 million, in 1991, 56 million and in 2001, 75 million. It is expected that in 2025 their population will be more than 175 millions. Their proportion in the population has gone up.

State-wise dependency ratio in totality is high in rural areas as compared to the urban. The total (DRY + DRO) dependency ratio in 1991 was 1000:794 in which 122 were old persons. It is also important to note that almost 40 percent of them are below poverty line.

A large portion of the aged is that of widows and widowers. The proportion of widowers is almost three times less than that of widows.

If, on the one hand, the population of the aged, say 60 years plus population has increased over the successive decades, on the other hand, the traditional family/community-based support systems for the aged have not only weakened but showing signs of complete collapse. This has seriously affected the situation of senior citizens in society. Neither they have the earlier position of importance in the family and community, nor are they looked after the way it was done earlier. This is because with the spread of modernization and industrialization the roles and status of old people are on the decrease.

Indeed, not unlike 'desertion' of women, desertion of old parents has shot up as a serious problem, to the context that state like Himachal Pradesh had to enact laws extending the scope of the provision of maintenance of deserted women by their husbands, to parents abandoned by their sons. The Government of Maharastra and to some extent Goa too, have prepared a Bill on similar lines. The right of parents without any means to be supported by their children having sufficient means has been recognised by Section 125(1)(d) of the Code of Criminal Procedure 1973, and Section 20(3) of the Hindu Adoption and Maintenance Act, 1956. Evidently, the problem is getting more acute in the regions and sections of society prone to migration in search of work and employment. Apparently, the problem must be more acute among the asset-less labouring class who cannot earn beyond their own survival. No doubt, the syndrome manifests among the middle classes also where the tendency of neglect of the old parents may be more due to 'selfishness'.

Old age is characterized by diminished physical and psychic activity and a plethora of problems. Broadly, we can divide the problems of the aged in three categories, as health problems, economic problems and socio-psychological problems.

The common health problems are blood pressure, pulmonary disorders, diabetes, orthopaedic and cardiovascular problems, mental problems like depression, anxiety, etc.

Except the few aged, who retire from organised sectors and get some retirement benefits, the plight of the aged in the unorganised sectors is worse, because they practically do not get anything to fall back.

Some of the socio-psychological problems faced by an aged persons are isolation, alienation, loneliness, powerlessness, dependence, feeling of boredom, lack of emotional response from family members, etc.

From the above, it is clear that the large-scale institutional support and facilities are required to properly look after the aged. The Constitution of India (Article 41) recognises that elderly people need special assistance. Item No.9 of the State List and Item 20, 23 and 24 of Concurrent List relates to old age pension, social security and social insurance and economic and social planning. Several institutional measures and welfare benefits are there, but these appear far too insignificant in the face of the huge magnitude of the problem. It is significant to discuss here what has been done for the aged over the years.

The most important and general problem of the aged is related to access to health and medical facilities. Most of the aged persons are deprived of this facility. The superannuated employees of the organised sector get usual medical facilities but persons of the unorganised sectors have problems to get proper medical attention due to poor economic conditions. Most aged people have to rely on general government hospitals, primary health centres and on some charitable hospitals for medical treatment. The aged have a special medical need but in most of the hospitals a geriatric unit does not exist. Elderly people also find it difficult to afford expensive medicines.

Superannuated employees of the organised sector get social security and public assistance in the form of pensioner benefits, GPF, gratuity, etc. At the time of superannuating they get some money. The situation of the aged of unorganised sector is very precarious. In this sector social assistance to the aged is available only under the Old Age Pension (OAP) Schemes. Eligibility and criterion of the aged differs from state to state. The quantum of assistance and outlays also vary from state to state. Inter-state variations in OAP coverage can also be seen. The assistance amount is insignificant to cater the needs of the aged.

The importance of the institutional care is realised especially for the poor and destitute aged. At present, most of the institutional care in the form of Old Age Homes is run by voluntary organisations. There are 1018 Old Age Homes (OAH) in India today; 118 homes are exclusively for women. The maximum number of OAH is in Kerala — a total of 186 in numbers (obtained from HelpAge India, New Delhi, 2004). The membership of these homes imposes different types of eligibility conditions. Except for few, most of the homes are not only overcrowded but also mismanaged with poor facilities.

Voluntary organisations are also running Day Care Centres (DCC) to fulfil the psychological needs (needs for empathy and sympathy, urge for assistance and belongingness, etc.) of the aged. These Day Care Centres are very useful but limited in number.

The concerned citizens may derive some satisfaction from the fact that there is a heightened cognition of the problem of the aged at the policy level and efforts are being made to work out the operational details of the 'National Policy', Moreover, there is a national policy of everything, but the impact of these policies is far from encouraging. The main thrust appears to be on 'coordination' among the different departments and the government departments and NGOs. But the basic question that comes is what is there to coordinate in terms of programmes and services?

Apparently, the entire old age population cannot be lumped together. It falls in different categories to be identified by residential status, e.g., rural-urban, gender, social and economic class, level of social security entitlement, family support structure. To put it very briefly there are old age people who enjoy the basic economic security and their needs are essentially socio-psychological. There are others and unfortunately they are in an overwhelming majority, who probably may not be beset by psychological problems but lack the basic economic security and immediately land in destitution after they lose their earning capacity. Unfortunately, the country has not been able to put in place a Social Security System for mass of the unorganised labour, the artisans and workmen, excepting those in the organised sector. An urgent and long-term strategy is required to tackle the possible problems of the population ageing. Not only this, the growing problems of the elderly persons have also be properly looked into.

II

It is obvious from the above that the problems of ageing shall become clearly visible very soon in India's population. Though, Sociologists in India have started writing on elderly persons during 50s itself. Yet the studies were very few. In recent years a number of studies have taken place on the problems of elderly persons, ageing and old widows, etc. but still more in-depth studies are required to understand the various facets of ageing. There is a paucity of reliable data on the conditions of aged persons. Keeping all these in mind the idea of writing a book on India's elderly came to my mind during discussions in the World Congress of International Sociological Association at Brisbane, Australia in 2002.

Here the author has edited several papers—theoretical and empirical—of eminent scholars of the field on diverse themes so that one can clearly understand the status of elderly persons in India. These papers are grouped into three broad categories, i.e., perspectives, empirical studies and rehabilitation.

I. Sobha and M.S.N. Reddy in their paper, 'Healthy Ageing: Concepts, Problems and Prospects' try to present the comprehensive exposition of the ageing question from the point of view of not only the challenges but also of worries. They have tried to highlight the societal and cultural pre-requisites and obstacles towards active, successful and healthy ageing.

Sociologically speaking, ageing is a series of transitions from one set of social roles to another, which is structured by the social system rather than mere biological one. Aditya Keshari Mishra and Bikram Keshari Mishra have made an attempt in their paper 'Sociology of Ageing in India: Perspectives and Policy Options', exclusively from the sociological perspective to understand 'ageing'. They also tried to outline a brief literature on the existing legislative as well as the policy measures and finally propose a policy option for the future prospect of the elderly individuals.

Sushila Jain in her paper'Globalisation and the Aged' has tried to analyse the challenges of globalisation and its impact on aged persons. She is of the view that due to economic and social challenges aged have become marginalized. Children want to move out to the wider world with relatively more attractions for jobs in info-tech, biotech, pharmaceuticals and software engineering, etc. as these are the demands of the present day. Therefore, information revolution that brings about basic changes even if they occur over a relatively long period of time necessitated the need of a successful restructuring of the ageing process.

A.R.N. Srivastava in his paper 'The Aged: Their Problems, Social Interventions and Future Outlook in the Western U.P.' has presented the findings of his empirical study on 440 respondents of eleven districts of Uttar Pradesh. They were chosen randomly from the urban population of aged living in non-institutional homes. The study reveals that over 75 percent aged have independent households and also extended-family types. In the cases of independent households, decision-making process is regulated by the aged themselves but in the cases of dependent household only the non-financial issues were discussed with them. It is very surprising to know that majority of the aged persons have no serious health related problems. Majority of the aged persons would like to help members of their family in one or the other way. The attitude of the family members towards the aged is also found positive.

A.K. Joshi, the author of the book, in his empirical paper 'Rural Aged: Living Arrangements, Problems and Care' has tried to portray the living conditions of the rural aged of Varanasi district. The adequacy of the social security measures has also been examined by him. He has found that majority of the aged prefer to live in their own/ancestrol homes with their sons. The quality of housing and the facilities are generally poor. They do not get food according to their dietary requirements. The conditions of the single living aged are the worst. The main problems of the aged are related to means of survival and health. Majority of the aged feel that they are neglected by the family members. Upper caste aged have better status as they live in extended family and also they remain the owner of the entire landed property till their death and obviously this influences the attitude of the family members towards them. The aged persons who have no income are treated miserably. The author is of the view that large-scale institutional support and facilities are required to properly look after the rural aged especially for the poor and destitute aged.

D.P. Saxena in his empirical paper on 'Bio-psycho and Social Aspects of Ageing' strongly argued that the right approach to handle ageing problems was to have a co-ordinated, integrated and a comprehensive base, i.e., sociological perspective approach. Another objective of his study was to examine Emile Durkleim's assumption of social bond/community bond. It was observed by Saxena that most of the respondents were immune from the ageing problems due to their closeness with the social bond/community bond in old age.

N. Audinarayana and N. Kavitha in their paper on 'Living Arrangements of the Widowed and Currently Married Women in Tamilnadu State' argue that due to several factors the living arrangements of the elderly have been severely affected by disturbing the multi-generation familial co-residence and compelling them to live by themselves as an elderly couple or alone (if never married/ widowed). Besides this phenomenon, in the recent period, the population of widowed women has started to increase slowly because of the longer life expectancy of women than men on an average. In the absence of clear social security policies for elderly women they have to face more problems than men. It is suggested that the government may provide safety and near family environment either through old age homes or institutions to the aged particularly for widowed or widower and also monetary support to them.

Ganesh a Somayaji in his paper 'Transition, Transformation and Re-socialisation: A Biographical Approach to the Elderly Question' has made an attempt to demonstrate the dimensions of 'the elderly question' with the help of a biographical approach. He has made an attempt to sharpen this approach by adding autobiographical touch to the issue by reconstructing the social worlds of the elderly of his own household, village and caste (Brahmin). It was found that the whole locality is greying. Their problems of re-socialisation vary in accordance with living arrangements. The elderly couples who are staying together are in a better position than those who are living single. Almost all of them have regular sources of income. Socio-psychological problems are not there but still most of them are worried about their future when they reach the 'old age' stage. Frequent quarrels, out-migration of young and adult members and non-availability of workers to carry out agricultural work are some of the problems. The factors of personality and social transformation are at the root of these problems.

Vighnesh N. Bhat in his paper on 'Social Construction of Ageing: An Empirical Study of the Perception of the Urban Elderly', tries to examine and analyse some important issues concerning people's perception of the ageing process in their day-to-day life and ageing in the immediate societal surroundings in the typical Indian set up. He has used the paradigm based on the sociological conception of 'social construction of old age'. The study sample consisted of 150 middle-class elderly individuals from three wards in Shimoga City (Karnataka), selected on the basis of stratified random sampling method. The results have clearly demonstrated that 'old age' is not simply a matter of accumulated years and decrease in physical capabilities. Rather, it results from the popular perception to a considerable extent, it is a set of expectations and beliefs—among both the young and the old—that are socially contrived. The impact of the western values have knocked off some of the erstwhile Indian ethos about the elderly in the Indian family and in the public space. Hence in India today, old age is a stigmatised social status and role expectations are ideologically constructed. There is an urgency to carefully consider measures to better the scenario so as to lessen the future pungency of this enigma.

Anupma Shah and Uma Joshi in their paper on 'Ageing Women from Low Socio-Economic Status' try to analyse the problems of the elderly women, perceptions of their family members regarding health, economic, security worth, status and psycho-emotional security and the social welfare services available for them in Baroda City. It was found that the majority of the ageing women had presented a sad picture about their life. The plight of poor old women seemed to be worsening because of added problem of widowhood, which ushers in new problems of lowered status and lessened financial support. The authors have presented the future actions for the aged and also several recommendations for the care and welfare of the ageing persons.

Rameshwari Pandya and Priti Shah in their paper 'Problems of Elderly Widows of Baroda-Gujarat' try to analyse the problems of elderly widows residing in Vadodara in the year 2001-2002. The study is based on 125 widows. Three interdependent problems of the widows namely psychological, social and financial were examined by the authors. With regard to the awareness among widows regarding government widow pension scheme it was found by them that the majority of the respondents had low awareness.

K. Rethi Devi in her paper 'Elderly Abuse in the Family' tries to identify the type of abuse directed towards the elders. She has tried to analyse the relationship between sex, occupation, income of the elders and their abuse and also tried to identify the chief abuser. Her study is based on 50 elderly respondents of Kannankurich village, Salem

District of Tamilnadu. Her study reveals that almost all the aged experienced one form of abuse (i.e., neglect, lack of attention, denial of freedom, food and health care, etc.) in the family. It was also found by her that the females are the chief abusers viz. daughter-in-law and daughter.

Chandra Paul Singh in his paper 'Depression: A Major Hazard in Work Participation of Senior Citizens' has tries to analyse the physical and mental decline of the elderly. He is of the view that mainly elderly are suffering from the problems of depression only due to non- or under-utilisation of their capacities, talent, knowledge and experiences. He has suggested some measures like proper treatment and prevention of depression like proper planning, etc. before retirement.

Damodaran Shivkumar in his paper on 'Older Persons and Social Work Treatment' presents the birds eye view of the population characteristics of older persons and methods and techniques of social work treatment. According to him social work treatment is an important technique of professional social work. It has an important role to play in the betterment of older persons.

Jasmeet Sandhu and Tripti Arora in their paper on 'Institutionalised Elderly in Punjab—A Sociological Study of an Old Age Home' have presented the institutional arrangements and facilities being provided by an old age home at Amritsar. The study is based on the information received from the 45 inmates of the old age home. It was found that the inmates despite having been driven out of their families either out of compulsion or out of choice were enjoying their institutional life.

Finally, Umesh Kumar Singh in his paper on 'Voluntary Agencies and Care of Aged' tries to examine the role of four major voluntary organisations of Varanasi in the care of older persons. The study finds that the voluntary agencies in Varanasi/Kashi are playing a positive role in the care of the older persons. They are serving the cause of the older persons in their search for solace and salvation at the fag end of life.

ACKNOWLEDGEMENTS

I am grateful to many people who have contributed significantly to the successful compilation of this book. In particular, I thank Dr. Michael Fine (Department of Sociology, Macquarie University, Sydney, Australia), Dr. Andress Hoff (Oxford Institute of Ageing, University of Oxford, UK), Professor Ofra Anson (Faculty of Health Sciences, Ben-Gurion University of Negev, Israel) Professor Anoop Chandola, Arizona State University, U.S.A., and Dr. Tetsuo Ogawa (Oxford Institute of Ageing, University of Oxford, UK) for their constant support and encouragement. My gratitude to them cannot be expressed in few lines.

I am also thankful to all the contributors for this edited version. Their apt response has made this work transformed in the shape of a book. My heartiest gratitude also goes to Professor Tulsi Patel, Professor P.K.B. Nayar, Professor B.N. Juyal, Professor S.K. Bhattacharya, Professor Vighnesh Bhat, Professor R. Shankar Professor K.N. Singh Yadav and Professor M.S.N. Reddy who helped me in many ways to enable me to complete this scholarly work.

I would also like to express my gratitude to all the faculty members of the Department of Sociology, Banaras Hindu University.

Finally, I take this opportunity to offer my deepest regards to my revered father, Mr. A.S. Joshi and thanks to my wife, Dr. Vibha Joshi (Lecturer, Department of Economics, Vasanta College for Women, Rajghat Fort, Varanasi). I would also wish to place in record my affection to my son Abhinav and daughter Apoorva who spared me from all parental obligations and kept me occupied with pen and paper.

At this important moment of life, I wish to remember my mother, Late Krishna Rani Joshi who had always been an eternal source of inspiration and guidance to me. I wish she would have lived to see my work published.

August 2, 2005 **Arvind K. Joshi**

Varanasi

CONTRIBUTORS

Dr. I. Sobha is Associate Professor in the Department of Womens' Studies, Sri Padmavathi Mahila Visvavidyalayam, Tirupati Andhra Pradesh. She has conducted several research projects funded by UGC. She has published over thirty-five research articles in reputed journals. She has published two books entitled, "Educated Working Women in Andhra Pradesh" and " Welfare Services for Women and Children".

Prof. M.S.N. Reddy is a Professor (former Head) in the Dept. of Sociology, Sri Venkateshwara University, Tirupati, Andhra Pradesh. He has over thirty years of teaching and research experience. He has been involved in conducting research projects funded by UGC. He has published over thirty research articles in reputed journals and presented over forty papers in national and international conferences /seminars.

Aditya Keshari Mishra is pursuing Ph. D. in Sociology at the Department of Sociology, School of Social Sciences, University of Hyderabad (Central), Hyderabad, Andhra Pradesh. Currently, he is working on "The Role of Local Communities towards Biodiversity of Conservation" for the purpose of doctoral thesis. His areas of interests are Sociology of Development; Sociology of Science and Technology; Sociology of Environment and Sustainable Development; and Non-Governmental Organizations and Development. He is the author of many referred or invited articles published in both national and international journals and also in magazines.

Bikram Keshari Mishra is pursuing Ph. D. in Sociology at the Centre for the Study of Social Systems, School of Social Sciences, Jawaharlal Nehru University, New Delhi. His specialized areas are Sociology of Gender; Sociology of Work/Profession; and Sociology of Education. Currently, he is focusing on "Women and

Work" for the pursuit of his doctoral thesis. He has written several articles and book reviews, which have been published in journals of both international and national standard and also in magazines and newspapers.

Dr. Sushila Jain is currently working as Associate Professor (Former Head of the Department) in the Department of Sociology, University of Rajasthan, Jaipur, Rajasthan. She has published several articles and research papers in the journal of repute.

Prof. A.R.N. Srivastava is the former Head and Professor of Anthropology in the Department of Anthropology, Allahabad University, Allahabad. He did his Ph.D. from Arizona State University, USA. He has completed several research projects including one major project on Ageing. He has published several papers and books. Currently he is visiting Faculty at the Centre of Cognitive and Behavioural Sciences, University of Allahabad.

Dr. Arvind Kumar Joshi is currently working as a Reader in the Department of Sociology, Banaras Hindu University, Varanasi. He has participated in several national and international seminars. He is co-convener of the R.C. 19 (Age and Social Structure) of the Indian Sociological Society and also Executive Committee Member of the R.C. 11 (Sociology of Ageing) of the International Sociological Association. He has published two more books and several articles/research papers and book reviews.

Prof. D.P. Saxena is a former Head and Professor of the Department of Sociology, D.D.U. University, Gorakhpur, UP. He was the recipient of the Royal Economic Society's (London) Fellowship in 1957. He has actively participated in several national and international seminars. He was invited by several universities (under UGC sponsored Lecture Series) to deliver special lectures. He has conducted two UGC major research projects in which one was on 'Ageing Among the Senior Citizens: A Sociological Study of the Problems of Ageing Among the Superannuated University Teachers, Superannuated Civil Servants, Elderly Lawyers and Doctors' He has published one book on 'Rururban Migration in India' (Popular Prakashan, Bombay, 1977) and has several papers/ articles in national and international journals.

Prof. N. Audinaryana is currently working as a Professor and Head, Department of Population Studies, Bharathiar University. He has specialization in Nuptiality, Fertility, Women's Studies. He has published 60 papers in various international and national journals and edited books. So far he has been involved in 8 minor/major projects including the one on "Status and Well-being of the Elderly in Tamilnadu", funded by the Population Investigation Committee, United Kingdom.

Dr. N. Kavitha is currently working in the Dept. of Population Studies, Bharthiar University as a Research Assistant in South India Fertility Project, Phase-II.She has specialised in the matter related to Reproductive Health of Women. She has published a couple of papers in the referred journals. Got a small Grant from the PARKE'S-Foundation, United Kingdom, to meet the field expenses of her research work.

Dr. Ganesh a Somayaji is currently working as a Reader and Head in the Department of Sociology, Goa University where he teaches current debates in social theory and philosophy of social sciences. His areas of interest for research are Sociology of Language, Enterprise in Food and Social Gerontology. He has actively participated in several national seminars. He has edited one book and has several papers/articles in the journals of repute.

Prof. Vignesh N. Bhat is Ph.D. (Sociology) from Pittsburgh (U.S.A.). At present he is a Professor and Chairman in the Department of Sociology, Kuvempu University, Shankaraghatta, Karnataka. He has published 11 books (including 7 books in Kannada) and 42 articles/papers published in national and international referred journals. He has submitted 7 Research Reports to ICSSR, ISRO (SAC), LMRF, Delhi/Karnataka Government. He was the recipient of Andrew Mellon Fellow, University of Pittsburgh, U.S.A., 1982. He was UGC Associate, Indian Institute of Advanced Studies, Shimla.

Anupama Shah is a former Dean, Faculty of Home Science and Head of the Department of Home Science, Extension Communication. M.S. University, Baroda. She has teaching experience of more than 35 years. She is the consultant to several Departments of Home Science. She has authored several books and published several articles and papers in the national and international journals. She has completed one major and 10 minor research projects. She specializes in the non-formal education, audio-video education and evaluation.

Uma Joshi is currently working as a Professor and Head, Department of Home Science, Extension Communication, M.S. University,

Baroda. She has a teaching experience of more than 20 years. She has guided several M. Sc. students in the areas of vocational guidance, women and family welfare, communication and curriculum. She was the co-investigator and director of research project funded by UGC, ICSSR and Ford Foundation. She has published several papers in the journal of repute.

Dr. Rameshwari Pandya is currently working as a senior Lecturer in the Department of Home Science Extension and Communication, M.S. University, Baroda. She is the Coordinator for Urban Extension Centre "PRAGATI" run by the Dept. She has co-authored two books and contributed more than 50 articles to academic journals and chapters in two books along with several Booklets and Monographs.

Priti Shah did her M. Sc. Home Science (Dissertation) under the supervision of Dr. R. Pandya.

Dr. K. Rethi Devi is currently working as a Reader in the Department of Sociology, Mother Teresa Women's University, Research and Extension Centre, Madurai, Tamilnadu. She has published several articles and papers in the reputed journals.

Dr. Chandra Paul Singh is currently working as a Reader in the Department of Social work, Kurukshetra University, Kurukshetra. He was formerly a Project Officer in Urban Basic Services Programme, a joint project of UNICEF and Government of India. He has been actively engaged in research on elderly and working with communities infested with alcoholism, drug abuse and resulting health hazards. He has also published a number of research papers and his recent book is "Alcohol & Drug Dependence among Industrial workers."

Prof. Damodaran Sivakumar worked as a Social Work Scientist since 1967 with different designations in Government service. He was the research guide of Kerala University since 1997.He has prepared and presented 110 research papers and interviewed 18000 persons for different studies. He has participated in several national and international seminars/conferences/workshops. He has received Hony. Professor award in social work and population studies 1978. He is associated with more than 40 Professional Organizations in India and other countries.

Prof. Jasmeet Sandhu is currently working as Professor of Sociology at Guru Nanak Dev University, Amritsar, Punjab. She is the author of "Sociology of Fertility" and co-editor of "Sustainable Human Settlement: The Asian Experience". She has been the Head of Department and Editor of Guru Nanak Journal of Sociology. Her areas of interest include Social Demography and Gender Studies.

Tripti Arora is a Ph.D. student at the Department of Sociology, Guru Nanak Dev University, Amritsar.

Dr. Umesh Kumar Singh is currently working as a Lecturer in the Department of Sociology, V.S.S.D. College, Kanpur, U.P. His areas of interests are Social Gerontology, Sociology of Death and Dying. He has participated in several national and international seminars/ conferences and has published several papers in national journals and chapters in edited books.

PART–I
PERSPECTIVES

1

HEALTHY AGEING: CONCEPT, PROBLEMS AND PROSPECTS

I. Sobha and M.S.N. Reddy

Introduction

Over the past fifty years, mortality rates have declined in developing countries raising the average life span from around 41 years in 1950 to almost 62 years in 1990. According to WHO, this average life span is expected to reach 70 years by 2020.One of the main features of the world population in the 20th century has been a phenomenal increase in the elderly population in both the developed and developing countries. Approximately among the 580 million elderly (60 years and above) in the world, around 355 million live in developing countries. The number of elderly world wide by 2020 is expected to cross 1000 million with over 700 million of them in developing countries. The population of those who are 60 and above constituted 5.66 per cent of the total population in 1951 in the case of India. India had 25 million persons over 60 years in 1961 and 33 million in 1971. The figure rose to 40 million in 1981. In 1991, the figure further increased to 56 million constituting 6.5 per cent of the total population. The population of the aged was predicted to become 76 million by 2001, forming 7.6 per cent of population and nearly one-seventh of the world elderly. By 2020, the number may rise to 124 million, which means 11 per cent of the population will be over 60 and only 25 per cent of the population will be under 15 years. Increase in longevity does increase the aged population, but the concern is how active this populations?

Population ageing has been occurring much faster in developing countries, due to rapid fertility decline and increasing life span through medical interventions, providing effective treatment and prevention of diseases that used to be fatal. This rapid growth of ageing population has become a serious challenge to public health globally.

Ageing is a natural process, spanning the life period from conception through Birth — Infancy — Childhood — Adolescence — Adulthood — Old Age to Death. Each of these stages has unique characteristics and vulnerabilities requiring special attention to ensure optimum health during each stage. Concerted efforts are on the agenda to provide for mechanisms leading to active ageing, but translating them into action is the need of the hour.

The Physical and mental health in each stage influences the further stages in life span, which ultimately leads to the active aged population if proper attention is paid for the health care needs of individuals at each stage.

Dramatic influence in medical and health care facilities due to scientific and industrial advancements has brought about an increased longevity for the human race. However improved and advanced may be the achievements in the world of health care, there is no denying the fact that an advancing age and increased longevity are often accompanied by psych-social problems for the elderly. While medical and health care facilities can and do treat bodily afflictions, they do not have solutions to the problems of the mind and soul. Active ageing does not depend only on physical health but also on the psycho-social wellbeing of the individual. Treatment of the mind and the soul requires concerted inputs into addressal of the root causes for emotional upsets, noticeable behavioural changes and difficulty in coping with the stress and strain of advancing age.

Rapidly increasing aged population is one of the biggest political and socio-economic issues in the present day world. The discussion on this issue is problem centred and seems to include several controversial statements. The ageing population is both a threat and a burden but also a great challenge and opportunity. The gerontological theories — whether activity or disengagement oriented, whether functional or critical seem to support this variety and also the discordance of attitudes and visions.

The aim of the present paper is a comprehensive exposition of the ageing question from the point of view of challenge but also of worries: to highlight the societal and cultural pre-requisites and obstacles towards active, successful and healthy ageing. This article is a review of the problems and prospects to understand the multitude of active, successful and healthy ageing. One of the issues that is often taken up, is the age question: generations and age cohorts are seen in serious confrontation against each other more so than for instance different kinds of families — and it seems that age has became one of the core issues in welfare redistribution.

Accordingly the paper presents the introduction of the concepts of active, successful and healthy ageing and continue the logic of social and cultural capital and deals with the way in which ageing can contribute to development, focussing on the welfare of the aged themselves ending up to ponder their impact on active ageing.

The question then arises: Whether these active elderly who have good education, knowledge and experience in their field of work can contribute to the community and country? If yes, then what and how? Are their any impediments to their being thus utilised? Can some thing be done about it, in case there are preventable drawbacks? If yes, what? If not why? All these are important questions to which the attention is drawn in the ensuing discussion particularly in the area of active, successful and healthy ageing.

Multi-disciplinary Nature of Ageing

The study of ageing is multi-disciplinary, composed of three kinds of ageing: biological, psychological and social, (Int. Enc. of the Soc. Sci. 1968: 177). As the number of elderly people in Europe and North America grew large enough to justify another branch of medicine, a "new specially, called gerontology from the Greek geron (an old man) became a respected science" (Milne and Milne, 1968: 213), Tibbits (1960) sees Psychological age in terms of the individuals adaptive capacities and social age in terms of social habits and roles.

"The idea that individuals develop and age with variations around an average trend was a powerful conceptual innovation of the early nineteenth century". (Int. Enc. of the Soc. Sci. 1968: 177), but with the increasingly global and mobile population, the validity of the perceived "average trend" may be called into question as may be the notion of "normal life cycle of events", with the adults moving forward in time, successively making educational and occupational choices, marrying, having children and advancing in occupation and then retiring (Int. Enc. of the Soc. Sci. 1968: 178-179). Even the name gerontology has as reference point "an old man". And the linear progression through the life cycle stages fits the "traditional male" better than it would the "traditional female". There are cultural differences in the degree to which legal restrictions and social pressures limit certain social groups-career choices even to day. How then should we look at age and ageing?

What is Age, Old Age and Ageing?

How can we study an area in which the subject matter is so poorly defined? While "age" one of the basic demographic facts, it is also one of the "most complicated and complicating of data" (Hardy, 1997: 98). "The state of current research on ageing is data rich but theory poor", according to Birren and Bengston (1988: IX). A theoretically adequate definition of the age concept is still missing. Another major problem is that "research consists of a large number of studies and perspectives" (Kenyon, 1988. 3). Viewing the theoretical developments in Psychology, Schroots, (1996: 742) states that "there are three foci-the aged, the age, and ageing" each with their own conceptual problems. Ageing is an integral part of human condition, because of its phenomenological nature and theorists have overlooked the need to define "old", "older" "elderly". Even grammatically, it is incorrect to speak of "older people" without defining "older than whom", yet it is done all the time. Although there is no universally accepted thresh-hold at which people are labelled "old", societal age norms do in fact exist.

Concept of Gerontology

The term gerontology is derived from the Greek word "geras" meaning "old age" and 'logos' referring to the study of the subject. The term gerontology is very broad and encompasses the psychological, socio-economic and physiological aspects of old age. Social gerontology is concerned with reciprocal relationship between the individual and society. The term Geriatrics deals with causes and remedies of physical pathology in old age. Senescence, a biological term refers to the physiological aspect of growing old; Gerontocracy refers to Government that is ruled by elders. Ageing is discrimination against individual on basis of old age. The term gerontophobia is used to designate the fear of growing old or fear of hatred of the aged. The term ageing refers to the process of growing old (James, E, Birren, K, Warner Schaie, 1996, 6-10).

History of Gerontology and Geriatrics

Ignatz Z Nascher, the father of modern geriatric medical research and practice, coined the word 'Geriatrics' in 1909 and gave a new name in the medical field, the field was still called ageing and apparently unnoticed until N.A. Rynikov the originator of the term outlined the nature of this new discipline. Gerontology aims at the investigation of the conditioning causes of old age as well as the study and careful description of the regular progress of the changes in behaviour peculiar to age. Despite the fact the research and publication of studies on various aspects of ageing grew rapidly in the late 1920s and 1930s, the discipline of gerontology was not formally recognised nor was the name used in any form until 1940. In 1945, the gerontological society was organised and in 1946, the Journal of Gerontology made its first appearance (Sati, P.N. 1988).

Edward J. Stieglitz in his work on 'Geriatric Medicine' (1954) used the expression of social gerontology. He divided gerontology in to three major areas, namely, (i) Geriatric medicine, (ii) Biology of senescence, and (iii) Social gerontology. All economic and cultural factors of ageing such as employment, retirement, chronic illness, housing, and education for senescence, marriage, family attitudes towards the aged, social attitudes, cultural maturation and international aspects of maturing population comprise social gerontology. (Sati,P.N., 1988). The growing interest and attention of social scientists in 1940s and 1950s to gerontology led to the creation of an Inter-University Training Institute in Social Gerontology in 1957 (Frank L.L, 1946). The publication in 1948 of Social Science Research Council's Planning Report, Social Adjustment in old age edited by Otto Pollak marked another transition from concern about the aged to the study of ageing as a process. At the end of 1950s, a multi-university consortium projected three volumes documenting the scope, methods and conceptualisation of studies on ageing. These volumes constitute an excellent bibliographic coverage of studies on ageing prior to their publication and document the principal characteristics of studies of ageing. (Sati, P.N, 1988). Duke and Chicago concentrated on adaptation in late life, conceptualised on morale, mental health or life satisfaction. The dominant perspective, which emerged in these studies, was that social integration in late life is not only possible but also probable and that social integration predicts morale. The exception to this perspective was of course Cumming and Henry's (1961) concept of disengagement. Irving Rosow's Social Integration of Aged, states that the probability of social interaction of older persons is significantly affected by the availability of age peers as similar social status. (Sati, P.N, 1988).

Towards Active Ageing

In view of the global dimension of the aged, the United Nations organised the World Assembly on Ageing in Vienna in 1982 as a forum to launch an international action programme aimed at guaranteeing economic and social security to older persons as well as providing them with opportunities to contribute to national development. In the documents circulated during the conference and in the recommendations entitled 'Vienna International plan of Action on Ageing' (United Nations, 1982). The World Assembly on ageing among other measures sponsored the idea of active ageing as an important strategy for the adjustment of the ageing in modern societies (V. D' Souza: 1993, 54 (13), 333-44). The Vienna International Plan of Action on Ageing lays great stress on creating conditions which enable the ageing to live with their close relatives as long as possible. Article 17 of the Vienna International Plan of Action points out humanitarian issues related to specific needs as health and nutrition, housing and environment, family, social welfare, income, security, employment and education of the elderly. From the development point of view, society should guarantee to all persons regardless to age, the right to belong participate and contribute. The recognition of inter-dependence between the development of ageing and that of society would make it evident that the social resources invested in the betterment of ageing instead of a drain on the economy are on the contrary a productive investment having both tangible and intangible benefits. (Indian Journal of Social Work, 1993, 54 (13), 333-44).

Active ageing accordingly deals with the way in which ageing can contribute to development, focussing on the welfare of the aged themselves. Countering the disengagement theory, the active ageing has some similarity with the 'Activity Theory' but with a wider connotation. Unlike the activity theory active ageing implies attainment of certain objectives on the part of the elderly such as economic security, sense of purpose and meaning in life and integration in the community and society. Active ageing embraces a very broad perspective including the inter-relationship between the humanitarian and development needs of the elderly and those as the society. (United Nations Activities >United Nations Logo for the International Year of Older Persons= Bulletin on Ageing, 1998, No. 1, p. 11).

The United Nation's Official logo for the year of older persons: I YOP 1999 (1-10-1998 to 31-12-1999) is meant to represent vitality, diversity and interdependence as well as movement and progression. Vitality refers to the increased ability as mind and spirit made possible by healthy life styles as people age. The combination of vitality and diversity is seen as heralding both >a new age for old age 'and the reality of > old age in a new age = This draws attention to the independence and interdependence of the generations, which create a dynamic and reciprocal exchange and caring. This ideal of reciprocity is reflected in the theme for the year 'towards a society for all ages' (United Nations, New York 1997, Department for Policy Co-ordination and Sustainable Development, Older Persons in Countries with Economies in Transition, Designing a Policy Response, 126-31).

Successful Ageing

Marjatta in her paper "Successful Ageing Dependent on Cultural Social Capital?"(2001) opines that the increase of elderly population has aroused discussions and debates on several age-generation-related issues, such as political, social, cultural and medical. The idea behind this is to tackle with changing position of elderly people in society, especially concerning their power and autonomy. It also deals with the cultural and social resources the elderly people have in the modern society. The viewpoint arises from Pierre Bowrdieu's theories, which deal with different kinds of resources (capital) that influence people's position in power structures and social life. Three different kinds of capital are important when dealing with successful ageing and wellbeing: Cultural, social and symbolical. Though economic capital plays an important part in this respect it is seen more dependent on the other three than as an independent resource. The social capital comprises, for instance, social net works, organisations, family etc and the norms, rights and obligations arising from them. Social capital is based on interaction, reciprocity and trust, and thus can be owned only as long as one can be active in social contacts. Social capital is also the source of symbolic capital. The capital is needed in legitimising the value and importance and social meaning of other forms of capital. These values are the targets of negotiations and fights that take place in social interaction. The cultural capital can be viewed as a social status: the more one has cultural capital, the easier it is for him/her to own symbolic power in social interaction.

Successful ageing can be taken from the viewpoint of society and individual. It is born and created in the interaction between these two in a certain cultural setting. Thus successful ageing cannot be totally individual or social and its features are dependent on both levels, what is successful from society's point of view, may not be successful to individuals, what is successful in certain culture, may not be successful in another, and what is successful for one person may not be successful to another. It should also be noted that, as a concept, successful ageing contains more than mere healthy ageing.

Notwithstanding, the modern society denies the value of the cultural capital of elderly people. By this devaluation, the symbolic power of the elderly people as a group diminishes. The present mechanisms of symbolic capital tend to legitimise mainly the work-related, active mid life position and activities. They also seem to emphasise the value of social capital leaning only on these qualities. Thus, they operate as lessening the social capital of the elderly. Their own social activities and networks are losing their symbolic value. Through these processes the elderly population are divided by gender, the activities and networks typical to women's life course are undermined, and a retirement may become too big a change to men.

Coping in old Age

Old age poses a particular momentum in one's life when not only physical sensory-motor conditions decline, but more specially, one is confronted with multiple social and psychological challenges, such as the loss of friends frequent marginalisation from work positions, the fear of imminent diseases and impairment, the approach of death and so on. Questions as to the possibility of a healthy and enjoyable old age often involve disputable interchanges among different areas, like biological models of human ageing tend to emphasise the decline of human capacities, where as psychological models tend to consider that human capacities can open to learning and adaptation even when sensory-motor adjustments perish (Labouvie-Vief, 1982). To become old involves facing challenges. Recent works on old age has pointed out the psychological demands that have to be met in having to adjust oneself to different and difficult conditions of living. (Messy, 1992; Veyset. 1989). Nevertheless, not all the individuals are prepared to deal with such demands adequately. Thus, the question is what makes some old people abler than others face the challenges of the ageing process? What sort of "competence" is useful as one gets old? What are the chances, and then one could ask, of an enjoyable and fulfilling old age?

In their paper "Coping in old Age", Lucia Rabello Decastro and G. Rabello Decastro (2001) have proposed to understand coping mechanisms at old age are held to be the result of a life long process which enables old people to better adjust themselves to the multiple challenges of ageing process. Two case studies in the form of life histories are presented and analysed in order to illustrate how through out one's lifetime inner resources and potentialities can be restrained or expanded. Further, it is argued that cultural dispositions can legitimate a view of the self as multiple so that individual can fare better in managing the challenges the old age thwarts.

Coping mechanisms is thus fundamental at advanced stage when diverse and multiple challenges affect human lives. To grow old means to face and cope up with the finitude of human condition, the physical deterioration and the threat of helplessness, dependency and loneliness (Hess, 1987). Perhaps, it is one of the most challenging moments of human existence, which supports the idea of an enjoyable and satisfactory old age results from life long process of dealing with hardships, which may be regarded as opportunities for expanding inner resources.

Healthy Ageing

Healthy ageing dwells on the fact that though ageing is a natural, inevitable and inexorable phenomenon, one can find better way to live it positively and actively. The term "Healthy Ageing" is often used to emphasise that ageing is not a disease. In other words ageing period should be as healthy as possible and reasonably meaningful confirming to the WHO slogan. "It is not sufficient to add years to life but the more important objective is to add life to years". In India and other countries, aged people are described as old and senile. In recent years several positive terms are being used to describe them as senior citizen, elderly, third age individuals and individuals in the twilight of their life. Who are aged individuals? All individuals of 60+ are elderly. This is the cut off point prescribed by the United Nations. Recent studies conducted in physiology, bio- chemistry and epidemiology have confirmed that all aged individuals cannot be put in one homogenous group. They can be categorised in to "young-old" between the age of 60 to 75 years, "old-old" between 75 to 85 years and "very old" between 86 years and above. The first stage categories are physically active and mentally alert, and in most cases they are not dependent on others while the second and third categories need support and help. Numerous scientific studies have confirmed that the life span of Homo-Sapiens is possibly around 120 years. With better health care and better standard of living there is no reason why man will not cross hundred years and more. Throughout the world, attention is now being focused on the elderly of tomorrow and in which the health promoting behaviour for ensuring healthy ageing should be initiated.

Elderly and Community Mental Health

The question then arises whether those elderly can contribute to the community and country at large? S.K. Verma and Ashima Nehra (2001) in their article "Elderly and community Mental Health" feel that the growing population of elderly (both young elderly and old elderly) every where but particularly in a developing country like India has to be seen as a boon in disguise. They are not only the consumers of mental health services of the country but can be real producers of community mental health services, and must be seen in that light, particularly in view of the limited resources in trained man-power. Their vast experiences over the years need to be harnessed in the years to come, if the dream of "Health for All" by the year 2000 A.D. may be achieved. Why let go waste such a huge reservoir of experiences in various fields just because of our own faulty attitudes towards them and their problems? It we do not utilise such an available rich resource, then who is to blame? And why cry over limited resources? It is high time to over come these draw backs and sooner it is done the better it would be better for the community.

Community mental health appears as an abstraction. It can be seen through various manifestations indicating positive mental health of the community. The positive indications are level of co-operation among its various individuals, families, groups, units, institutions as manifested in sharing experiences, happiness, even grief, in sharing community achievements, healthy interpersonal relations, medical facilities, law and order as well as in absence of negative indicators like wars, conflicts, social discrimination on the basis of caste, religion, sex, etc. (ICMR Report, 1997). These constitute what is known as quality of community life (QCL) and it is here the elderly can contribute much through Governmental and non-Governmental agencies and even at one's own individual levels.

Role of Elderly

Elderly through creative use of leisure, through constructive leisure time activities, can serve the community they live. These are so far untapped, massive resources in a developing country (Verma, 1981, 1982, 1983). The older elderly can help their younger ones in preparing for retirement from active and strenuous activities (service, business etc). However, some non-governmental organisations like Red Cross, Helpage, Clubs, religious groups and individuals are making rich contributions in this area. The elderly groups need to do it in a better, organised way and more and more elderly need to join, in further enriching the quality of community life.

Hospital based, as well as community based, health services need these helps, where the illiterate rural masses of India may be lost when they first come for help. Government offices and courts are other such places where a helping and guiding hand of the elderly is necessary. Adult education and community programmes like family planning, banking loan facilities for agriculture, Medicare, child and maternal health care etc. are other areas in which the elderly can contribute. Guidance and counselling services can be made possible where education about common diseases, sex-education, marital counselling, counselling for alcohol and drug addicts etc. can be other areas of their activities. Lectures, camps, seminars etc. can be arranged for the rural and urban population regarding health and health care. Some persons have abnormal fears about ageing and relating to elderly — these need to be removed in a helpful and therapeutic atmosphere. Older elderly/senior citizens can come forward in this area of gerontophobia. More studies in this area are needed, which is described as auto gerontology (study of the aged by the aged for the aged) and all should strive to contribute. Besides, the help by the aged need not be limited to elderly only (Verma, 1996-97)

Conclusion

In the light of the above discussion it is high time that we change our attitudes and ways of modern life. Joint families where elderly also contribute as a useful member is welcome, respected and cared for — not abused should once again be a norm rather than an exception. The elderly on the other hand, need also change their attitudes, leave ideas of being head of family and of being for even in the decision-makers and accept and regard the view points of younger generation — even if they differ regarding the utility and sustainability of their new ways of 'modern life'. The 'generation gap' has to be reduced if not removed (which seems to be impossibility). Tolerance to different view points, values, behaviour has to be created and perpetuated, and if this has to be achieved and elderly returned to respective 'own homes' instead of 'old age homes' may go all the way to ensure towards sustainable active, successful and healthy old age.

Strategies for Healthy Ageing

1. Healthy ageing alone leads active ageing; health of the older people depends on the prevailing economic, political, social, cultural, educational and physical environment. This multi-dimensional supportive environment needs to be planned and developed by the individual, family, community, and institutions, NGOs, Governments and International Organisations for the welfare and care of the aged.

2. Promotion of health is the most important part of the total health care of the aged. To maintain and promote health during old age, it is vital to prevent diseases and disability. Early detection and appropriate care should follow when preventive measures taken up, 50 percent or more of all the health problems are preventable. Positive attitude towards life coupled with exercise and good nútrition makes a big difference in your over all quality.
3. Ageing process varies from community to community depending upon factors like-ethnic and culture, climatic conditions, geographic location, family size, gender, genetic background, disease experience in life, nutrition, infections, life style and education. Those who formulate ageing programmes should consider these factors in developing the activities.
4. Ageing starts from the day of conception and, therefore, the active ageing activities should be initiated early in life and not when people are sixty plus. In India, unfortunately, women have lower life span than men. This is mainly due to inappropriate treatment given to female foetus, girl child and women during the reproductive phase. All these factors should be considered in formulating active ageing programmes for women in addition to what is done for the men.
5. If the older people are enabled and encouraged, they can be a valuable asset to the family and to the community. They are not an economic and social burden to the family and the community. Old age is prone to develop chronic diseases like diabetes, Cardio-vascular problems, cancer, mental disorders, arthritis and disability of vision and hearing etc. Appropriate care need to be provided to older persons to meet these conditions effectively, older people could be both receivers and providers of care.
6. With increasing urbanisation and individualism, more and more nuclear families are coming up. This is bound to have adverse affect on the life of the aged. Family system which was supportive of old people is fast disappearing, requires readjustment in life situation and inter-personal relationships. This readjustment can improve the psycho-social well being of the aged.

7. The elderly keeping normal health to reasonable extent should conceive and develop an activity to spend their time productively by using their wisdom and experience to the extent possible which enables them to age actively.
8. Active ageing requires a firm foundation of good health derived from healthy life styles since childhood. Apart from caring for physical health, participation in activities with in and out side the household contributes to the optimal approach and attitude towards active ageing.
9. To facilitate participation of older persons in the economic life of the society by creating conditions conductive to employment. The right of older persons to employment should be based on ability to perform the work rather than the chronological age.
10. Organisational frame work and programmes at central and state level should be accepted for implementation including setting up of:
    (i) National Board for senior citizens.
    (ii) National Institute for senior citizens

    Formulations of policies and special programmes for schemes such as construction of homes for the elderly, maintenance of the destitute elderly in homes, day-care centres to improve the quality of life as elderly, foster care services for them etc; and constitute a committee for welfare of senior citizens at the state level.
11. The financial and other social support should be provided thorough Government and Non-government organisations especially to the lower income groups to maintain their elders.
12. The aged should be encouraged to form their voluntary organisations and cooperatives, which should be helped by the Government under their programmes as grant-in-aid for undertaking social services.
13. Certain measures like preferential allocation of land for Group Housing Societies for the elderly. House building advances need to be integrated in the National Housing Policy.
14. Senior citizens should be asked to serve the public cause in their individual capacities. They may provide on the spot assistance to victims of crime and accidents and provide

useful information for crime detection and prevention. Services of the senior citizens in villages should be linked with rural development of the remote areas.

15. Further, necessary infra structural facilities of transport, health and other services, travel concession by all modes of transport, recreational activities and day-care centres to interact with persons with commonality of interests and discuss common problems which may lead to alleviation of emotional problems of the elderly.
16. To cope with emergent medical and psychological problems greater emphasis needs to be given on geriatric medicine both in teaching and practice for geriatric assessment.
17. Facilities on education and training should be available for doctors, para-medical personnel and social workers from voluntary and governmental circles to impart training in geriatrics and gerontology covering all aspects of old age ailments. Families should also be oriented on health and nutrition needs of the elderly and ways to meet them through specially brought out literature, book lets and mass-media.

BIBLIOGRAPHY

1. Ageing & Society: The Indian Journal of Gerontology, Calcutta, Vol. IX, No. 1 or 11; Vol. X, No. 1 & 11; Vol. XII, No. 1 & 11 and Vol. XI, No. 111 & IV (1999, 2000, 2002, 2001).
2. Birren, J.E and Bengston, V.L (Eds), 1988, Emergent Theories of Aging, New York: Springer Publishing Company.
3. Bourdieu Pierrs (1980, 1983, 1986), The Forms of Capital, in John G. Richardson (Ed, Hand Book of Theory and Research for the Sociology of Education, New York, Green Wood Press.
4. D'Souza, V, (1993), "The Concept of Active Ageing", Indian Journal of Social Work, 54 (13), 333-34.
5. Frank. N; Magil, Jaclyn Rodrignez (Eds), International Encyclopaedia of Psychology, Vol. 1 London, Filz Roy Dear born Publishers, 1996, 105-106.
6. Frank, L.L, 'Gerontology', Journal of Gerontology, Michigan, Ann Arbor, 1946, 1 (1) (1-12).
7. Hardy, 1997, 1998 (Ed), "Studying Aging in Social Change", Conceptual and Methodological Issues, Thousand Oaks, CA

Publications, Helpage India-Research and Development Journal Vol. 6, No.3, June-Sep 2000.

8. Hess, N (1987), King Lear and Some Anxieties of Old Age, The British Journal as Medical Psychology, Vol. 60, 3,209-215.
9. Iswar Modi (2001) (Ed), "Ageing — Human Development", Rawat Publications, Jaipur & New Delhi.
10. Irudaya Rajan, U.S., Mishra, P. Sankara Sarma (1999), "India's Elderly — Burden or challenge", Sage Publications, New Delhi, Thousand Oaks, London.
11. James, E, Birren, K, Warner Schaie, Hand Book of Psychology of Ageing (4th edition), Mergret Gatz and Timothy (eds) Newyork, Aademic Press, Pandiego, 1996: 6-10.
12. James, E. Birren, K. Warner Schaie, "Hand Book as Psychology of Ageing (1st edition), Van Nostrand, Reinhold: Lilton Educational Publishing Inc. 1977: 95.
13. Kenyon, G.M (1988), "Basic Assumptions in Theory of Human" in Emergent Theories of Ageing, ed. by T.E. Birren and V.L. Bengston, New york. Springer Publishing Company.
14. Lucia Rabello de castro and G. Rabello de castro (2001), "Coping in Old Age" edited by Iswar Modi on "Ageing — Human Development" (2001).
15. Labourvie-Vief (1982), Individual Time, Social Time and Intellectual Ageing, in T. Hareven and K. Adams (eds.), 'Ageing and Life Course Transitions: An Interdisciplinary Perspective, London, Tavistock.
16. Messy, J (1992), "A pessoa l dosa nao existe (Sao Paulo ed., Aleph).
17. Milne and Milne, 1968, 'The Ages as Life', New York, Harcourt Brace & World, Inc.
18. Marjatta Marin (2001), "Successful Ageing-Dependent on Cultural and Social Capital" (Ed) Ishwar Modi in "Ageing-Human Development", Rawat Publication, Jaipur & New Delhi.
19. Ramamurti, P.V., "Life Satisfaction in the Older Years", Indian Journal of Gerontology, Jaipur (Rajasthan), Vol. 2, Nos.3 and 4, 1970.
20. Reymond, J, Corsine, Bonnie, D. Ozaki, Encyclopaedia of Psychology, Vol. I, John Wiley & Sons, Inc 1984: 39-40.
21. Sati, P.N (1988), "Retired and Ageing People", Delhi, Mittal Publications.
22. Schroots, J.J.F., (1996), "Theoretical Developments in the Psychology of Ageing", The Gerontologist, 36 (6), 742-48.
23. Sobha, I. And Reddy M. S. N. (2002), Care of the Aged: Institutional Support, Paper Presented at the International Symposium and XI

Biennial Conference of Association of Gerontology, India, M S Ramaiah Medical College, Bangalore, September.

24. Sobha, I. (2000), How Do The Aged Live? Ageing and Society, Jan-March & April-June, Vol. X Nos. I & II.
25. Tibbits, C (1960) (Ed), 'Hand Book of Social Gerontology, Societal Aspects as Ageing', Chicago University Press.
26. International Federation of Ageing, 1992, The Report of the First Conference on Ageing, Pune.
27. Veysset, B. (1989), Dependence et Vieillissement (Paris.L' Harmattan).
28. Venkoba Rao, A. (1989), 'Psychiatry of Old Age in India' published by Torrents Lab Pvt. Ltd, Ahmedabad and Sun Pharmaceutical Industries, Bombay.
29. Verma, S.K and Ashima Nehra (2001), "Elderly and the Community of Mental Health' (Ed) by Ishwar Modi in Ageing—Human Development (2001), Rawat Publications, Jaipur & New Delhi.
30. Vijayakumar, S. (1995), Challenges Before the Elderly: An Indian Scenario, New Delhi, M.D. Publications Pvt. Ltd.

2

SOCIOLOGY OF AGEING IN INDIA: PERSPECTIVE AND POLICY OPTIONS

Aditya Keshari Mishra &
Bikram Keshari Mishra

> *"...Towards a society for all ages' – a society that does not caricature older persons as pensioners, but sees them as both agents and beneficiaries of development"*[1].

Introduction

The root metaphor of our Indian cultural heritage has been eroding from the Indian soil due to various processes such as: westernisation, urbanization and industrialization – in a single word, modernization. Families have instigated to break up, and social support and respect for the elderly is in constant decay. At this juncture, the scientific understanding of this issue is a compulsory task for the academicians as well as the development practitioners.

The multifarious dimensions of ageing in India can sociologically be thought to be a series of transition from one set of social roles to another and such roles are structured by the social system. According to Bhatia (1983), "age and ageing are equally related to role-taking, value orientations and modes of behaviour of a person the expectation of which varies at different age-stages of members of a society". It may be mentioned that the process of ageing is not uniform for all individuals in the society. Thus, a change in the life of the old age, which is considered to be the *sanyas ashram* of the Hindu *ashram* theory, is influenced by the biological as well as the social and cultural systems. However, in recent times, the status and role of the old age population have been diminished due to the technological developments that have colonized the outlook of the youths. While contemplating on the issue of the 'aged', the ideas that haunt our imagination are quite complex as well as intriguing. Some argue that the elderly individuals are in a state of 'decay'. It implies that their role in society seem to be redundant and obsolescent for our contemporary times. In other words, they rarely have any function/role to contribute to our times. On the other hand, it is also believed that elderly persons are the guardians of our generation, preservers of the joint families, foundation of experience and knowledge, and resource of traditional values, norms and cultural practices. Thus, at this juncture, sociologists should be engaged in this debate in providing sociological perspectives on the transitional state of affairs of the elderly persons and advocate alternative approaches also for their emancipation to mainstream life.

Background

While the phenomenon of 'ageing' has been widely recognized in developed countries in India during the late 1960s, the Indian Gerontological Association (IGA) with a group of young and enthusiastic scientists from different branches of knowledge has brought this issue to the limelight for academic discussion. According to Lawrence Cohen (2003), "since the 1970s, gerontological writing in India has been dominated by a powerful and seldom challenged narrative of the decline of the Indian joint family and the consequent emergence of old age as a time of difficulty". Prior to industrialization, it was observed that the cultural heritage of Indian society was given the leadership roles and powerful positions of decision-makers and advisors in the joint family and community to aged persons, as their knowledge and experience were considered to be of great value in the proper functioning of society (De Souza 1982; Bhatia 1983; and Mishra 1987). Furthermore, according to Mishra (1987), the technological breakthrough due to industrialization, westernisation, and urbanisation has neglected the ascribed statuses by weakening the unity and integrity of the joint family and caste group that leads to the negligence of the role and status of the elderly persons. Moreover, the emergences of achieved properties like wealth, education etc., in distorted forms, has colonized the state of mind of the youths by adopting the individualistic value of the West. According to Ambedkar (1990), the issue relating to old age is a result of the conflict between the traditionalism of the old individuals and the uncritical eagerness of youths towards the Western values (Raju 2002). In fact, there has been a diminishing value of the aged population in contemporary Indian society. As a result, it articulates to the emergence of ageism, which believes in inequality, prejudice and discrimination against aged.

It is against this backdrop that the present paper makes an attempt to understand 'ageing' in India exclusively from a sociological perspective. It also undertakes to outline a brief literature on the existing legislative as well as the policy measures and finally, proposes some suggestions towards the future prospect of the elderly individuals of India. The problem of ageing can be seen through the following variables.

The Sociological Turn

It seems the discipline of sociology has been almost insouciant to the category called the aged. The 'aged' is about a vulnerable population, which is usually overlooked in our discipline; it is about a population, which is always at risk. No wonder, sociology has been enriching itself by encompassing and integrating new domains of discourse from time to time. From ecology to the Dalits, youth to feminism, though interrelated, it is constantly renewing itself. That is, perhaps the precise attribute of sociology for which August Comte called it a 'dynamic sociology'. Thus, the central methodological question that still remains unresolved is: should sociology make an attempt to construct a discourse for the aged, which would address all the issues confronting the aged? It goes without saying that the literature available on "ageing" in our discipline is very sparse. Thus, perhaps it becomes a methodological imperative for sociologists to build up a systematic discourse on gerontology for a panoptic understanding: their crisis, contribution as well as problems and possibilities. Of late, Social Gerontology, a branch of Gerontology, has started to focus on ageing from the socio-cultural aspects.

A Social Process

Ageing is a by-product of physical, psychological and social processes. While contextualising the process of ageing, the main thrust of the sociology, both as a discipline and a movement, is to reflect on how and to what extent transformations in the society and of the individual life influence each other, as individuals of different age categories pass through social system-institutions, values and norms. Sociologists specify three interrelated processes of ageing: physical, psychological and social. First, the physical ageing refers to the internal and external physiological changes that take place in the individual body. Second, the psychological ageing is understood as the developmental changes in mental functioning – emotional and cognitive capacities. Third, the social ageing focuses on the changes such as: how individuals are viewed, what individuals expect of themselves, and what is expected of them from others that individuals experience over the various age categories. However, sociologists are paying attention to the socio-economic and cultural antecedents of the process of ageing. Furthermore, ageing does not mean what an individual is able to act rather it facilitates what he/she is expected to act, permitted to act or prohibited from acting.

A Socially Determined Category

Every society uses age categories to divide this ongoing process into stages or segments of life. These life stages are socially constructed rather than inevitable. Age, too, is a production of social category. At any point of life span, age simultaneously denotes not only a number and a mixture of physical characteristics but also a set of social constructs, defined by the norms specific to a given society at a specific point in history. Think about childhood, for example. When you were growing up, childhood was a distinct period of life with particular activities designed especially for your age group: television programmes, movies, school, music etc. Thus, a specific period of life, be it infancy, childhood, adolescence, adulthood, middle age or old age is influenced by the structural entities of a given society. Therefore, ageing is not to be considered the mere product of biological function rather a consequence of socio-cultural factors.

Moreover, what is important about ageing, then, is how a society uses it to put people into categories. As a classificatory tool, age is important in three ways. First, like sex, age is an *ascribed* status or characteristic, which is, based on attributes over which we have little or no control. Second, unlike sex, a specific age is always transitional – constantly moving from one age to another, beginning life at zero and ending with a certain number at death that is regulated by societal expectations of age-appropriate behaviour. These transitions also assume that conformity is rewarded whereas deviance is punished. Third, although in every society some age groups are more powerful, rich and respectable than others; the unique aspect of ageing is that everyone can expect to occupy various positions throughout life on the basis of his or her age. The equation is very simple – all of us, at certain time, were powerless infants, and in course of time, the power and influence change as we move from one age category to another. Thus, the definition of ageing is socially caused.

Sociological Perspectives on Ageing

One of the branches of sociology i.e. Sociology of Gerontology or Social Gerontology focuses on what it means to age in society; that is, personal concerns and social issues associated with ageing and the ways in which these themes are influenced and at the same time influence the society in which we live. Thus, according to the sociologists and other social scientists, ageing, looking through the lens of sociological imagination, as devised by C. Wright Mills is not an individual problem rather a widespread issue that is faced by both the developed and underdeveloped nations as a whole. The process of ageing can be approached from four distinct perspectives: functional, symbolic, conflict, and emancipation.

First, the functional perspective argues that the elderly persons having knowledge, wisdom and experience help in the continuation of social norms, values and traditions. Hence, negligence of aged individuals needs to be rectified, according to the social situations. For example, the case of National Agricultural Technology Project (henceforth NATP), which has been initiated by the Ministry of Agriculture, Government of India with the financial assistance from the World Bank and is running with the assistance of the National Institute of Agricultural Extension Management (MANAGE), Hyderabad, in 28 districts covering seven States: Andhra Pradesh, Bihar, Jharkhand, Himachal Pradesh, Maharashtra, Orissa and Punjab. The project aims at mobilization and organization of different farmers' or women farmers' groups at grassroots levels in order to develop and disseminate various agro-based technologies to the farmers'/ women farmers' interest groups (Mishra 2004). It has been observed that although the youths participate in a large number, the aged persons, however, occupy the advisory-cum-central positions at grassroots, block and district levels. The reason is that the youths consider the aged members as more experienced and efficient than them in the concerned field.

Secondly, the conflict perspective assumes that the ageing is problematic for the society. According to this perspective, as the individuals become aged, it leads to the diminishing of power, prestige and privileges, unless these have been maintained by himself or herself. It argues that the wealthy and powerful individuals have blocked efforts to help the aged because they think spending for aged does not serve their personal interest. Moreover, it points out that the aged individuals, in course of time, lose their memory power and physical strength; thus, their role should be minimized. For example, the case of Yuva, one of the Bollywood blockbusters of 2004, directed by Mani Ratnam, lays down the significance of youths in the present day Indian politics. The central crux of the movie portrays that the youths must join politics, if the Nation has to survive and prosper. And, finally, the movie ends with its expected slogan. The youths have started taking the power from the hands of the aged, particularly those who have involved in corruption. But, the sociologically significant question is how the youths perceived politics and students' movements in the contemporary scenario. What I do believe is, that politics and students' movements are positively correlated. Critically examining, the youths want to redefine the knowledge system in relation to the students' movements and politics both at the level of educational institutions and at the level of the State.

Thirdly, the symbolic perspective examines the symbols and definitions that people use to communicate with one another, symbols that provide people with their view of the world. According to this perspective, all individuals with their features and characteristics, which are the reflections of their age, become the symbol of their respective age groups for others. Generally, the youths are considered to be smart, courageous and sportive. On the other hand, as Henslin (1990) mentioned that old persons are seen as weak, indolent, calm etc. Thus, we tend to perceive both others and ourselves according to the symbols our culture provides.

Fourthly, the emancipation perspective is an alternative to above three perspectives for two reasons. First, it abandons the approaches, proposed by the above theoretical perspectives. And, secondly, it gives priority to the liberation of the aged from the exclusion of social, economic and political participation in the society. In fact, the emancipation perspective is defined as creation of a sense of social identity of aged in one extreme, and, an instigate to social, economic, political welfare of the aged individuals on the other extreme. In essence, the emancipation perspective provides relative privilege in socio-economic, political and psychological aspects of aged through the construction of a sense of age consciousness, which leads to the provision of social security.

Ageing in India: Some Reflections

The aged population in India is currently the second largest in the world. In modern times, for all practical purposes the individuals who are above sixty years of old are considered to be aged or 'senior citizens' of the State. In academic research, retirement age is often taken as an index of aged status. Chronological age of fifty-eight or sixty is considered the beginning of old age. However, existence of mass poverty, growing trends towards nuclear family, greater life expectancy and deterioration of cultural values and norms are engendering stumbling blocks on the part of the aged to cope with the changing environment (Bhatia 1983). As a result, the aged population in India is accompanied by a series of problems in their day-to-day life. The major areas of problems, faced by the aged individuals are: income generation, health, use of free time, social security, social participation, dignity and respect and so on. These problems are because of the following reasons namely, geographical and cultural differences, red-tapism and disproportionate socio-economic facilities to urban and rural areas in terms of education, sanitation, health and housing. As a result, the Government of India has undertaken some legislative and policy measures for the welfare of the aged.

Existing Programmes on Ageing

Much progress has been made in the quality and quantity of the service of the ageing in India in the last five decades. However, improvements have been uneven in the urban areas that avail the best advantage of modern advanced technological package in contrast to the rural one. While much of the emphasis has been given to care for women and child, the government has played a least role for aged except formulating certain legislative and policy measures. Here, a brief attempt has been made to understand the constitutional and the legislative and the policy measures pertaining to the welfare of the aged population of India.

Constitutional Provisions

The welfare of the aged has been enshrined in the Constitution of India. The item 9 of the State list and items 20, 23 and 24 of the Concurrent List speak of the provisions of age pension, social security, social insurance, economic and social planning, and relief to the disabled and the unemployed. The Article 41 of the Directive Principles of State Policy expresses "the State shall make effective provision for securing the right to work, to education and to public assistance in case of unemployment, old age, sickness and disable ness, and in other cases undeserved wants, within its limits of economic development and capacity". Fundamental Right, Article 16 (2) emphasizes on equal opportunity in matters of public employment. Article 47 of the Indian Constitution points out the raising of the level of nutrition and the standard of living of its people and improvement of public health.

Legislative Measures

Coming to the category of legislative measure, the retirement benefits (GPF & PPF) are provided to those who served the Government and the public undertakings.

- The Employees Provident Funds and Miscellaneous Provisions Act, 1952 (amended in 1996) provide for economic security to persons or their families in the event of retirement or even death before retirement.
- The National Social Assistance Programme came into existence on 15th August 1995 and one of its programmes is the National Old Age Pension Scheme that is implemented through the Panchayats and municipalities. Presently, all State Governments and Union Territories are implementing the old age pension scheme under the State sector.

Policy Measure

The emergence of National Policy on Older Persons, 1999, a collaborative pursuit of both public and private agencies along with the 'Third Sector', which aims at the well-being of the aged focuses on the areas of financial security, health care and nutrition, shelter, welfare and other needs of the senior citizens and provides protection against abuse and exploitation. Moreover, he National Council for Older Persons on 18th October 2002 and 7th February 2003 emphasizes on the following areas: uniform age of 60+ for extending facilities/benefits to senior citizens; financial security; health care and nutrition needs; food security and shelter; and highlighting the role of media[2].

However, the empirical implications of the measures through legislation and policy measures have not achieved their desired goals. The result is that the rich used to receive more and perhaps better services than the poor, although the poor are deserving and downtrodden (Hess, Markson and Stein 1998). Moreover, owing to the physical, socio-economic, psychological and the influence of uncritical western philosophy like 'individualism', out of their practical experience and research endeavour, an innumer able number of social scientists report that there is degradation in the social status as well as economic conditions of the aged population in India. In fact, the living conditions of the aged individuals in Indian society are influenced by a series of factors such as caste, religion, education, health condition, dependent on the chief earner of the family, living standard of the adult members of the family and the process of migration (Raju 2002 and Mishra 1987). Furthermore, the unconditional power, prestige and privileges that older people used to enjoy in joint families are being gradually eroded in the society. Thus, there is an urgent need for the restructuration of the existing legislative and policy measures.

Reading Future Options

In India, as stated above, the living standards of the aged are influenced by the following factors: physical, social, economic and psychological. Thus, any attempt towards the welfare of the aged community should be taken into consideration the above-mentioned factors. Moreover, any policy should include the poor, vulnerable and neglected segments of the society. In a concrete sense, as Farah (2004) mentions, the policy option should recognize the following four objectives:

1. To bring about every individual to an equal and common platform in order to launch any measures and provide equal opportunities for basic amenities like food, shelter, health care facility etc.
2. To provide equal socio-economic opportunities to everybody by removing all sorts of discriminations that operates at societal level.
3. To ensure the institutional and regulatory mechanism for discrimination.
4. To mainstream the marginalized sections of the society.

Here, an attempt has been made to propose some suggestions for the development of the longstanding issue relating to 'ageing' in India. Moreover, these suggestions will act as critical inputs into the process of developing an appropriate policy measure for the welfare of the aged individuals.

- India lives in her villages. Furthermore, Indian economy is primarily an agrarian-based economy. She is characterized by the existence of longstanding variations, such as, rural-urban dichotomy; rich and poor difference; the unequal distribution of updated technological facilities etc. Hence, any proposed measure undertaken by the government should take into account these factors. In this context, the first and foremost thing is that the government should adopt a provision of social security measure irrespective of rural and urban, caste and class so on and so forth. Here, the social security measure believes that the State should make itself responsible for ensuring a minimum standard of material welfare to all its citizens.
- The aged individuals should be encouraged to form Self-Help Groups (SHGs) so that they can organize themselves and to provide services to their fellow senior citizens. Moreover, it will facilitate a sense of 'age consciousnesses among the aged individuals.
- Apart from the improvement of health care system, the effective way of dealing with the elderly is to improve the economic condition of the elderly population. Thus, there is a need to formulate an alternative employment opportunity

for the aged; at least those who have efficiency to work after retirement, whereby they can increase their bargaining power in contemporary competitive society.

- In recent times, the process of 'participation' seems to be the buzzword in every sphere of intellectual discourse. Thus, along with the youth, the aged need to participate instead of staying in isolation in all the communitarian or societal or development activities. This participation is expected to bring about the developments of equality, efficiency and effectiveness, which ultimately lead to mainstream life.
- There is also a need to revive our normative structure of the society. Owing to the influence of distorted form of modernity, the philosophy of 'individualism' has colonized the mental state of the youths. Thus, efforts should be promoted in order to tackle this situation.
- There is also a need to introduce the institutional support in order to address the structural problem of ageing. This institutional set up will deliver training programmes, oriental course, and mass campaign against the attitude towards ageism. On the other hand, it will also conduct various research works pertaining to the problems relating to ageing and will also find out the possible solutions.
- Advocacy, research, involvement of voluntary agencies, training opportunities for gerontological workers, awareness building and a close networking between the old aged population with the national and international agencies should also be developed.
- Finally, the emergence of collaborative effort made by the public and private agencies along with the 'Third Sector' and also the public at large will address effectively the conditions of ageing. This multi-agential strategy is based on interactive-bottom up approach and active participation of stakeholders.

Towards Conclusion

The emergence and the persistence of the issue of 'ageing' in Indian society comprise a series of factors. In brief, the major antecedent to the issue of ageing is the changing aspects of Indian social structure, which includes family pattern, adoption of individualistic values by youths, migration etc. From a sociological point of view, ageing, a social process is not an offshoot of the mere biological aspect rather a by-product of larger socio-cultural milieu. In this context, agency seldom works whereas structure drives every agency in its own way. Thus, it is indispensable that the policy interventions should take notice of the socio-economic conditions of the aged individuals. Hence, the liberation of ageism does not imply a collaborative effort, undertaken by the public and private institutions along with the involvement of NGOs and community at large but it also depends on the freedom from the shackles of 'individualism' and the 'self', which will retrieve cognitive tradition of Indian civilization.

(N.B.: The authors are grateful to Prof. E. Haribabu, Department of Sociology, School of Social Sciences, University of Hyderabad, Hyderabad, and Dr. Avijit Pathak, Associate Professor, Centre for the Study of Social System, School of Social Sciences, Jawaharlal Nehru University, New Delhi for their constant support and encouragement).

NOTES

1. UN Secretary-General Kofi Annan, 1st October 1998, available at: http://www.un.org/esa/socdev/ageing/ageless.htm.
2. Available at: http://socialwelfare.delhigovt.nic.in/nationalpolicy.htm.

REFERENCES

Basu, D. D. (1989), *Shorter Constitution of India*. New Delhi: Prentice-Hall of India.

Baum, M. and Baum, R. C. (1980), *Growing Old: A Social Perspective*. New Jersey: Prentice – Hall, Inc.

Bhatia, H. S.(1983), *Ageing and Society – A Sociological Study of Retired Public Servants*. Udaipur: Arya's Book Centre.

Cohen, L. (2003), *'Old Age and the Global Economy of Knowledge'* in V. Das (Ed.). *The Oxford India Companion to Sociology and Social Anthropology*, Vol. 2. pp. 956-973. New Delhi: Oxford University Press.

Coleman, J.W. and Cressey, D. R. (1987), *Social Problems*. New York: Harper & Row Publishers.

Crandall, R.C. (1980), *Gerontology: A Behavioural Science Approach*. Philippines: Addison-Wesley Publishing Company, Inc.

De Souza, A. (1982), *'The Social Organization of Ageing Among the Urban Poor'*, *Social Action*, 32(1).

Farah, F. M. (2004), *'Population and Social Development Policies'*, *Health*, Vol. 29 (06).

Hens, B.B., Markson, E.W. and Stein, P.J. (1998), *Sociology*. New York: Macmillan Publishing House.

Henslin, M.J., (1990), *Social Problems*. New Jersey: Prentice Hall.

Macionis, J. J. (1998), *Sociology: The Basics*. New Jersey: Upper Sadale River.

Mills, C.W. (1976), *The Sociological Imagination*. New York: Oxford University Press.

Mishra, A.K. (2004), *'Globalization and Agricultural Extension Reforms: A Study of National Agricultural Technology Project in Orissa'*, Unpublished M.Phil Dissertation, Submitted at University of Hyderabad, Hyderabad.

Mishra, S. (1987), *Social Adjustment in Old Age*. Delhi: B.R. Publishing Corporation.

Raju, S.S. (2002) *Health Status of the Urban Elderly: A Medico-social Study*. Delhi: B.R. Publishing Corporation.

3

GLOBALISATION AND THE AGED

Sushila Jain

Introduction

The concept of globalization is one that has become widely used in debates, in politics, business and media over the past few years. A decade ago, the term 'globalization' was relatively unknown. Today it seems to be on the top of everyone's tongue. Globalization refers to the fact that we are all increasingly living in 'one world', so that individuals, groups and nations become more interdependent.

Sociologists use the term globalization to refer to those processes, which are intensifying worldwide social relations and interdependence. It is a social phenomenon with vast implications, it should not be thought of simply as the development of worldwide networks — social and economic systems that are remote from our individual concerns. It is a local phenomena too, one that affects all of us in our daily lives. It is changing the way the world looks, and the way we look at the world. By adopting a global outlook, we become more aware of our connections to people in other societies. We also become more conscious of the many problems the world faces at the start of the twenty first century. The global perspective opens our eyes to the fact that our increasing ties with the rest of the world means that our actions have consequences for others and that the world's problems have consequences for us.

Globalization—Its Meaning

Anthony Giddens, in a book On the Edge: Living with Global Capitalism identifies many meanings of globalization; firstly as:

(i) The world wide communication revolution.

(ii) Secondly, he refers to what he terms the 'weightless economy'; by this he means the new 'Knowledge economy', with financial markets at its leading edge.

(iii) Thirdly, it refers to a post — 1988 world, that is world after the fall of communism and

(iv) Fourthly, it refers to transformations happening on the level of everyday life.

Globalization — Its Impact on Aged

A general concern about the worldwide phenomena of increase in the aged population has existed for many years now. On the global level the phenomena of population ageing was first highlighted in 1982 when the United Nations organised the first world conference on ageing in Vienna. In the present times the proportion of people who are sixty-five or over is steadily increasing. At the same time, the issue of the social importance of ageing is one that ranges much more broadly. For what old age actually is- the opportunities it offers and the burdens it carries - is changing dramatically. Gerontology, the study of ageing and the elderly, concerns itself not only with the physical process of growing old, but also with social and cultural factors concerned to ageing.

Two rather contradictory processes are involved here. On the one hand, older people in modern societies tend to have lower status and less power than they used to have in premodern culture. In these cultures, as in non-western societies today, old age was believed to bring wisdom, and the older people in any given community were commonly its main decision-makers. Today, increasingly age normally brings with it something of its reverse. In a society undergoing constant change, as ours is, the accumulated knowledge of older people often seems to the young no longer valuable store of wisdom, but simply behind the times.

On the other hand, however older people today are much less prone to accept ageing as inevitable process of the decay of the body. Here once more we can trace the impact of the nature of socialization. The ageing process was once generally accepted as an inevitable manifestation of the ravages of time. But increasingly, ageing is not something taken for granted as natural. Advances in medicines and nutrition have shown that much that was once regarded as inevitable about ageing can either be countered or slowed down. On average, people live to much older ages than was true over a century ago, as a result of improvements in nutrition, hygiene and health care.

Globalization is a complex process, which has diverse meanings and facts. These meanings are important. Challenges of globalization are (a) economic and (b) social, leading to marginalization of the aged. Retrenchment of personnel and its implications for the aged and in terms of certain kind of positive and negative freedom, new opportunities in terms of the potential for self fulfilment.

Definitional Problems and Conceptualisations

Different definitions and conceptualisations of ageing have been employed by scholars from time to time, usage of the term 'Elderly' is common both in popular and academic discourses. The use of such blanket term to encompass a forty year range has contributed to the popular stereotype that the elderly constitute a homogeneous social group: one of the most persistent and potent images of ageing is that all older people are alike.

Old age denotes a specific stage of life in a tripartite division of the life cycle, i.e. phase of preparation, followed by the one of productive activity in economic/income generating terms, and finally the stage of retirement. The chronological criterion for classifying an individual or a collectivity as "aged" or "elderly" is generally employed for administrative purposes for example, pensions, retirement, insurance and the like. Here, old age is identified by the transition from the salaried work to retirement.

No definite criterion is fixed by biologist to consider a person old, and for administrative purpose each country tends to carry its age limit for working. The definition of the term "elderly" or "aged" has undergone modification over the passage of time. Ancient Chinese scholars delineated seven phases in a man's life and Pythagoras in the sixth century B.C. compared human life to the seasons. In both cases, old age was deemed to be beyond 60 years (Stub, 1982). Some societies still treat 40 or 50 years as marking the transition into old age.

In Western industrialised nations the typical onset of old age is reckoned as 65. Worach - Kardas (1982) argues that age must be viewed as a socio-cultural category as much as it is a chronological and biological phenomenon, and advocates a life-course perspective in which youth, middle age, and old age are studied as separate entities with their own distinctive problems and processes.

Dutt (1986) says the term ageing signifies the progression of changes in bio-chemical processes. The factors, which cause the ageing process, are mainly environmental, genetic, mutation and free radical theory. Dutt endorses the view that the chronological age is a poor predictor of functional ability. The age of 60 has been adopted by the census of India for the purpose of classifying a person as old.

Old age is determined by cultural norms prevailing in a society. In Indian society, marriage of one's children, particularly of a son, heralds the beginning of old age for women far more clearly than do a specified number of years. Accordingly, role expectations change for male and female members in a household.

Old age is depicted positively in terms of wisdom and the potential for spiritual growth. For some, wisdom and serenity are positive aspect of old. The best things about old age include freedom to do and to be what one wishes, i.e. freedom from responsibility and freedom from worry about other's opinions. The "elderly" or "aged" sustain positive self-concepts by narrowing their social contacts to avoid exposure to people who would reject them on account of ageing.

On the other hand, old age is also depicted negatively in terms of physical decline and decrepitude. Elderly people are characterised or stereotyped as ill, tired, mentally slow, self pitying, unhappy and unproductive. They are often depressed by feelings of loneliness and alienation. The negative content of the conditions of old age derives from the relationship of individuals and society; the absence of a role, the isolation from the significant social life, the marginality in family relationship and the lack of commitment, partly induced, partly forced on old people. Their problems include a feeling of material insecurity or dependence, and attenuated intergenerational relationships. The aged are also said to be losing gradually their decision-making authority. Elders suffer from a sense of dispossession that reflects loss of roles and status, as they are deprived of the earlier identities defined by parental or employment functions. The hardest part of being old is declining health and lack of finances, threat of dependence, and the loss of beloved ones.

Concept of Ageing

Some scholars like Partha N. Mukherji (1972) distinguish between biological and sociological or psychological age. He says, biologically a person may be old, but if he possesses a youthful mentality, sociologically and psychologically speaking, he should be included in the younger generation. Dutt (1986) says, the term ageing signifies the progression of changes in the biochemical processes, which determines structural and functional alterations with age in the cells and non-cellular tissues and, hence, in the whole organism. The prime factors which cause the ageing process as known today are: environmental; genetic mutation; and free radical theory. He also endorses the view that chronological age is a poor predictor of functional ability. Some 80 years old function as well as the 40 years old and some 40 years old perform like the average 80 years old. While there are no definite criteria fixed by biologists to consider a person old, for administrative purposes each country fixes an age limit, which defines a person as such. The Indian census, for example, has adopted the age of 60 for classifying a person as old.

However we may broadly classify the development of age classes as:

- Era of dependence, socialization and education.
- Era of independence, maturity and responsibility.
- Era of personal fulfillment.
- Potential for self fulfilment in terms of positive as well as negative freedom and responsibility.
- Era of elderly ageing: to be further divided into two types:
  (i) The effective elderly (60-75 years), also called young old.
  (ii) And elderly in need (above 75 years), called old.

Theories of Ageing

Several theoretical approaches have been advocated by scholars in their efforts to understand the phenomenon of ageing. Since the time when there ensued a lovely debate between the proponents of the activity and disengagement theories, the field of social gerontology has been studied by such diverse points of view as socio-environmentalism (Gubrium, 1973), continuity theory (Atchely, 1971), the age stratification approach (Riley, 1971; Riley, Johnson and Foner, 1972) symbolic interactionism (Marshal, 1980); exchange theory (Dowd, 1975); modernism theory (Cow gill and Holmes, 1972); and political economy (Olson, 1982).

Activity and Continuity Theories

Social integration and participation are regarded as necessary criteria for satisfactory ageing in order that lost roles are replaced with other types of behaviour. Proponents of these theories contend that older people have social and psychological needs similar to those of younger people or to themselves when they were middle aged. Successful ageing requires finding new ways of being involved, to compensate for losses of retirement or the death of long-time friends — in plain words, efforts not to let previous life space Shrunk. Research evidences highlights the inadequacy of the activity theory as an interpretation of ageing.

Disengagement Theory

A second theoretical approach to the understanding of the process of ageing is the disengagement theory. The proponents of this theoretical approach (Cumming, 1963; and Cumming and Henry, 1961) contend that as people grow older they have less energy, and sustain a diminishing number of interactions (as well as types of roles) with other persons. As they retire from work, lose of dear ones and experience deteriorating health, they become more egocentric, this theory propose that the elderly person and society undergo a process of mutual withdrawal which is explained as a natural and inevitable procedure of functional benefit both to the individual and to society. Thus, lowering of activity levels and involvement in social interaction are regarded as indicators of 'correct' ageing. Cumming and Henry's theory has met with expensive criticism and has been described as the geriatric euphemism of social death (Platt, 1972: 133-150).

Exchange Theory

To Dowd (1980) this approach suggests that the lives of elderly people are shaped by the relative power resources of the social actors involved. "Thus although exchange theorists recognize that old people in modern society tend to be disadvantaged because they generally possess less power resource than young people, these theorists also recognize that there are expectations: individuals often manipulate in innovative ways the few resources they do possess. Thus, although the long term 'exchange' views recognizes that possession of resources also lead to power in social relationships, the short term view appreciates the creative ability of humans to use resources in unique ways". (Dowd 1980:19) Dowd argues that older people form a cohesive age stratum through their sharing of certain attributes (e.g., their exclusion from work roles). In old age, age interests once again become dominant. Age status becomes a permanent identity. There is no age stratum to move to play an increasing vague role. Furthermore, social relations are 'lifted' from their physical context; the people one considers to be close can be just as close at a distance. New technology contributes to increasing the tempo of social life and shrinking of world. The pace of social life is increasing and spatial distances decrease in importance. The world is collapsing 'inward' towards us.

In principle, the process of globalization affects all parts of social life, but it is particularly relevant in discussions around the changing life style of aged. The most immediate effect of this process of globalization and individualization is that the traditional ties are becoming less important, young people no longer follow in their parent's footsteps; they have other needs and desires than those of their aged parents. These needs and desires do not necessarily collide with those of their parents, but they are not identical and risk of conflicts exists. And unlike the power, prestige and respect they commanded in the traditional societies, they find their positions threatened. Furthermore unlike the traditional societies where every work and occupation was conducted under their supervision and guided wisdom, they increasingly find themselves unfit, and incapable of keeping up to the pace to new information technologies and heterogeneous life style.

Second main concern of elderly people is retaining independence, freedom of movement and the ability to participate fully in the social world. However, there are great variations between elderly people in their material resources and their access to emotional and health support. These differences can influence the ability of the elderly to maintain their autonomy and overall well being.

Class, gender and race are important influences on the experience of ageing. As an example, ageing is a gendered phenomenon. Women tend to live longer then men, making old age highly 'female'. The later years are heavily influenced by experiences earlier in life, because of domestic and childcare responsibility; women on the whole participate less than men in paid labour. They also receive lower levels of pay. Studies reveal that elderly women have lower personal income than men and also suffer inequalities in other resources such as housing and vehicle ownership. The discrepancy in vehicle ownership may not seem a major concern, but it can significantly restrict women's overall mobility and their access to health care, shopping and contact with others. With increasing age women suffer more than men from disability. This means that they require more assistance and support than men.

Thirdly, as far as the aged members are concerned, the family is a vital institution because they spend most of their time there. It provides them a feeling of togetherness, security and moorings in an increasingly dynamic, fast growing and anomic society. However, due to rapid socio-economic changes and the pressures of modernisation, the traditional family structure is now changing and it is becoming increasingly difficult even for the joint family to discharge its role of taking care of its elderly members. Several extraneous demands are in the way in doing this, shortage of space, high expenditure on children's education and equally huge Medicare costs are resulting in the ability of the nuclear family also to meet the demands of its elderly members and consequently resulting in their marginalization. Women's work outside home prevents them from taking care of the elderly during day time in many families, as was done in earlier times, out migration of the young also leaves the elderly alone in the family. Some of them have no resource to fall back upon. It has extended the period of unproductive life of the aged, and increased the financial and physical strain of the family in caring them by several more years than was the case previously. This compels the younger members to seek employment outside home to augment the family income, thus leaving the elderly with no one to attend on them.

Overall, the elderly tend to be more materially disadvantaged then other segments of the population. Retirement results in the loss of income that may cause a significant drop in elderly people's standard of living. Thus we may say that as people age, they face a combination of physical, emotional and material problems that can be difficult to negotiate.

There is a need for good physical functioning, positive mental health and material security as intergenerational relationships are being disturbed. Children want to move out to the wider world with relatively more attractions for jobs in info-tech, bio-tech pharmaceuticals and software engineering etc. as these are the demands of the present day.

Common Structural Variables in Ageing

The commonly identified individual contextual factors, which should make difference to the elderly are:

Age

Even among the elderly the greater the chronological age the greater are likely the problems of the elderly, particularly in the areas of health and familial environment.

Sex

Sex is an important differentiating factor in the general condition of health and in the specific types of problems faced by the elderly in the role change and role performance. At a general level one is aware that females tend to continue in their traditionally defined "work" roles at home much longer than men in their formal work setting and as such tend to suffer less with regards the void in social relationship and time as compared to their counter parts, males.

Marital Status

The state of being married is a positive factor for adjustment in the old age. For the male the presence of his wife means minimally the presence of the major caregiver at the level of physical care and psychological support. For the female the state of being married is culturally all important and the death of her husband may also affect to a degree her authority in the family and make her fully dependent upon her son/s. The implication of being a widower or widow need to be studied in terms of its influence on familial status, sense of dependence and intrafamilial social transaction generally.

Economic Condition

Individuals with a secure and sufficient income during old age are likely to face less economic and psychological problems because of their ability to meet their needs, the ability to afford supportive services and sense of security that this brings.

Occupational Status

Chance of continued occupational involvement even after the normal age of "retirement" varies a great deal on whether one has been an employee or self-employed person and this in turn make for a difference in the kinds of problems and challenges one face with age.

Family Structure

Individuals may live in unitary or joint households or even in non-household situation as independent individual or individuals in institution. These differences may strongly affect individual's life.

Social Background

Do differences in religion, caste, community make for differences in life philosophy and coping with life's challenges in old age?

These are a few of the background characteristics which would serve as independent variables, the presence or absence of such may make considerable difference in facilitating or hindering the ability of the elderly individual to cope with the stresses and problems of aging.

Patterns of Adjustment

The concept of "adjustment" is very common and very old. Its goal has been described as "satisfaction" and "smooth switch over from one status to other".

Good adjustment is achieved primarily through a balance between the "expected" and "enacted" roles. When the role-playing individual attaches more value to one particular role than is expected/demanded of that role, the "role counter" does not appreciate it and it leads to role conflict. Adjustment is a balanced performance of all roles in conformity with the role demands. When a person is able to make a smooth switch over from one role to another and his role behaviour is in consonance with the role expectations, and his role does not obstruct the performance of other's role, the person succeeds in integrating the various roles into an ordered sequence of roles, leading to adjustment. Good adjustment means that the person feels that he is neither over performing nor under performing a role in relation to the demands of the role. Symbolically, thus adjustment may be described in terms of role demand and role performance.

Thus "balance in environment" tried by the aged as a process of adjustment may be used as the focus of their development process.

Criteria of Adjustment

Criteria of adjustment refer to standards and norms employed to assess the degree and quality of personal and social adjustment of the aged. The focus of this sociological framework to analyse their family and social adjustment may include such areas of analysis-

(i) *Family Adjustment*

- (a) Satisfaction with the sibling treatment.
- (b) Satisfactory relationship with wife and other family members, other than siblings in the family.
- (c) Satisfaction with home life

(ii) *Social Adjustment*

- (a) Favourable attitude towards social participation with others known/unknown.
- (b) Effective relationship with Social realities and situations.
- (c) Ability to get along with other persons.
- (d) Successful adjustment with different groups and subgroups.
- (e) Possession of socially desirable attributes. (Description of self as sociable, likeable, popular and able to get along with different kinds of people etc.)

(iii) Economic/Financial Adjustment

(a) Re-employment/no employment conditions and satisfaction.

(b) Motivation in seeking re-employment.

(iv) Political/Social Work Interests

(a) Leisure time activities.

(b) Religious beliefs and practices.

(c) Participation in voluntary organisations.

(v) Problems and Stresses

(a) Financial / Occupational.

(b) Familial, Neighbourhood.

(c) Health problems.

(d) Insecurity, loneliness and emotional support problems.

The Future of Ageing

In a society that places a high value on youth, vitality and physical attractiveness; older people tend to become invisible. Recent years, however, have seen some changes in attitudes towards old age. Older people are unlikely to recover the full authority and prestige that used to be accorded to elders of the community in ancient societies. Yet as they have come to comprise a larger proportion of population, older people have acquired more political influence than they used to have. They have already become a powerful political lobby.

The later years of life can be seen as a time of great opportunity and even celebration provided aged people acquire new outlook towards the life. With their positive mental outlook and good physical shape of body these individuals can continue to grow, learn and explore. Travelling, pursuing further education or developing new skills, doing small jobs in family, helping grand children with their education and their by keeping themselves well occupied and busy. A few suggestions for personal growing and healthy well being of the aged may be outlined as:

(i) Face new opportunities, challenges and experiments

(ii) Adopt to the uses of new technology

(iii) Maintain creativity in its new forms

(iv) Seek avenues for volunteerism and intergenerational activities

(v) Maintain social contacts and

(vi) Continue with spiritual activities through various media.

Thus to conclude information revolution that brings about basic changes even if they occur over a relatively long period of time necessitate the need for a successful restructuring of the ageing process. To face these new challenges and to adapt to the uses of new technology, one needs to get involved in active learning and creativity in a new form, which also requires mechanisms to seek avenues for volunteerism and intergenerational activities.

BIBLIOGRAPHY

1. Akhtar, S.S. and Pestonjee, D.M. (1963), A Study of Employees Adjustment Within and Outside Work Situation, Indian Journal of Social Work, Vol. XXIII, No.4, January.
2. Bali Arun P.: (1999), Understanding Greying People of India. Inter-India Publications.
3. Birren, J.E. (1964), The Psychology of Aging, New Jersey, Englewood Clifs: Prentice Hall.
4. Cowgill, D.O. (1974), Aging and Modernization: A Revision of the Theory, In Gubrium, J.F. (ed.), Late Life: Communities and Environmental Policies. Springfield, II: Charles C Thomas, pp.167-197 (H.16).
5. Cowgill, D.O., and Holmes, L.D. (eds.), (1972), Aging and Modernization, New York: Appleton - Century Croft.
6. Cumming, E. (1963), Further Thoughts on the Theory of Disengagement, International Social Science Journal 15, 377-393.
7. Dowd. J.J. (1975), Aging as Exchange: A preface to Theory. Journal of Gerontology 30: 584-594.
8. Dube, S.C. (1955), Indian Village. London: Routledge & Kegan Paul.
9. Dutt, S.K., (1986) Aging Nutrition, The Hindustan Times, No. 24.8 Sept. 27 Vol. LXIII.
10. Desai, I.P. (1964), Some Aspects of Family Change in Mahuwa. Bombay: Asia Publishing House.
11. Desai, K.G. (1982), Aging in India. Bombay: Tata Institute of Social Sciences.
12. De Souza, Alfred (1982), The Social Organization of Aging Among the Urban Poor, New Delhi: Indian Social Institute, pp. 7-8.

13. Gangrade, K.D. (1988), Crisis of Values: A Sociological Study of the Old and the Young. In Bose, A.B. and Gangrade, K.D. (eds.), The Aging in India: Problems and Potentialities. New Delhi: Abhinav Publications.
14. Gangrade, K.D. (1989), Emerging Conception of Aging in India. Eastern Anthropologist 42(2): 151-69.
15. Gore, M.S. (1968), Urbanisation and Family Change. Bombay: Popular Prakashan.
16. Giddens A. and Hutton W. (2000b), On the Edge, London Ionathan Cape.
17. Gore, M.S. (1997), Studying Problems of Aging Sociological Bulletin, Vol. 46, No.1, March.
18. Kapadia, K.M. (1996), Marriage and Family in India. Bombay: Popular Prakashan.
19. Pihlblad, C. Terence, and Robert L. McNamara (1965), Social Adjustment of Elderly People in Three Small Towns, in Rose, Arnold M., and Warren A. Peterson (ed.), Older People and their Social World, Philadelphia; F.A. Davis & Co.

PART–II
EMPIRICAL STUDIES

4

THE AGED: THEIR PROBLEMS, SOCIAL INTERVENTION AND FUTURE OUTLOOK IN THE WESTERN U.P.

A.R.N. Srivastava

INTRODUCTORY BACKGROUND

Introduction

This research paper falls within the area of "Social Gerontology"—a sub field of the sociological discipline that is a relatively new but is developing fast little researched in Indian sociology and social anthropology. Social gerontology concentrates on cultural and economic factors of ageing, employment, retirement from the active services, and chronic illness among the aged, and family attitudes towards older people. It is to be noted that the terms like 'ageing', 'aged', 'elder', 'gray population' among others are often used by the gerontologists to describe persons having distinct characteristics at a point of time in a life span.

In India old stage roughly corresponds to age group 55-60 years and beyond. This is a very crucial stage in one's life span because person's social obligations, privileges and expectations towards his/her obligations, privileges and expectations towards his/her immediate kin groups undergo a reciprocal change. Demands and expectations of older from the younger and in turn their attitudes and obligations enter new dimensions and have resumed special importance in human relationships.

For our immediate purpose 'sixty' years has been considered as the cut off point. In other words, persons of 60 years and above have been considered to constitute "old persons"

Some Studies on Ageing in India

Over the past three decades specialists in the disciplines of Sociology, Social works, Psychology, Public Administration, Social Medicine and Mental Health have contributed to the unraveling of dynamics associated with the aged people in India. We briefly review a few specific studies having some bearing on the present research.

Desai and Naik[1] studies problems of retired people of Greater Bombay, which marked the systematic beginning of sociological study on old age in the country. Victor S. D'Souza published a paper entitled "Changes in Social Structure and Changing Roles of Older people in India". The same author took the same theme again in 1981 and wrote a comprehensive paper on the "Changing Social Scene of the Aged in India"[2]. In 1973 Delhi School of Social Work took a project on "The Study on Aged in India".[3] About the same time Soodan had published "Ageing in India" on the basis of field work data related to "Old pension Scheme in Uttar Pradesh".[4] This was an evaluation study of retired persons of Uttar Pradesh.

Again in 1978 K.G. Desai completed a research project on "Social Situation of Aged in India"[5]. During 1975-80 a few sociologists completed a few Ph.D. Dissertations on elderly people specially retired and nearing retired working in organized sectors. Some of these dissertations are now available in published form[6].

The United Nations had declared the year 1962 as the year of the Aged. Its focus was to draw the attention of the people on the problems of the aged in respective countries. This year saw a very important publication "Ageing in India" based on a national seminar organized by the Tata Institutes of Social Sciences. Several papers are enclosed on aspects of gerontology in India. The volume was edited by K.G. Desai[7]. Desai in the foreword note to this volume dwelt on "the need of examining the problems of the elderly in India". Included in this volume are papers on: "Demographic Aspects on Ageing in India"[8], Health Problems of the Aged[9], "Health services for the Aged in India – An International Perspective[10], "On Some Aspects of Ageing in India"[11], "Social Aspects of Ageing"[12], "Social Welfare Services for the Aged in India"[13], "Illness among the Aged"[14], Research Reports – "Situation of the Aged.[15] It is to be noted that among the authors of these papers some had already initiated studies on aged in India during late seventies.

In recent years, some studies have been completed on specific topic related to aged in India. Mention may be made on Bhatia[16], R. Verma[17], Sinha[18], Chadha, Shah and Mahajan[19] and Sinha[20]. This study may fulfill some gaps in the study of ageing in Uttar Pradesh.

Aged Population in India

Over the decades in the country our total population is increasing, and so also the proportion of the aged in the population is increasing. According to the *Census of India,* (1981), the total population of aged in the country was around 42 millions (4.2 crores). In 1971 it was about 28 millions stated differently, in 1971 only 5.12 per cent of country's population was 60 years and above; in 1981 this percentage rose to 6.4. In the past two censuses the proportion comes around 7.5 per cent.

The above clearly indicate the trend that the number of aged in coming decades would increase significantly. The demographers have projected around 80 millions aged population in India by the 2020 A.D. It is interesting to note that this projected figure is almost equal to the population of a few European nations viz. Germany.

For our immediate purpose 'sixty' years has been considered as the cut off point. In other words, persons of 60 years and above have been considered to constitute "old persons" go pay pf students away teaching.

II

Aged Population in India

Over the decades in the country our total population is increasing, and so also the proportion of the aged (60 yrs. phase) in the population is increasing. According to the *Census of India (1981)*, the total population of aged in the country was around 42 millions (4.2 crores). In 1971 it was about 2.8 millions. Stated differently, in 1971 only 5.12 per cent of county's population was 60 years and above; in 1981 this percentage rose to 6.4. In the past two censuses the proportion comes around 7.5 per cent (75 millions in 2001).

The above clearly indicates the trend that the number of aged in coming decades would increase significantly. The demographers have projected around 177 millions aged population in India by the 2025 A.D. It is interesting to note that this projected figure is almost equal to the population of a few European nations, viz., In sociological terms. Population aging is profound, having major implications for all faces of making.

Differential Aged Population

A comparative look at the distribution of the population over 10-year period in terms of broad age-groups makes it clear that there has been an increase of aged population both in urban and rural areas. As per figures in rural areas the increase is 28.8 per cent in urban areas it is 45.7 per cent; overall an increase of 31.76 per cent is apparent. When proportion of old to general population is considered we get that in 1971 rural areas had a higher population of persons 60 years and above that the urban areas (4.3%); in 1981 the proportion of aged to general population was 4.6 per cent for urban area. Percentage has reached 6 per cent in urban areas during 1981-2001.

Sex Ratio

For the aged population we find 112 in 1991, 110 in 1981, and 109.1 in 1971. In other words, more males over 59 years are residing in urban areas.

Marital Status

Less than 3 per cent of both males and females in the 60+ age group found to be 'never married. Further, the proportion of widows in the 60+femalses population is almost three times the proportion of widowers in the 60+ male populations. The main reason for this difference is that males who loss their wives remarry to a much greater extent than the women, who loss their husband. In this respect difference between rural and urban areas is very little.

Longevity

Life Tables prepared by demographers clearly indicate that since the turn of the present century longevity after 50 years in India has been increasing. As of estimated figure, a person of age 50 years could expect to live for another 19.5 years. This is an index of having more aged in India in coming decades. Improved health standards, lower infant mortality, and growing medical facilities have contributed to the longevity of people in general and above 50 years particular.

Aged Population in Uttar Pradesh

Among all states in the country, Uttar Pradesh is the longest in terms of its population. As per Census of 2001, 16.44 per cent India's total population resides in U.P. It had centered of a little over 138 million (13.8 crores) in 1991. A significant population of this population belongs to the persons of 60 years and above.

In 1981, nearly 20 million persons were recorded residing in urban areas of U.P.; of this, a little over one million persons were of 606+year's age-groups. This constitutes 5.4 per cent aged population of U.P. urban areas.

A comparison of Census data clearly indicates a decreasing trend in the percentage of population in descending order of age brackets. In other words, of the total aged population of urban U.P., nearly 42 per cent is of persons of 60-64 years age group, and nearly 19 per cent is of 70-74 years age group. Less than one per cent is of 95-104 years age group in urban areas of the state.

Aged Population in Western U.P.

Since this research addresses itself to the study of aged in the urban plain areas of western U.P. it is relevant to present some population statistics on 11 sample districts. Because of non-availability desired census data (1991 and 2001) the analysis presented below is based on the Census data of 1981.

Out of 63 twenty of them fall in plains of western Uttar Pradesh. From these, eleven districts were purposely selected for the present study. They are: Allahabad, Ferozabad, Agra, Mathura, Bijnore, Aligarh, Meerut, Dehradun, Moradabad, Bareilly and Bullandsahar.

Distribution of Aged Population in Sample Districts

Table 1 presents the distribution of population in eleven selected districts of this study. For a proper understanding of this situation the distribution has been recorded under age-group categories formed on the basis of age intervals, viz. 60-64, 65-69, 70-74, 75-79, 80-84, 85-89, 90-94, 95-99 and 100-104.

Of all sample districts, Agra has nearly 14% aged person (51,060). A little less than this percentage is that of Meerut city. It is important to note that Mathura which is usually regarded as the city of older devotees has the lowest percentage of age population among the sample districts. (Many old persons are residing in Mathura temporarily hence they are treated as visitors to this holy place). Nearly 43% of the population falls within the age group of 60-64 years; twenty one per cent to 65-69; clearly the population decreases as we move on next age-groups.

However, in the last age group category (100-104 years), except for Agra, Mathura, Dehradun all other districts contain more persons than the preceding age-group. We may therefore conclude that these districts contain more persons of advanced ages.

III

The Problem and Objectives of the Study

The main objectives of the study are:

1. to look into the living conditions of the aged 60 years and above) belonging to urban ecology.
2. to examine into the role and status of the aged in the household and to study their inter-personal relations in family groups having one or more aged;
3. to study those progressive physiological changes which often accompany the old age vis-à-vis nutritional, health, and occupational factors which influence the process of ageing;
4. to study economic, health, socio-psychological problems of the aged;
5. to analyse the attitudes of the aged towards family and society;
6. to analyse the attitude of the family members towards the aged;
7. to analyse the level of participation among the aged in family's community's and welfare organizations;
8. to study the coping mechanism available to the aged facing problems within the family and community;
9. to suggest ways and means which elderly people can adopt to make themselves useful and in contributing to the service of the society.

Research Design

The research technique employed in the present study is of "social survey approach" usually following in applied researches in sociology.

The Universe

The universe of the study consists of persons of age groups 60 years and above residing in urban areas of twenty districts of western Uttar Pradesh. The universe of old age population is characterized by mutually quasi-self-supporting aged population and dependent aged population.

Sample

Keeping in view the problem and objectives of study at hand we have drawn samples from the urban population of aged living in non-institutional homes. In a study like this it is difficult to meet the scientific requirement of having appropriate number of cases in the sample set alone the ideal of testing each unit of population. Because of the nature of universe we have followed 'incidental-cum-purposive' sampling technique and selection of sample is made on above basis coupled with them willingness to make themselves available for interviewing. Scientific and research considerations led us to fix a target of selecting 450 persons. (Eleven districts of western U.P., which were chosen for study were pieked up randomly assuming that they could represent the state and admit no bias.

Regarding the procedure followed in selection household samples we have followed non-probability method. In other words, our sample is purposive. In the present situation because of non-availability of complete units of universe it has been rather very difficult to draw sample using the random method.

Tools for Collection of Data

The main tools employed in the present survey are *interview-schedules* and *observations*. In order to get the interview-schedule completed by the sample of aged people the method of informal discussion was resorted to in cases where necessary. The responses were recorded either by the sample units (respondents) themselves or by the investigator. Care was taken no distortion entered to cause error-variance. Items of Interview-schedule were carefully prepared and pre-tested. Over five dozen case studies were also prepared.

IV

Discussion & Finding

Keeping in view the general and specific objectives stated above, data were collected from 440 respondents of eleven districts of Uttar Pradesh. By and large our respondents were in normal condition. Because of paucity of space relevant statistical data are presented in fewer tables in the Appendix I, would briefly refer to statistical data drawn from tabulated figures. Since my purpose is to provoke interest in the consideration of gerontological dimensions, I will present findings in order of the objective set out above.

OBJECTIVE FIRST

To Look into the Living Conditions of the Aged in Urban Areas

The study reveals that over 75 per cent aged have independent households, whereas the remaining 25 per cent live in dependent households. Most of the aged lives in Extended-family-types. Some of course prefer to live in nuclear family. (Refer Table 1).

Majority of the aged is found residing in flats and kucha-pucca mixed houses. In these housing types the number of rooms varies from two to four. Most of the aged has independent rooms with facilities like water taps, electricity and toilet. Many aged have own houses.

OBJECTIVE-SECOND

To Look into the Role and Status of the Aged in the Household as well as their Interpersonal Relationships

Status and role are conceptually inter-related concepts, which signify one's social position and role played by the member in the group. In context of the present study we have inferred the social position of the aged in terms of decision inferred the social position of the aged in terms of decision making process in the household and common issues of conversation services rendered by the persons, reasons for their liking or disliking household members.

Table 1
Living Arrangements of the Respondents

Sl. No.	Question Items	Total No. of Eleven Districts	%
1.	Alone	22	5.00
2.	Nuclear variety (H/W or both with unmarried children)	104	23.64
3.	Extended variety		
	1. Joint Family (H/W or both with).		
	(a) Married sons and their spouses.	268	60.91
	(b) Married brothers and their spouses.	4	0.90
	2. Composite Extended variety. (H/W or both with)		
	(a) Married daughter and their spouses	22	5.00
	(b) With married sister and their spouses.	10	2.28
	(c) With other relatives	6	1.37
	(d) With non relatives	4	0.90
	Total	440	100.00

The study reveals that in cases of independent house-hold, decision making process is regulated by the aged themselves whether the matter concerns social issues or children's future career, but in the cases of dependent household mostly the responsibilities rest with the person concerned. Interpersonal relationships among the members of dependent households are of general nature. In other words, matters related to non-financial issues are discussed with the aged persons but when in matters wherein finances are involved they are not consulted. (Refer Table 2).

OBJECTIVE-THIRD

To know Health Problems of the Aged

Deterioration in general physique, problems with vision and hearing, pain in joints are the frequently occurring disorders of the aged. Majority of the aged people has no problem with regard to quantity and quality of note that more than half of the aged population did not have serious problems with their health. During the past three years they were seldom required to seem medical care. However, about 40% of the aged people reported to be suffering from some or the other minor disorders, such as occasional blood pressure, coughing, mild diabetes or symptomatic jaundice, etc. This corroborated our observation of Respondents during the field study (Refer Table 3).

Table 2
Common Issues For Family Conversation

Sl. No.	*Question Items*	*No.*	*%*
1.	Domestic	151	25.46
2.	Health Problem	45	7.59
3.	Economic	43	7.25
4.	Religious	34	5.73
5.	Political	28	4.72
6.	Social	93	15.68
7.	Job related	18	3.03
8.	Education	25	4.21
9.	Coming Problem	18	3.03
10.	Career	08	1.35
11.	Entertainment	30	5.06
		17	3.87
12.	Different topics	83	14.00
	Total	593	100.00

Table 3
Respondents' Activities (Daily Walk)

Sl. No.		*Question Items*	*No.*	*%*
1.	A	No.	176	40.00
2.	B	Occasionally	31	7.05
3.	C	Yes	283	52.95
		Total	593	100.00

OBJECTIVE-FOURTH

To Examine Problems of the Aged

In this study various problems related to aged persons' economic, health, social and psychological conditions are discussed.

The study reveals that about 70 per cent of the aged sample had immovable property (Refer Table 4). Some retired aged, at the time of data collection had not received their provident fund etc. from the government or other bodies they had been serving. Therefore they had to depend on other sources income for their livelihood. 70 per cent aged have bank accounts. Their income patterns are varied (Refer Table 4.1). Problems related to the health of aged people have already been discussed above.

Table 4
Respondents' Assets

Sl. No.	*Question Items*	*No.*	*%*
1.	No Property	127	28.86
2.	Property	313	71.14
3.	A- Plot	62	15.08
	B- Land	75	18.25
	C- House	271	65.94
	D- Others	03	0.73

Table 4.1
Income Pattern of The Respondents

Income Group (Rs.)	*No.*	*%*
001 - 1000	95	26.60
1001 - 2000	106	24.09
2001 - 3000	43	9.75
3001 - 4000	38	8.64
4001 - 5000	33	7.50
5001 - 6000	30	6.82
7001 - 8000	22	5.00
8001 - 9000	12	2.73
9001 - 10000	10	2.27
10000 - up	27	6.14
No. Response	24	5.45
Total	440	100.00

Aged with dependent children are worried about their dependents' employment and marriage. Some aged are found unhappy with the behaviour or their own sons and daughters. Children are perceived as not paying adequate attention to them. "Younger generations do not like to spend time with older people." This is the general opinion expressed by the aged people who were interviewed for the purpose of this study.

It is relevant to note that some of the aged do not get adequate sleep without any physical or pathological reasons but due to the fact that they think much about the problems of their family and keep anxious. In other words, the present environment pf the household is not perceived, by the aged, congenial for living a happy life. Some of them feel depressed and alienated in the household. (Table 5).

Table 5
Reasons for not Living with Own Relatives

Sl. No.	*Question Items*	*No.*	*%*
1.	Alone	03	3.57
2.	Division of property	32	38.09
3.	Not lived in family	18	21.43
4.	Banishment	02	2.38
5.	Attitude deference	05	5.59
6.	Members living outside	17	20.24
7.	Personal health	02	2.38
8.	Left the place	01	1.19
9.	Economic	02	2.38
10.	Barren	02	2.38
	Total	84	100.00

OBJECTIVE-FIFTH

To Analyse the Attitude of the Aged Towards Family and Society

The present study reveals that majority of the old persons like to help members of the family in more than one ways. About 55 per cent aged have stated that they could be useful to the family in matters of household economy. Others feel that they can render their assistance to children education, and physical labour involving household chores.

The attitude of the ageing population towards society and the problems that infest it viz., corruption, rising price, violence, social injustice, unemployment, casteism, atrocities, and many other facts of social evils are reflected in Table 6. These are expressed in the form of their views towards each of these.

Forty per cent old people felt that in years to come the social situation will deteriorate rather than improve. In this way they hold apathetic attitudes.

OBJECTIVE- SIXTH

To Analyse the Attitude of the Family Members Towards the Aged

What family feels about the aged is an important issue. In this study the opinion was sought from those heads of the households in which older people were residing. It was found that 60 per cent

Table 6
Respondents' Perception of Social Problems

Sl. No.	*Problems*	*Total Preferences*		
		Ist	*IInd*	*IIIrd*
1.	Poverty	27	34	28
2.	Corruption	27	28	29
3.	Price Increase	41	29	31
4.	Injustice	21	26	23
5.	Decline in Moral Value	21	26	21
6.	Communal Riots	25	27	26
7.	Violence and Terrorism	17	24	20
8.	Illiteracy	25	25	24
9.	Unemployment	34	21	26
10.	Defective Education Policy	16	15	13
11.	Lock of Religious Activity	09	18	09
12.	Casteism	29	26	24
13.	Pollution	09	10	17
14.	Drug Addiction	07	09	18
15.	Population Increase	33	23	22
16.	Child Marriage	03	06	16
17.	Cruelty with Women Including Dowries	37	31	29
18.	Wrong Reservation Policy	30	34	36
19.	Others	29	28	29
	Total	440	440	440

heads stated their relationship with the aged people as "normal". About 15 per cent heads expressed their relation with old members of the family as "bad". About 25 per cent however, opined having good relationship with the older persons. In this connection some case studies were prepared to ascertain the specific views of the members of those household in which aged couples were living with married aged- couples, have been living independently although they had married sons. (These cases in narrative form have been included in case studies). Below a few lines have been extracted from the case studies, which reflect the views of the present generation towards older people.

1. "They have lived enough, now it is the time for them to live alone and allow us to enjoy our lives..."
2. "...the older people must compromise those who do not will suffer...."
3. "They are unproductive dead wood...they must take rest now..."
4. "...they are vegetables, one must care them".

5. "...consigning the age to old age home would not serve.. " They should not be left in isolation away from the family. The present generation must realize this."
6. "...they are the best persons to serve as guides..."
7. "...Employed sons should not claim hose-rent allowance if they are living in parent's houses. In such cases HRA should be given to age parents."
8. "Younger generation should not demand share in the income from their parents' property during their life time.
9. "...Members of younger generation must not demand the property of parent..."

OBJECTIVE-SEVENTH

To Examines the Extent of Participation Among the Aged on Familial, Community and Social Efforts

Reference to the services rendered by the old person has already been made earlier under objective-5. Specific services which older people are ready to offer are listed below.

Around six per cent population likes to involve themselves in household activities normally undertaken by their wives sons and grandsons. A significant percentage is of persons who wish to help family members in all possible ways, when and if required (Refer Table 7).

Table 7
Services Rendered by Respondents to the Family

Sl. No.	*Question Items*	*No.*	*%*
1.	Alone	22	5.00
2.	With wife/husband	111	25.23
3.	With son	85	19.32
4.	With daughter	28	6.36
5.	With grand son	71	16.14
6.	With grand daughter	45	10.23
7.	With brother	14	3.18
8.	With sister	01	0.23
9.	With daughter-in-law	20	4.54
10.	With nephew	10	2.27
11.	Others 1	33	7.50
12.	Others 2	00	0.00
	Total	440	100.00

More than one fourth of the aged population has a wide friend circle; therefore, they like to share activities with friends in the neighborhood. About 10% of the old people are prepared to help the society through various organizations and association. In other words, they very much like to get associated with voluntary teams and organizations to assist adult literacy programmes, educating slum dwellers, helping blinds in becoming self-dependent and undertaking, helping blinds in becoming self-dependent and undertaking to do and participate in other community-services related activities.

Some of the old people like to keep themselves involved in those activities or which they had been doing earlier, e.g. teaching, supervising the jobs of others and doing accountancy. A few people like to become legal advisors and homeopath doctors. Few old persons however like to spend time by themselves that is listening to radio, watching TV, reading magazines, smoking and drinking as also travelling.

OBJECTIVE-EIGHTH

To Analyse the Coping Mechanism Available to the Aged Facing Problems within the Family and Community

Older persons from unhappy households prefer to live in old-age centers if made available to them. It is to be noted that except in Mathura, in none of the districts included in this survey, have facilities of old-age-homes are available. Cases of older couples living in rented houses or with distant relations in separate households may be considered as institutional-old-persons. It is to be noted that in majority of cases such older persons do own houses but they were rented to others. In this was living way from their married sons is one of the mechanisms through which older people cope with the domestic problems of joint households. Other coping mechanisms are employing non-skilled persons as assistants, proceeding pleasant behaviour towards the members of the household and minimizing their expectations from others including children.

OBJECTIVE-NINETH

To Examine the ways and Means which Elderly People Employ to Serve Society for its Benefit

On the basis of finding with respect to the objectives of the study we can infer that aged people can worth society by their services in a number of ways. Some specific programmes for serving the society have been noted but not reported here. The old could help the society in some following ways:

1. Helping in marriage negotiations,
2. by proving family-counseling,
3. by helping in literacy projects,
4. by helping the blind and reading out books to them,
5. by doing sitting or running baby crèches,
6. by visiting the lonely and helpless in hospitals,
7. by doing social forestry in urban areas,
8. by helping to rehabilitate drug addicts.

SUGGESTIONS AND RECOMMENDATION

For the Aged

1. Utilizing various methods of audio-visual media such as newspapers, radio, T.V., V.C.R., etc. older people should develop awareness that they can and need to work for themselves. Financially sound and physically fit persons of older age-group can organize small groups work teams in their localities to help other fellow of their age group and contribute their bit to the service of society and community in larger interest.
2. In accordance with the current trends older people should be made to know how to adjust and compromise with the younger generation. Many know about this but some do not.
3. Concerned persons should provide information in respect of all social welfare schemes launched by the government and voluntary agencies in their localities.

For the Government Agencies

Although the government has provided some support and services to older persons other than the monthly pensions, some special facilities need to be created for the entire aged population. These facilities and services could be as below:

(i) Special counters at banks, post offices, railways, bus-stands, hospitals and judicial courts.

(ii) Opening of geriatric wards in government medical colleges and hospitals with specialists, provision should be made exclusive service for the aged people on certain days of the weeks as they cannot stand in the queue. The aged need be given cheaper medical treatment, if not free.

(iii) Except for the very old persons all others must do some works according to their capacity. Pension should be restricted to the very old only.

(iv) National Policy for the Aged should be formulated.

(v) Special aids be provided to the voluntary agencies working exclusively for the aged.

For the Voluntary Organizations

Voluntary organizations must come up with some concrete programmes for the "growing aged population" in the country. Some suggestions in this regard are as follows:

1. In smaller cities 'Day Care Centers' (DCC) be opened for the aged. Some DCC may be converted into homes for aged, if required.
2. Voluntary organizations should establish Hobby centers (HC) in different localities.
3. Some organizations should bring out the publication of weekly or monthly magazines for children and old persons. New generation must respect elders and the old must know and accommodate the views of the young.
4. As for as possible voluntary agencies should allocate the tasks to aged persons according to their capabilities and potentiality for their own benefit and to keep them engaged.
5. Voluntary organization should keep it in view that they are not doing just routine services to the aged but their effort is to know what the aged can do for the society and for them. In other words, in their programmes participants should include both young and old learners and teachers.

Suggestion for the Professional Researchers

Micro studies related to the old age problem of societies at various levels should be undertaken all over the country. Some of the suggested problems for investigation are as follows:

1. Psychology of the aged.
2. Problem for single and childless couples,
3. Efficacy of the services for the aged,
4. Health and nutritional studies,
5. Profiles of case studies of widows and widowers,
6. Recreations problems of the aged,
7. Evaluation of old-age-benefit programme.

NOTES & REFERENCES

1. Desai, K.G. and Naik R.D.: (Ed.) Problems of Retired People in Greater Bombay. *Ageing in India,* Tata Institute of Social Sciences, Bombay, 1982: 123-139.
2. D'Souza Victor S.: Changes in Social Structure and Changing Roles of Older People in India. *Sociology and Social Research,* 55. 1971.
3. Delhi School of Social Work; *Study of the Aged in India.* University of Delhi, 1973.
4. Soodan, K.S.: *Ageing in India,* Calcutta: T.K. Mukerjee Minerva Association (Pvt.) Ltd., 1975.
5. Desai, K.G. and Bhalla, R.: *Social Situation of the Aged,* Tata Institute of Social Sciences, Bombay, 1978.
6. Mishra, Saraswati: *Social Adjustment in Old Age* (A Case Study of Retired Government Employees Living in Chandigarh, Unpublished Ph.D. thesis, University of Punjab, 1976.
7. Desai, K.G. (Ed.): *Ageing in India.* Tata Institute of Social Sciences, Bombay, 1982.
8. Bhende, A.A.: Demographic Aspects of Ageing in India *in Ageing in India,* 1982, 99 3-18.
9. Pathak, J.D.: Health Problem of the Aged; Medical Research Centre, Bombay Hospital Trust Bombay. *In Ageing in India,* 1982, pp. 32-42.
10. Sahni, A.: Health Services for the Aged in India: An International Persepective". *In Ageing in India,* 1982, pp. 54-68.
11. Parthasarthy, N.R.: On Some Aspects of Ageing in India, *Indian Journal of Social Work.*40 (4) 1980, pp. 381-368.
12. Ranade, S.N.: Social Aspects of Ageing in India *in Ageing in India.* 1982, pp. 80-88.
13. Bose, A.B.: *Social Welfare Services for the Aged.* P.R.E.M, Division, Ministry of Welfare, Government of India, *Ageing in India* 1982, pp. 109-116.

14. Sharma, U.: Illness Among the Aged, Ph.D. Thesis, Lucknow University, 1975.
15. Desai K.G.: Research Report Situation of the Aged in *Ageing in India*, 1982, pp. 140-142.
16. Bhatia, H.S. *Ageing and Society* (A Sociological Study of Retired Public Servants). The Arya's Book Center, Udaipur, 1983.
17. Verma, R.: Personality Change and Adjustment in Ageing, Ph.D. Thesis, Banaras Hindu University, 1980.
18. Sinha, J.N.P.: *Problem of Ageing*, Classical Publications, 1989.
19. Mahajan, A. Chandha N.K. and Shah S.: Leisure Time Activities Among the Aged; A Comparative Study, Utkal University, 1991.
20. Sinha, Suman Rani: Olders in Allahabad District: A Sociological Study, A. D. Phil. dissertation, Allahabad University under the synopsis of A.R.N. Srivastava, (1995). Its Hindi version has been published by K.K. Publications, Katra, Allahabad in 2001.

5

RURAL AGED: LIVING ARRANGEMENTS, PROBLEMS AND CARE

Arvind K. Joshi

Introduction

The definition of the 'aged' peoples varies from country to country but there is one similarity that all over the world the population of the aged is increasing relative to the level of development. In India too, the population of the aged, i.e., those of the age group of 60 years and above, is on the increase. In 1971, they were 28 millions and in 1981, 42 millions, in 1999, 56 millions and in 2001, the figure stood at 75 million. It is expected that in 2025 their population will be of the order of 177 millions.[1]It is obvious that a 'grey wave' may soon sweep over the country. Not only this, but by 2050, the number of older persons in the world will exceed the number of young for the first time in the history.[2]

If, on the one hand, the population of the aged say 60 years plus population has increased over the successive decades, on the other hand, the traditional family/community based support system for the aged has not only weakened but started showing signs of complete collapse.

Population ageing is affecting every single individual of the society. The UN Report in its major findings has rightly pointed out that :

(i) "The steady increase of older age group in national populations, both in absolute numbers and in relation to the working age population has a direct bearing on the inter-generational and intra-generational equity and solidarity that are the foundations of society,

(ii) Population ageing is profound, having major consequences and implications for all facets of human life. In the economic area population ageing will have an impact on economic growth, savings, investment and consumption, labour markets, pensions, taxation and inter-generational transfers. In the social spheres, population ageing affects health and health-care, family composition and living arrangements, housing and migration. In the political arena, population ageing can influence voting patterns and representations."[3]

The age dependency ratio and the life expectancy at birth have been gradually increasing in India. The current demographic scenario indicates that mortality has declined significantly and continues to show signs of further decline (Refer to Table 1).

Table 1
Life Expectancy At Birth In India

Census Year	*Sex*	*Expectancy at Birth*
1951	M	32.5
	F	31.7
1961	M	41.9
	F	40.6
1971	M	47.1
	F	45.6
1981	M	54.8
	F	52.0
1991	M	60.8
	F	61.7
2001@	M	62.4
	F	63.4

@ Projected by RGI in Family Welfare Programme in India Year Book 1996-97, Central Bureau of Health Intelligence, Ministry of Health and Family Welfare, Government of India, New Delhi, 1998. *SOURCE*: Census of India, 2001.

The increasing population of the elderly makes it clear that the problems of ageing shall become visible very soon in India's population. On the other hand, the study of Gerontology and the study of Sociology of Ageing are in its infancy in India. Sociologists, demographers, economists and policy makers, etc. have started to think about the various problems, strategies and policies to adopt for the steadily increasing elderly population. Several studies have been conducted in Indian context also, for example, Bose and Gangarade (1968)[4], Sharma (1969,1971)[5], Vishwanathan (1969)[6], Singhi (1970)[7], D'Souza (1971,1984)[8], Desai and Naik (1973)[9], Vatuk (1975,1980)[10], Soodan (1975)[11], Parthasarthy (1980)[12], D'Souza, A (1982)[13], Bhatia (1983)[14], Dak and Sharma (1987)[15], Punia et.al. (1987)[16], Mahajan (1987)[17], Mehta (1987)[18], Nagla (1987) [19], Rajeshwar Prasad (1987)[20], Sangwan (1987)[21] Basu and Basu (1987)[22], Shayam (1988)[23] Gulati (1989)[24], Rajan (1989)[25], Sarkar (1989)[26], Sarin (1990 [27], Kumar S. Vijaya (1991)[28], Mahadevan, et al (1992)[29],Dhillon (1992)[30], Yadava et.al. (1996)[31],etc. The Ministry of Welfare, Government of India had also sponsored studies on problems of the aged in 1990. The studies have been completed by several scholars[32] (like Khan, Muthayya and Aneesuddin, Hussain, Shah and Joshi, Upadhyay, Gurumurthy, Nayar and Shanthakumari, Mukherjee, Mishra, Dandekar, Sinha, Sati, Raja, Ahmed, Srivastava) of various important Universities and research institutes in various Indian states. Kohli[33] has compiled the findings of these studies.

In this empty nest stage[34] of the life cycle, the person's social obligations, privileges and expectations undergo a change.[35] In other words, we can say that old age is a shift in an individual's position from active social participation to significant decline in role performance and from economic self-sufficiency to economic dependence.[36] The lack of economic power in the hands of the old led to many intra- familial conflicts. The aged feel lonely, dependent and marginalized. At present, ageing has become a social problem because socio-economic shifts are affecting the ability of the family to continue with traditional care giving role towards elders.[37] The declaration of 1982 as the International Year of the Aged by United Nations and the year 2000 as the National Year for Older Persons by the Government of India shows the seriousness of the problem of old age the world over.

Aged commanded great respect due to the traditional norms and values of Indian society. Choudhry[38] is correct in saying that 'it was indicative of the gratitude of the younger generation towards their parents and grandparents for bearing and rearing.

Another rationale for the respect and regard for elders was their wisdom and experience, which was supposed to rub off of the next generation.'

In the traditional Indian society the better status of the elderly was due to the value system, which contains the following features.[39]

(i) Reverence for age in an Indian family;

(ii) Premium on wisdom and experience of the elderly as opposed to knowledge and information;

(iii) Strong joint family system and sound protection offered by it;

(iv) Pride in parenthood and grand parenthood and great expectations from the children;

(v) Claim for love and affection from immediate relations;

(vi) Respect for the institution of marriage and disapproval of divorce;

(vii) Contentment in old age; and

(viii) Looking beyond in search of peace and faith in God.

The Hindu Joint family system has a built in mechanism which helps prevent some of the problems of the elderly, it provides "the common hearth funda'" which ensured social security to them and took proper care of them. They were the heads of the households and played a dominant role in various spheres of life. They were considered to be the pioneer in every walk of life. In the agrarian societies they were the patriarch and executive head of household by virtue of the ownership of land and their being the lighthouse of knowledge, wisdom, sagacity and experience. Due to this in rural India an aged person occupies a vantage position in the family domain and even in community affairs. The elderly persons generally constituted the traditional panchayat, though mostly they were men. So long as they maintained normal health according to the culturally prescribed norms, they virtually dictated terms for all the socio-economic and cultural matters. The aged were never considered as liabilities.

But now the situation has undergone a big change due to several factors. In joint families too, the situation is altogether different now. There is a growing tendency among new generation to deviate from this traditional attitude. Not only this the institution of joint family has started disintegrating rapidly due to recent changes in social values, social structure and economy resulting from industrialization and urbanization and consequent mobility. Poverty, unemployment, under-employment and inflation have rendered the family members unable to discharge their duties to the aged. This has seriously affected the situation of senior citizens in society. Neither they have the earlier position of importance in the family and community, nor are they looked after the way it was done earlier. Aged people are looked upon as useless, non-productive, rigid and burdensome. Not only this, the desertion of old parents has shot up as a serious problem. Evidently, the problem is getting more acute in rural regions and sections of society prone to migration in search of work and employment. Apparently, the problem must be more acute among the asset-less labouring class who cannot earn beyond what is required for their own survival in the short run.

Objectives

The aims of the present study are:

(i) to portray the living arrangements of the aged in rural settings;

(ii) to understand their various problems such as the economic, health, socio-psychological, etc; and

(iii) to examine the adequacy of the social security measures.

Universe and Sampling

An urbanising rural area Sewapuri in the proximity of Varanasi city was purposely selected for the study.

Socio-economic Background of the Study Area

The Sewapuri Block of the Varanasi District lies between the Varanasi city and Bhadohi, the premier carpet industries centre in eastern U.P. The direct road link between Varanasi and Bhadohi runs east -west through the block area from one end to the other. Two other link roads, i.e., Kalika Bazar-Thathra on the G.T. Road and Jansa-Rameshwar link the Block villages with important Highways. These communication lines especially Varanasi-Bhadohi road, have visibly transformed the entire block area. The impact of the road links and other infrastructure facilities is clearly visible on village settlement pattern, economy, and occupational structure and on other institutions.

Due to factors like faster growth of population and increasing demand for non-agricultural purposes, land has been excessively over- burdened. Therefore, availability of agricultural land per cultivating household is very low. Thus, there is a preponderance of uneconomic, marginal and tiny land holdings. On the other hand, landlessness has also increased. This has negatively affected the agro-based economy of the area. Land holding pattern is not suitable for capitalistic farming and employment generation in agriculture. In this area, there is geographical constraint for agricultural modernization and the presence of socio-structural constraints has also important consequences. The majority of larger land holdings are possessed by the traditionally non- cultivating higher castes, viz., Bhumihars and Rajputs in particular. Evidently, they do have the capacity to raise capital for modern farm machinery and better technology but face the problem of labour and lack of appropriate attitude as well.[40] Their new generation, especially the educated ones are reluctant to do agricultural operation.

The agrarian relations still carry on the hangover of the old feudalistic order. The trend observed is that the traditional agricultural labourers, mostly dalit (oppressed class) have shifted to carpet weaving, or to silk sari weaving. Their place has been taken by inter-state migrant labour for which the landowners have a distinct preference. There is a significant activity in the household industry sector that is mainly inter-related with Bhadohi-based carpet weaving industry, Lohata-based Banarasi sari weaving and wire-knitting industry, etc. Rural industrialization is affecting several aspects of day-to-day life. Owing to all these factors the nature of land use is changing fast especially along the roadside villages, both along the G.T. Road and the Varanasi-Bhadohi Road. String of rural market centres has developed. At present, there are 10 rural market centres operating. However, the work and wages available in the industrial sectors are irregular and low. Thus, in spite of these changes, the labourers continue to remain poor.

Sampling

The study was conducted in the five villages, namely Gajepur, Haribhannpur, Odarhan, Uparwar and Danupur of Sewapuri

Block. These villages were at random selected for investigation. For the purpose of this study men who have attained the age of 60 and above are considered elderly. We have used the Census method and visited all the families (total number was 843) to find out the number of elderly population. We identified 580 aged persons: 310 male and 270 female. Their percentage in the total population of the 5 villages (7213 persons) comes to 8.04, which is higher than the national average. Further, on consideration of availability of respondents during the rather short span of field data collection, in all 260 elderly persons (all males), so identified could be interviewed.

Data Collection

Both primary and secondary sources of data were used for the purpose of the study. Secondary data was collected from the available published and unpublished material on the aged, i.e., Census reports, UN Reports, Reports of different NG0s, Project Reports, etc. Empirical data were collected with the help of semi-structured interview-schedule by the researcher himself. It took on an average two hours to complete one interview-schedule.

Major Findings

We can put together the major findings of this study under different headings as per the objectives framed for this micro study.

Personal Background of the Respondents

In rural India, caste system still dominates the socio-cultural life - the functions, status, opportunities etc. of the villagers. The upper caste people have larger land-holdings, joint families, comparatively better education and a different culture of thinking and behaviour. On the other hand, people of lower caste posses low social economic status, nuclear family, sometimes broken family also and several other handicaps and obstacles towards greater vertical mobility. Many of the poor aged persons continue to do hard and labour-intensive work for their survival.

Cent per cent respondents of this study are Hindus. Caste- wise we can classify them into three broad categories (See Table 2).

It is obvious from the table that 28.1 per cent respondents belong to the general or upper castes, 51.9 per cent backward castes and the rest of the respondents (20%) belong to scheduled castes.

Table 2
Caste Wise Distribution of the Respondents

Caste	*Frequency*	*Percentage*
General or Upper Castes (Brahmin, Kshatriya, Bhumihar, Kayastha, Bania, etc.)	73	28.1
Backward Castes (Yadava, Kurmi, Koiri, Gaderiya, etc.)	135	51.9
Scheduled Castes (Chamar, Dhobi, Paasi, Mushar, etc.)	52	20.0
Total	260	100.0

The profile of the aged population that emerges is that a majority of them (51.2) were of the age group of 61-65 years; 24.5 per cent were of the age of 66-70 years; 15.0 per cent were of the age of 71-75 years; 7.7 per cent were of the age of 76-80 years and 1.6 per cent was of the age of above 80 years.

The large majority (71.5%) were found to be married and still have their spouses alive, 28.0 per cent were widowed (and only 0.5 per cent were remarried). None of the respondents were divorcee or deserted.

The illiterates comprise 52.2 per cent, 15.3 per cent were simply literate, 16.3 per cent were middle school, 8.1 per cent were matriculates, 7.1 per cent were intermediate, 1.0 per cent were graduates.

Family members' behaviour is also associated with the economic contribution of the aged. The aged people who are contributing through pension and/or other retirement benefits or doing business or agricultural work or engaged in some sorts of economic activities are considered as 'assets' and they command respect and are looked after fairly well by the others in the joint family. On the other hand, the persons who have no income are treated miserably. In majority of the cases, they have to face negligence and seclusion: Due to economic compulsion, a large percentage of the aged has to engage him in economically gainful work that is beyond their physical capacity.

As far the occupational background, 9.2 per cent were in Government service, 43.9 per cent were labourers, 41.8 per cent were doing agriculture and rest (5.1%) of them had other occupations. At present, 18.3 per cent respondents were totally dependent on other family members due to the old-old age. The rest of the respondents, who are still working despite their old age, are earning meagre amount per month, but as it often happens in the rural economy, excepting for those in service/pensioners, their contribution to family income is not accounted for.

Landed property is an important factor in keeping the family together. As such the joint family tradition is still stronger among the property-owning higher castes than in landless lower castes. Among the former, the head of the family remains the owner of the entire property till his death and this influences the attitude of the family members towards him; he generally receives proper attention and care from the members.

Cent per cent respondents owned some landed property in the same village where they were living. But the average area owned is less than a *bigha* (i.e., less than 0.66 acres). Cent per cent of respondents owned house [pukka (59%), semi-pukka (31%) and jhopari (thatched) (10%).

Living Arrangements of the Aged

It is found that the majority of the aged (99%) preferred to live in their own/ancestral homes and also with their sons. Cent per cent aged were residing with their families in their own houses but the quality of housing is generally low. Tap water and toilet facility were available to only less than 5 per cent in the houses. They (90%) had the practice of defecating in the open fields. They got water from public hand pump or well. Electricity is there in the houses of about 40 per cent of the respondents.

Due to several factors like migration, family disputes, economic necessities, etc. family is disintegrating in the rural areas. In our study we have found that almost in equal proportions (46.5%) aged persons were residing in nuclear and joint families. 7 per cent aged were living in intermediate families. The joint families are there but in most of the families, only parents and their married son(s) and his/their wife/wives and offspring were residing together. It was found that 5 per cent aged widowers were living singly. Their condition was the worst. Since they were getting food from one or another son, they were put in the intermediate family.

Problems of the Aged

Ageing is not a problem in itself but it becomes a problem due to several socio-economic factors. The main problems of the poor rural aged are related to means of survival and health. The aged also felt socio-psychological problems.

Table 3
Distribution Of The Respondents According to Health Problems@

Problems	*Percentage*
Impaired Vision	92
Hearing Problems	10
Dental Problems	69
Chronic Cough	31
Respiratory Disease	21
Debilities	90
Asthma	11
Arthritis	47
Insomnia	7
Prostate Problem/Urinary Trouble	48
Piles	12
Filarial	5
Diabetic Problems	10
Gastric	25
Cardiac Problems	5
T.B.	3
Cancer	1

@ The total pf percentage is more than 100 as several respondents were suffering from more than one disease/problems.

It is obvious from Table 3 that common health problems among the rural aged are impaired vision (mostly due to Glaucoma, diabetes (due to poor diet and age), dental problems, enlarged prostrate, arthritis, etc. Only one elderly person was found suffering from cancer.

The most important and general problem of the aged is related to access to health and medical facilities. Most of the aged persons are deprived of this facility. They have problems of access to proper medical attention due to poor economic conditions. They have to rely on government hospitals at Varanasi or primary health centres in the Block, or on some unqualified private medical practitioners in the area. The poor elderly people also find it difficult to afford expensive medicine. Needless to say that any medical expenses to be incurred for the aged are usually considered especially burdensome.

Old age and ailments are often synonymous. It has been observed that majority (90.2%) of the aged were in need of medical attention. They have reported steady deterioration in their health conditions over the years. It is very strange that 35 per cent of them have never visited hospitals for their health related problems. The aged take their illness with stoicism. On the other hand, proper medical facilities are not available in the villages under study.

It is true that there is a nexus between economic stringency and nutrition and Medicare. Except the few aged respondents (9.2%) who retire from organized sectors get some retirement benefits, the plight of the rest of the respondents (agrarian, labourers, artisans, etc.) is deplorable. They are neither getting proper nutritious diet nor medicate.

Most of the respondents (89%) got poor man's food, that is, *roti/chawal* and sometime *bhaji*. They did not get food according to their dietary requirements but it was found that they got sufficient food in terms of quantity. 74 per cent respondents did not get milk at all. Only about 5 per cent respondents get seasonal fruits like mango, papaya and guava, etc. from trees owned by them. Though most (79%) of the respondents are non-vegetarians, only 10 per cent get non- vegetarian food whenever they desire to have it.

Socio-psychological Problems

Family members behaviour is associated with the economic contribution of the aged. The aged persons who are totally dependent are treated miserably. Due to economic compulsion, a large percentage of the aged have to engage them in economically gainful work that is beyond their physical capacity. But it is not a matter of economic compulsion alone, because neglect of the aged is observed also among those who have no such compulsion. It is the individualist philosophy taking hold of the minds of the emerging rural elite. In contemporary Indian society, there is a steep deterioration in social values and permeation of materialism in every walk of life. Villages are not exceptions; several factors have brought significant changes in social life and value system.

It was found in our study that most of the respondents (85%) are facing various socio- psychological problems. The majority

(60%) among them feel that family member neglect them. Their advice is not taken or given due importance in matters of education of grandchildren, purchase of new property or adoption of new occupation. They get some importance only at the time of marriage negotiations, or in some caste-related matters. It is clear from the facts that the role of aged in decision-making is also diminishing. Majority (60%) of them consider themselves not important. The comparatively young among these aged (i.e., 60 to 65 years old) feel that they still enjoy importance in their respective families. Most of the aged feel it that family members deliberately avoid talking to them.

Martin (1989) [41] has observed that 'significant changes in the familial relations may take place with an increasing age, deteriorating health, the diminishing job opportunities, especially when an economic loss is involved. The family members and the society may feel the burden of the elderly when the elderly are unable to participate in economic activities but need an increasing amount of medical and health care[42].

About 30 per cent of the respondents are not happy as their son(s) are living separately with their wives and children. During interviews it came out that most of the respondents (85%) are not satisfied with the present state of life. They have mentioned several socio-psychological problems like isolation, alienation, loneliness, powerlessness, dependence, feeling of boredom, lack of emotional response from family members etc. Feeling of loneliness or existence of withdrawal symptoms have been found among the elderly because of their experience that they do not get due respect and care from the family members. Among them, 20 per cent of the respondents feel lonely because of death of spouse.

Leisure Activities, Habits and Social Life

Leisure activities decrease with age. It was found in our study that majority of the aged (70%) either spends most of their time with spouse or with their grand children. Grand children are the most lovable one to elderly person. Generally rural elderly people don't have any special leisure time activities except gossiping with wives, cohorts or talking and telling stories to grand children. Mostly the aged person engage themselves all the time with one or another household or agricultural work.

Only a few (25%) respondents read newspaper regularly. The others mostly illiterate elderly respondents generally get all the important news from the small tea or Pann shops of nearby areas from others. With regard to reading magazines it was found that almost none of them read it regularly. The reason might be it's less availability and also of its expensiveness.

Since majority of the houses are not electrified therefore, majority of the elderly did not watch TV at all. A few respondents listened to radio and transistor regularly. It was also found that the respondent's participation and involvement in religious and ritual activities are also not much. A few respondents do regularly go to nearby temples.

Most of the respondents (87%)are in the habit of smoking bidi, chewing Khaini (tobacco) or Pann etc. A few respondents drink alcohol too. Majority of the respondents (60%) feel that since they don't have their personal income therefore, they are unable to meet their certain personal needs and demands.

The majority (95%) of the respondents had no hope for a better future for the elderly. Yet a vast majority still believes that the family could help the aged. Whatever problems aged are facing they are blaming for it to their daughter-in-law. A few respondents (2%) who had indicated of having very strained relations with their family members (especially with daughter-in-law), still considered their own home as the best place to spend their remaining part of lives. No body is inclined towards changing their present residential setting due to socio-cultural reasons. Yet it is observed that there is an urgent need in the villages to provide institutional care to the poor and destitute elderly.

Majority (90%) of the aged respondents were of the view that government should play a major role and provide social insurance and other welfare services to all the elderly.

Social Security Measures

From the above, it is clear that the large-scale institutional support and facilities are required to properly look after the rural aged. The Constitution of India (article 41) recognizes that elderly people need special assistance. Item No.9 of the State List and Item 20, 23 and 24 of Concurrent List refer to old age pension, social security and social insurance and economic and social planning. Several institutional measures and welfare benefits are there, but these appear far too insignificant in the face of the huge magnitude of the problem.

The importance of the institutional care is realized especially for the poor and destitute aged. At present, most of the institutional care in the form of Old Age Homes (OAH) is provided by voluntary organization. There are 1018 Old Age Homes in India today[43] but these are located mainly in the urban centres. But every town or city does not have an old age home. Even Varanasi city does not have one. Interestingly, the Varanasi city had the unique institution of 'Mumukshu Bhavan', 'Ganga Labh', etc. where the aged religiously prepare for death, but these have declined and not changed accordingly with the passage of time. Voluntary organizations are also running Day Care Centres (DCC) to fulfil the psychological needs (need for empathy and sympathy, urge for assistance and belongingness. etc.) of the aged, These Day Care Centres are very useful but limited in number; not a single Day Care Centre is there in the study area, that is, in the Sewapuri block area.

For reasons of inadequacy of social security measures and retirement benefits, the elderly people have to depend and survive with the support of their sons. But their needs are not, as it has already been stated, properly attended to because of their being unproductive and not contributing anything to the main income stream and also to some extent the poor conditions of the sons.

In the National Policy of the Aged, the entire old age population has been lumped together. Evidently, it cannot be lumped together. It falls in different categories to be identified by residential status, e.g., rural-urban, gender, social and economic class, level of social security entitlement, family support structure.

The overwhelming majority in the rural areas, especially the *Dalits* and landless people lack the basic economic security and immediately land in destitution after they lose their earning capacity. Unfortunately, the country has not been able to put in place a social security system for the mass of the unorganised labourers, the artisans and workmen, excepting those in the organized sectors.

Note: This is the revised version of the Paper presented in the XVth World Congress of ISA, held at Britane, Australia, July 2002.

REFERENCES

1. Derived from the website of the *HelpAge India*.
2. *World Population Ageing (WPA)*, 1950-2050, United Nations, Department of Economic and Social Affairs, 2002, p. XXVIII.
3. WPA, *Ibid*, 1950-2050, p. XXVIII.
4. Bose, A.B. and K.D. Gangrade (1968), *The Aging in India: Problems and Potentialities, Citizenship Development Society*, Abhinav Publications, New Delhi, India, 16: pp. 132.
5. Sharma, K.L. (1969), Leisure-time Activities of Retired Persons, *Indian Journal of Gerontology*, Jaipur, Vol.1, 32-37.

——(1971), A Survey of the Happiness and Unhappiness in Old Age, *Indian Journal of Gerontology*, Jaipur, Vols. 3 & 4.

6. Singhi, N.K. (1970), Role of Sociologists in Gerontology, *Indian Journal of Gerontology*, Jaipur, Vol. 2 Nos.1 & 2.
7. D'Souza, Victor S. (1971), Change in Social Structure and Changing Roles of Older People in India, *Sociology and Social Research*, 55, pp.297-304.

——(1984), Preliminary Report on the *Role of Active Aging in National Development*, Chandigarh, Population Research Centre, Department of Sociology, Panjab University. (Mimeograph).

8. Desai, K.G. and R.D.Naik (1973), *Problems of Retired People of Greater Bombay*, TATA Institute of Social Sciences, Bombay.
9. Vatuk, S.H. (1975), The Aging Women in India: Self Perception and Changing Roles in Alfred D'Souza (ed.) *Women in Contemporary India*, Manohar, Delhi.

——(1980), Withdrawal and Disengagement as a Culture Response to Aging in India in Christine L.Fry (ed.), *Aging in Culture*, Praeger, A.J.F.Bergin Publishers Books, New York.

10. Soodan, K.S. (1975), *Aging in India*, Minerva Associates (Publications) Pvt.Ltd, Calcutta.
11. Parthasarathi, N.R. (1980), On Some Aspects of Aging in India, *Indian Journal of Social Work*, XL (4), pp. 381-388.
12. D'Souza, Alfred (1982), The Social Organisation of Aging Among the Urban Poor, *Social Action*, Vol.32, No.1, Jan-March, pp. 53-64.
13. Bhatia, H.S. (1983), *Aging and Society-A sociological Study of Retired Public Servants*, Arya Book Centre, Udaipur.

14. Punia, R.K. et al (1987), Problems of the Aged: A Study of Rural-Urban Differentials, in Sharma, M.L.and T.M.Dak edition, *Aging in India: Challenge for the Society*, Ajanta Publications, Delhi, pp.56-66.
15. Nagla, B.K. (1987), Aging and Health, in Sharma, M.L. and T.M. Dak edition, *Ibid.*, pp.193-206.
16. Sangwan, K.S. (1987), Retirement Problems of the Army Personnel, in Sharma, M.L. and T.M.Dak edition, *Ibid.*, pp. 161-169.
17. Dak, T.M. and M.L.Sharma (1987), Changing Status of the Aged in North Indian Villages, in Sharma, K.L. and T.M.Dak edition, *Ibid.*,pp.43-55.
18. Mahajan, A. (1987), *Problems of the Aged in Unorganised Sector*, Delhi: Mittal Publications.
19. Mehta, S.R. (1987), A Strategy for Health and Medical Care of the Aged, in Sharma, K.L. and T.M.Dak edition, *Op.Cit.*, pp. 222-227.
20. Rajeshwar Prasad, (1987), Problems of Aged in India: Some Reflections, in Sharma.K.L. and T.M. Dak edition, *Op.Cit.*, pp. 33-39.
21. Basu, A. and K. Basu (1987), The Greying of Populations: Concepts and Measurement, *Demography India*, Vol. 16, No. 1, pp.79-89.
22. Gulati, S.C. (1989), Demographic Determinants of the Ageing Process: A Cross Country Analysis, *Demography India* 18(1): 211-225.
23. Rajan, S.I. (1989), Ageing in Kerala: One More Population Problem, *Asia Pacific Population Journal*, Bangkok 4(2): 19- 48.
24. Sarkar, B.N. (1989), *Demography of Aged People*, Indian Academy of Social Sciences, Survey Research Centre, Calcutta, India, 16.
25. Sarin, M. (1990), *Women and Environment: Health for the Millions*, Voluntary Health Association of India, and 16,4: pp. 7- 9.
26. Yadava. K.N.S., Surendar S. Yadava, Sharma, C.L.N. (1996), A Study of Socio-economic Factors and Behavioural Problems of the Aged Persons, *Demography India*, Vol. 25, No. 1, pp. 21-34.

——Yadava, K.N.S., Surendar S. Yadava and Roberts, Ron E. (1996), Ageing and Health Hazards in Rural Northern India, *Health and Population -Perspectives and Issues*, 19(1): 1-18.

27. Mahadevan, K. et al (Ed.), (1992), *The Elderly Population in Developed and Developing World*, B.R. Publishing Corporation, New Delhi, India.
28. Shayam, M.D. (1988), Aged Females: The Most Deprived Among the Deprived, *The Indian Journal of Social Work*, XLLX (3): 69-86.
29. Vishwanathan, R. (1969), *Medical Problems of Old Age*, Current Technical Literature Company, Bombay, India.

30. Dhillon, P K. (1992), *Psycho-social Aspects of Ageing in India*, Concept Publishing Company.
31. Kumar. S. Vijaya (1991), *Family Life and Socio-economic Problems of the Aged*, New Delhi.
32. The Title of the Projects on Aged Sponsored by the Ministry of Welfare, Government of India, New Delhi are:

Khan, M.Z. *Voluntary Welfare Services for the Aged.*

Muthayya, B.C. and Aneesuddin, M., *Rural Aged: Existing Conditions, Problems and Possible Interventions* (A Study in Andhra Pradesh).

Husain, M.G., *A Study of the Problems of the Aged and Need for Social Intervention in the State of Bihar-Rural* .

Shah, Anupma and Joshi, Uma, *Ageing Women Belonging to Low Socio-economic Status (Gujarat).*

Upadhyay, R.K., *A Study of the Problems of the Aged and Need for Social Intervention in the States of Haryana and Himachal Pradesh.*

Gummurthy, K.G., *A Study of the Problems of the Aged and Need for Social Intervention (Karnataka -Rural).*

Nayar, P.K.B. and Santhakumari, *The Aged: Their Problems and Need for Social-Intervention (A Study in Kerala).*

Mukherjee, B.M., *The Aged: Their Problems, Social Intervention and Future Outlook in Madhya Pradesh (1).*

Mishra, H.M., *A Study of the Problems of the Aged and Need for Social Intervention in Madhya Pradesh (II).*

Dandekar, Kumudini, *The Aged: Their Problems, Social Intervention and Future Outlook for Maharashtra.*

Sinha, A.C., Senior *Citizens of Meghalaya: A Study of the Problems of the Aged and Need for Intervention.*

Sati, P N., *A Study of the Aged, Their* Problems and *Need for Social Intervention (Rajasthan).*

Raja, D.V.P., *The Aged: Their Problems, Social Intervention and Future Outlook in the State of Tamilnadu.*

Mirza, R. Ahmed, A *Study of the Problems of the Aged* and *Need for Social Intervention in U.P. (Eastern).*

Srivastava, A.R.N., *The Aged: Their Problems, Social Intervention and Future Outlook in U.P. (Western).*

33. Kohli, A.S. (19961, *Research in Social Welfare*, Anmol Publishers Pvt. Ltd., New Delhi.
34. Spencer, Metta, Foundations *of Modern Sociology*, Second Edition (1979), Prentice Hall, Inc., p. 357.

35. Srivastava, A.R.N., The Aged: Their Problems, Social Intervention and Further Outlook in U.P. (Western) in Kohli, A.S. (Ed.), *Op. cit.*, p. 403.

36. Raja, D. V.P., The Aged: Their Problems, Joint Intervention and Future Outlook in the State of Tamilnadu, in Kohii, A.S. (Ed.), *lbid*, p.377.

37. Raja, D.V.P., *lbid*, p. 377.

38. Choudhry, D.Paul, (1992), *Aging and the Aged, Inter-India Publications*, New Delhi Page 21.

39. Choudhry, D. Paul(1992), *Ibid*, p.58.

40. Singh, S.B. (2001), Service Centre Planning for Integrated Area Development of Sewapuri Block, Varanasi District, *Unpublished Project Report*, Funded by NRDMS, Department of Science and Technology, Government of India, p. 79.

41. Martin, L.G. (1989), Living Arrangements of the Elderly in Fiji, Korea, Malaysia and the Philippines, *Demography*, 26(4): 187-198.

42. Yadava, K.N.S., Yadava, Surendar S., Sharma, C.L.N. (1996), *Op. cit.*, p. 26.

43. See for details *Varistha Nagarik Needeshika*, HelpAge India (2004), New Delhi.

6

BIO-PSYCHO AND SOCIAL ASPECTS OF AGEING—A SOCIOLOGICAL PERSPECTIVE

D.P. Saxena

Introduction

The present study highlights the major findings of a UGC sponsored major research project in respect of a representative sample of 240 respondents of different categories like superannuated university teachers 42, superannuated civil servants 40, 60+ elderly lawyers 120, and 60+ elderly doctors 38 in an urban set-up of east U.P. The main dimensions of the study were biological, psychological and social aspects of ageing among the senior citizens. And all these dimensions were implicit in the SOCIOLOGICAL PERSPECTIVE APPROACH the main thrust of the present study on Ageing.

The Sociological theory assumes that age located individuals or groups of people are in the social structure and each age stratum is composed of people similar in life stage who tend to share capacities, abilities and motivations to age. Age is thus a basis of structured social inequality. There is interdependence — containing interplay between aging and social change. This is inevitable since society and individual are inseparable. The problems are aging are steadily increasing in their magnitude and are generally the outcome of physical, psychological, socio-economic and cultural factors. Hence the right approach to handle the aging problems is coordinated, integrated and comprehensive base, which is the unique feature of Sociological Perspective Approach to the ageing problems. The Sociological Perspective

Approach is based on Emile Durkheim's assumption of a SOCIAL BOND. According to Durkheim so long people of any gender, class or age remain well knitted with this SOCIAL BOND they can well control and defer Ageing and do not experience pinch of ageing problems. The moment they are away from OR cut off from this SOCIAL BOND they begin to feel fast ageing and fall victim of many aging problems as highlighted in the present study.

Meaning of Ageing

Age alone is not the cause of ageing. Ageing is what happens to an organism as time passes. It is the weighted product of the internal and external factors affecting organism is sequence that influence the changes we term AGEING.

At this point, it may be necessary to distinguish between two types of processes of ageing.

First there is ageing of the systems of body that change or deteriorate in the usual course of development with the passage of time. This may be called NORMAL AGEING.

Second is the other process of ageing that is the effect of ageing by aggravating and hastening it. In this way ageing is not a disease. It is the normal decaying of the organism because of wear and tear over the years as the self-repairing capacity becomes increasingly weak. Thus, what is perceived as ageing in an individual is the sum of normal and disease effects. With ageing the immune system becomes weak and the organism becomes increasing prone to infections and as a result, aging is hastened, thus setting a vicious circle. Ageing may be fast or slow depending on the state of social and physical health. It becomes a problem if it becomes fast. The reasons for slow and fast ageing relate closely to the social scenario.

DISCUSSION AND FINDINGS

Biological Aspects

In the present study although 65 respondents distributed as 12 (29%), 5(13%) and 15(%), respectively among the superannuated, University teachers, Superannuated civil servants, elderly lawyers and elderly doctors, reported no geriatric problem but the major ageing problem is physical health. As age advances body immunity is lowered. The wear and tear also causes dysfunction in organ system. Hence the superannuated and the elderly respondents generally develop some sort of biological trouble and need physical help. About 133 (56%) respondents of different categories such as (60%), 28(70%), 60(50%) and 20(53%) respectively for superannuated university teachers, superannuated civil servants, elderly lawyers and elderly doctors reported eye trouble.

The other geriatric problems hearing, eating and walking inside/outside the house respectively were reported by 8(30%), 11 (5%), 13 (5%) and 13 (5%) respondents (Table 1). In order to face these problems the respondents reported use of instrumental aids such as glasses, hearing machine, walking stick and denture, wheel chair and foot wear etc. respectively by 133 (55%), 8 (3%), 14 (6%) and 13 (5%) respondents (Table 2).

Table 1
Geriatric Problems

Respondents	*No Geriatric Problem*		*Geriatric Problem*									
			Seeing		*Hearing*		*Eating*		*Walking Inside (House)*		*Walking Outside*	
	F	%	F	%	F	%	F	%	F	%	F	%
Superannuated University Teachers	12	29	25	60	–	–	–	–	03	07	02	04
Superannuated Civil Servants	05	13	28	70	01	02	02	05	02	05	02	05
Elderly Lawyers	30	25	60	50	06	04	08	07	08	07	08	07
Elderly doctors	15	38	20	53	01	03	01	03	–	–	01	03
Total	62	26	133	56	08	03	11	05	13	05	13	05

Health Disease

Physical aging generally affects the general health of the respondents. Various diseases, debility and disability were reported by the respondents. We found 62 (16%), 45 (19%) and 15 (6%) respectively for health on the whole good, minor illness, general debility and physical disability. There appeared the general debility being the dominating feature of ill health (Table 3).

Although there were 62 (25%) respondents of pretty old age enjoying normal health but on the other hand there were 178 respondents suffering from different diseases. Their distribution

Table 2
Instruments Used in Geriatric Problems

Respondents	*No Need of Instrument*		*Glasses*		*Hearing Machine*		*Walking Stick*		*Denture*		*Wheel Chair*		*Foot wear*	
	F	%	F	%	F	%	F	%	F	%	F	%	F	%
Superannuated University Teachers	12	29	25	60	-	-	03	07	02	04	-	-	-	-
Superannuated Civil Servants	05	13	28	70	01	03	02	05	02	05	02	05	-	-
Elderly Lawyers	30	25	60	50	06	05	08	07	08	07	04	03	04	03
Elderly doctors	15	38	20	53	01	03	01	03	01	03	-	-	-	-
Total	62	26	133	55	08	03	14	06	13	05	06	03	04	-02

Table 3
General Health and Ailments of the Old

Nature of Health	*Superannuated Teachers*		*Superannuated civil servants*		*Elderly Lawyers*		*Elderly Doctors*		*Total*	
	F	%	F	%	F	%	F	%	F	%
On the Whole Good	12	28	05	12	30	25	15	39	62	26
Minor Illness	10	24	12	31	20	17	03	08	45	19
General Debility	20	48	18	45	60	50	20	53	118	49
Physical Debility			05	12	10	08			15	06
Total	42	18	40	17	120	50	38	15	240	100

was as 21 (9%), 30 (12%), 14 (6%), 52 (21%), 18 (7%), 21 (9%), 2 (1%), 5 (2%), 6 (3%) and 3 (2%) respectively for ENT trouble, arthritis, asthma, cardiac problem, blood pressure, diabetes, skin disease, psychiatric problem, stone in gallbladder, prostrate gland and others (Table 4)

Some of the ailing respondents claimed that they were unable to consult a doctor's proper treatment for several reasons such as reported by 39 (19%), 18 (8%), 11 (6%), 116 (57%) and 18 (9%) respectively for want of money, doctor fairway, no faith in doctor, faith in nature cure, etc. Those ailing respondents taking proper medical care were financed by their own children/grand children, government agencies and non-government agencies reported respectively by 113 (47%), 55 (23%) and 40(10%) respondents (Table 5).

Table 4
Diseases of the Old Persons

Respondents	*Superannuated teachers*	*Superannuated civil servants*	*Elderly Lawyers*	*Elderly Doctors*	*Total*	
ENT Trouble	02	04	05	10	21	09
Arthritis	07	03	20	–	30	12
Asthma	–	05	09	–	14	06
Cardiac Problem	12	10	30	–	52	21
B.P.	05	05	05	03	18	07
Diabetes	03	03	05	10	21	09
Skin Disease	–	02	–	–	02	01
Psychiatric Problem	–	–	05	–	05	02
Stone	–	01	05	–	06	03
Prostrate Gland	–	02	04	–	06	03
Others	01	–	02	–	03	02
No disease at all	12	05	30	15	62	25
Total	42	40	120	38	240	100

Table 5
Reasons For Not Proper Treatment

Respondents	*Superannuated Teachers*		*Superannuated civil servants*		*Elderly Lawyers*		*Elderly Doctors*		*Total*	
	F	*%*	*F*	*%*	*F*	*%*	*F*	*%*	*F*	*%*
Lack of Finance	5	12	04	10	30	25	–	–	39	10
None to Bring a Doctor Nor Take Him to the Doctor	5	12	03	07	10	08	–	–	18	09
Doctor Far Away	5	12	06	15	–	–	–	–	11	06
No Faith in Doctor	20	48	21	53	75	63	–	–	116	57
Faith in Nature Cure	07	16	04	15	05	04	–	–	18	09
Total	42	21	40	20	120	59	–	–	202	91

Psychological Aspects

The most alarming psychological tendencies developed in about 95 (40%) respondents of different categories considering self as unwanted, worthless creature and socially alienated. The reasons for such feelings were indicated as discontinuity of work/job/profession at the age of 60 years by 6 per cent, contemptuous attitude of family members by 27 per cent, no hope of economic support from any source by 5 per cent, loss of professional and social status by 2 per cent respondents (Table 6).

Table 6
Reasons For Feeling Unwantedness and Worthless by the Old

Reasons	*Superannuated Teachers*		*Superannuated civil servants*		*Elderly Lawyers*		*Elderly Doctors*		*Total*	
	F	*%*	*F*	*%*	*F*	*%*	*F*	*%*	*F*	*%*
Discontinuity of Work Job/Profession	05	12	09	22	–	–	–	–	14	06
Contemptuous Attitude of the Family Members	08	19	03	07	50	42	03	08	64	27
No Help or Economic Support From Any Source	–	–	01	03	10	08	–	–	11	05
Loss of Identity (Social and Professional Status & Power)	–	–	01	03	05	04	–	–	06	02
Not Having Such Feelings	29	69	26	65	55	46	35	92	145	60
Total	42	18	40	17	120	50	38	15	240	100

Worrying About Unpleasant Aspects of Life

In this respect most of the respondents were found worrying about unpleasant aspects of life. These aspects were nothing else but mainly psychological such as facing disrespect in own family as reported by 84 (35%), children away from the family by 110 (46%), loneliness by 64 (26%), social attention by 19 (8%), bad health by 80 (33%), dependency by 65 (27%), unwantedness by 30 (12%), non cares to help nor speaks consolatory words by 85 (35%), non cares personal feelings and whims by 80 (33%) and worrying all the time for having no son by 88 (37%) respondents (Table 7).

Table 7
Worry About Unpleasant Aspect of Life

Unpleasant Aspect of Life	*Superannuated Teachers*		*Superannuated civil servants*		*Elderly Lawyers*		*Elderly Doctors*		*Total*	
	F	%	F	%	F	%	F	%	F	%
Disrespect in Family	10	24	20	50	60	50	4	11	84	35
Away From Children/Grand children	20	48	25	62	40	33	25	66	110	46
Loneliness	10	24	15	38	35	29	4	11	64	26
Social Alienation	–	–	4	12	15	13	–	–	19	8
Bad Health	15	36	20	50	45	38	–	–	80	33
Dependency	5	12	20	50	40	33	–	–	65	27
Unwantedness	–	–	5	12	45	21	–	–	30	12
None Cares to Help and None Speaks Consolatory Words	5	12	20	50	60	50	–	–	85	35
None Cares Personal Feelings and Whims	5	12	25	62	50	42	–	–	80	33
Having No Son	10	24	23	57	55	46	–	–	88	37
Not Worrying for the Unpleasant Aspects of Life	10	24	–	–	–	–	20	53	30	12
Total	N	42	N	40	N	120	N	38	N	240

Discussion

Depression is a sort of psychological problem in old age with worries, tensions, feeling alienated from the family and dejected. The depression was reported by 5, 37, and 33 per cent respectively among superannuated University teachers, superannuated civil servants and elderly lawyers (Table 8). The chief reasons for the depression and its resultant problems were indicated as declining socio-cultural values by 10 per cent, frequent shift of dwelling place by 46 per cent and bereavement by 19 per cent (Table 9).

Wishes and Desires

As regards major wishes and feelings we found reporting about peaceful and content life by all the respondents, normal health, no dependency, no liability, sweet home and sweet words from

Table 8
Whether Feeling Depressed

Feeling Depressed	*Superannuated Teachers*		*Superannuated civil servants*		*Elderly Lawyers*		*Elderly Doctors*		*Total*	
	F	*%*	*F*	*%*	*F*	*%*	*F*	*%*	*F*	*%*
Yes	02	05	15	37	40	33	—	—	57	24
No	40	95	25	63	80	67	38	100	183	76
Total	42	100	40	100	120	120	38	100	240	100

Table 9
Reasons For Depression in Old Age

Reasons	*Superannuated University Teachers*		*Superannuated civil servants*		*Elderly Lawyers*		*Elderly Doctors*		*Total*	
	F	*%*	*F*	*%*	*F*	*%*	*F*	*%*	*F*	*%*
Declining Social Cultural Values	02	100	-	-	04	10	-	-	06	10
Frequent Shift of Dwelling Place	-	-	05	33	09	23	-	-	14	25
Thin Social relations with Others	-	-	06	40	20	50	-	-	26	46
Berevement	-	-	15	27	07	17	-	-	11	19
Total	02	100	15	100	40	100	-	-	57	100

their kith and kin, company of devotees of their own common sect and faith, ever-enjoying status and prestige in the family and society and no economic hardship, etc. (Table 10).

Social Cultural Aspects Religious Faith and Practices

One of the important hypotheses of the study was that those elderly respondents who had been continuously retaining their religious faith and practices regularly since long before superannuated or attaining 60 years of age and still continuing were considered as tied with the religious bond/social bond. And this helped them much in controlling and deferring early ageing and reducing aging problems if any.

In this respect we found 71, 70, 71 and 29 per cent respondents respectively among the superannuated university teachers,

Table 10
Major Wishes and Desire of the Old

Wishes and Desires	*Superannuated Teachers*		*Superannuated civil servants*		*Elderly Lawyers*		*Elderly Doctors*		*Total*	
	F	*%*	*F*	*%*	*F*	*%*	*F*	*%*	*F*	*%*
Peaceful and Contended Life	42	100	40	100	120	100	38	100	240	100
Ever Enjoying Social Status and Power	30	76	35	88	90	75	35	92	190	79
Company of the Devotees of the Same Panth	32	77	30	75	100	83	10	26	172	72
Normal Health	42	100	40	100	120	100	38	100	240	100
No Dependency	42	100	40	100	120	100	38	100	240	100
Absence of any Economic Need	10	24	35	88	90	75	—	—	135	56
No Liability	40	95	40	100	100	83	38	100	218	91
Sweet Home with Polite Tongued Members	40	95	40	100	100	83	38	100	218	91
No Serious Illness	42	100	40	100	120	100	38	100	240	100
Natural Death	42	100	40	100	120	100	38	100	240	100
Total	N	42	N	40	N	120	N	38	N	240

superannuated civil servants, elderly lawyers and elderly doctors were still continuing their religious faith and practices since long till present (Table 11)

In return of the above persisting faith they were godly blessed with social bond tie to the extent of 71, 50, 83 and 39 per cent respectively among the superannuated university teachers, superannuated civil servants, elderly lawyers and elderly doctors along with many other blissful effects such as normal health, no worries and tensions, enjoying full social status, full contentment, no emotional problem, no liability, no deprivation of any sort, sweet home with amiable relations with all and feeling fully secured and protected (Table 12).

In this way our hypothesis based on Emile Durkheim's assumption 'that so long as people of any class, age, gender and creed closely knitted with social bond did not feel much the pinch of ageing and its related problems is validatede.

Table 11

Worship and Performance of Religious Rites Before and After 60 Years of Age

Routine of Worship	*Superannuated Teachers*				*Superannuated Civil Servants*				*Elderly Lawyers*				*Elderly Doctors*			
	Before		*After*		*Before*		*After*		*Before*		*After*		*Before*		*After*	
	F	%	F	%	F	%	F	%	F	%	F	%	F	%	F	%
Regular	20	18	30	71	15	38	28	70	40	33	85	71	05	13	11	29
Often	10	24	–	–	10	25	–	–	40	33	–	–	12	32	–	–
Sometimes	05	12	02	05	12	30	06	15	25	21	10	08	12	32	15	39
Never Performing Any Rites	07	16	10	24	03	07	06	15	15	12	25	21	09	23	12	32
Total	42	–	42	–	40	–	40	–	120	–	120	–	38	–	38	–

Table 12
God's Blessings in Return of Worship

God's Blessings	*Superannuated teachers*		*Superannuated civil servants*		*Elderly Lawyers*		*Elderly Doctors*	
	F	*%*	*F*	*%*	*F*	*%*	*F*	*%*
Normal Health	25	60	22	55	80	67	15	25
No Worry and Misery	15	36	10	25	50	42	15	39
Enjoying Social Prestige	10	24	15	47	50	42	15	39
Contentment	30	71	15	47	90	75	15	39
No Emotional Problem	30	71	15	47	60	50	15	39
No Liability	20	48	10	25	50	42	15	39
Completely Secured and Protected	30	71	28	70	100	83	10	26
Sweet and Amiable Relations With All	25	60	25	63	75	63	15	39
No Deprivation of Any Sort	10	24	05	12	40	33	10	26
Tie with community Bond	30	71	20	50	100	83	15	39

Table 13
Nature of Family Relations

Respondents	*Nature of Relations*							
	Cordial		*Normal*		*Un-cordial*		*Very Strained*	
	F	*%*	*F*	*%*	*F*	*%*	*F*	*%*
Superannuated University Teachers	28	67	08	19	—	—	06	14
Superannuated Civil Servants	35	88	04	10	01	02	—	—
Elderly Lawyers	75	63	35	29	02	01	08	07
Elderly Doctors	30	79	05	13	—	—	03	08
Total	168	70	52	22	03	01	17	08

Changing Family Relations

Another impact of ageing was seen as the family relations of the elderly respondents. These changes were measured on four points, i.e., cordial, un-cordial, normal and very strained. Generally after

60 years of age family relations of the old remain neither cordial nor normal but in the present study strange enough that respondent even after 60 years of age belonging to middle class and higher middle class were found maintaining cordial relations. More cordial relations in the family were found to the extent of 67, 88, 63 and 79 per cent respectively among superannuated university teachers, superannuated civil servants, elderly lawyers and elderly doctors. Very strained relations were found only to the extent of 14, 7 and 8 per cent among superannuated university teachers, superannuated civil servants, elderly lawyers and elderly doctors. Besides, normal relations were also found to the extent of 29, 19, 10 and 13 per cent respectively among the superannuated university teachers, superannuated civil servants, elderly lawyers and elderly doctors (Table 13).

Generally the main reasons behind these changes in family relations were reported as contemptuous attitude of family members, conflicts, adverse relations and minimum relations respectively to the extent of 46, 17, 20, and 17 per cent but the dominating reasons of contemptuous attitude of the family members if distributed among category wise respondents we found the extent of 42, 50, 45 and 50 per cent among superannuated university teachers, superannuated civil servants, elderly lawyers and elderly doctors. Adverse relations were thought of disturbing family relations as reported by 15, 12 and 20 per cent among superannuated university teachers, superannuated civil servants, and elderly lawyers. Similarly 10, 12, 10 and 33 per cent respondents among superannuated university teachers, superannuated civil servants, elderly lawyers and elderly doctors considered the least minimum relations were responsible for unpleasant family relations (Table 14).

Views about Looking After the Old Age

The changing family relations in old age raised another related problem of the need for someone to look after in old age. In this respect about 89 per cent doctors said that they needed none to look after them in old age. The superannuated university teachers desired for being looked after in old age by their sons/grandsons and relative to the extent of 10 and 31 per cent respectively. Similarly superannuated civil servants preferred looking after in old age by their own sons/grandsons and relatives to the extent

Table 14
Reasons For Changing Family Relations

Respondents	*Contemptuous Attitude of Family Members*		*Conflict in Relations*		*Distant Relations*		*Minimum Relations*	
	F	*%*	*F*	*%*	*F*	*%*	*F*	*%*
Superannuated University Teachers	05	42	—	—	04	33	03	25
Superannuated Civil Servants	04	50	02	26	01	12	01	12
Elderly Lawyers	09	45	05	25	04	20	02	10
Elderly Doctors	03	50	01	17	—	—	02	33
Total	21	46	08	17	09	20	08	17

of 15 and 30 per cent respectively. Except the elderly doctors all other respondents desired especially own sons/grandsons to look after them in old age (Table 15).

Table 15
Old Persons Wishing to be Looked After by Whom

By Whom	*Superannuated University Teachers*		*Superannuated civil servants*		*Elderly Lawyers*		*Elderly Doctors*		*Total*	
	F	*%*	*F*	*%*	*F*	*%*	*F*	*%*	*F*	*%*
Sons/Grandsons	04	10	06	15	16	13	04	11	30	15
Relatives	13	31	12	30	30	25	—	—	55	23
None	25	59	22	55	74	62	34	89	155	62
Total	42	100	40	100	120	100	38	100	240	100

Loss of Prestige and Status in Family and Society

In this respect one group of respondents held the view that they were enjoying all the respect from the younger family members and the status of headship in the family even after 60 years of age while the other group felt the loss of former social status and power in the family and society after 60 years of age. Excepting elderly doctors claiming all the respect, status and power as usual most of the respondents of other categories reported loss of status and power after 60 years of age to the extent of 65, 60 and 64 per cent by superannuated university teachers, superannuated civil servants, elderly lawyers and elderly doctors (Table 16).

Table 16
Commanding Honour and Prestige In Family

Nature of command	*Superannuated Teachers*		*Superannuated civil servants*		*Elderly Lawyers*		*Elderly Doctors*		*Total*	
	F	*%*	*F*	*%*	*F*	*%*	*F*	*%*	*F*	*%*
Always	03	07	02	05	15	12	38	100	58	24
Sometimes	07	17	10	25	03	03	—	—	20	08
Often	05	12	02	05	25	21	—	—	32	13
Never	27	64	26	65	77	64	—	—	130	55
Total	42	100	40	100	120	100	38	100	240	100

Major Expectations from the Government

The senior citizens were to face many sorts of aging problems, which could be contained only with the help of the Government. Hence the senior citizens disclosed many of their expectations from the Government in order to face different types of aging problems.

Their major expectations from the government were in order of per centage as follows:

1. Separate counters at public places for the senior citizens (99%).
2. Subsidy in essential consumption goods and articles (88%).
3. Concessions and rebate, etc. in prices of the commodities of daily use (85%).
4. Mobile, dispensary reaching homes of all the ailing elderly (84%).
5. Separate geriatric ward in medical college, civil hospital and health centers (84%).
6. Remunerative engagement of senior citizens utilizing their expertise, skill, excellence and long experience (73%).
7. Membership in the committees and commissions for the welfare of senior citizens (60%).
8. Time-bound revision of pensions and D.A., etc. (34%).
9. Government sponsored Old Age Homes and Day Care Centers (21%) (Table 17).

Table 17
Commanding Honour and Prestige in Family

Major Expectations	*Superannuated Teachers*		*Superannuated civil servants*		*Elderly Lawyers*		*Elderly Doctors*		*Total*	
	F	*%*	*F*	*%*	*F*	*%*	*F*	*%*	*F*	*%*
Separate Counters for Senior Citizens in Public Places	42	100	40	100	120	100	35	92	237	99
Subsidy in Essential Consumption Goods and Articles	40	95	40	100	120	100	10	26	210	88
Concessions and Rebates, etc in Prices of the commodities of Daily Use	30	71	40	100	120	100	15	39	205	85
Mobile Medical Facility at Home for all the Elderly Persons	42	100	40	100	120	100	—	—	202	84
Separate Geriatric Ward in Civil Hospital, Medical college and Health Centers	40	95	40	100	120	100	—	—	202	84
Remunerative Engagement of Senior Citizens Utilising their Expertise, Skill, Excellence and Long Experience	40	95	20	50	90	75	25	66	175	73
Membership in the Committees and Commissions for the Welfare of Senior Citizens	40	95	20	50	50	42	35	92	145	60
Time Bound Revision of Pensions	42	100	40	100	—	—	—	—	82	34
Government Sponsored Old Age Homes and Day Care Centers	5	12	10	25	35	29	—	—	50	21

Conclusion

The problem of ageing are steadily increasing in their magnitude and are generally the outcome of physical, social, economic, cultural and psychological factors. Hence the right approach to handle aging problems was to have a coordinated, integrated and a comprehensive base, i.e., sociological perspective approach, the main thrust of the present study. Such a comprehensive and holistic standpoint of sociological perspective approach is highly needed in the present context covering multi facet aspects on aging and its relative problems among the senior citizens. Further this approach complemented studies on ageing based on other perspectives conducted so far in the country.

The next main objective of the present study was to examine Emile Durkheim's assumption of social bond/community bond. Accordingly those old persons well knitted with the social/ community bond were not to worry at all about aging because of it being controlled and deferred and feel lesser the pinch of relative ageing problems. In the present study it was found that most of the respondents were immune from the ageing problems due to their closeness with the social bond/community bond in old age. In this way many other tentative hypotheses were put to verification and found valid.

There is still a wide scope for the application of the sociological perspective approach and the tie with the social bond in respect of the ageing problems of large number of rural old persons and elderly widows in rural India.

REFERENCES

Agnihotri, Narendra Kumar, 'Problems of Old Age,' *Agra University Research Journals*, 24(2), July 1976.

Anantharaman, R.N., 'The Problems of Older People in a Changing Society,' *Journal of Madras University*, LIV. 2, 1982, pp.31-33.

Bhatia, H.S., 'Aging and Society: A Sociological Study of the Retired Public Servants,' The Arya Book Centre Publishers, Udaipur, 1983.

Bose, A.B. and K.D. Ganguli, 'Aging in India: Problems and Potential, Abhinav Publications, New Delhi, 1989.

Chanana, H.B. and P.P. Talwar, 'Aging in India: Its Socio-economic Implications,' *Asia Pacific Population Journal*, Vol. 2, No. 3, 1987, pp. 23-38.

Chandra Dave, 'Some Psychological Aspects of Aging,' Paper presented at the National Seminar on Psychological Aspects of Aging, Tirupati, 1983.

Chandra, Sekhariah, 'Problems of Issues in Aging,' Paper on International Seminar on Population Aging in India, University Department of Sociology, University of Kerala, Trivandrum.

Dhaon, J.K., et al, Some Bio-social Characteristics of Pensioners of Lucknow City, Health and Population, 6(2), 1983, pp.119-27.

De Souza, V.S., 'Changes in Social Structure and Changing Role of Older People in India, Sociology and Social Research, Vol. 55, Nos. 4 & 5, April 1974.

Desai, K.G. and Rekha Bhalla, 'Social Situation of the Aged,' Tata Institute of Social Sciences, Bombay, 1978.

Dandekar, Kumudini, 'The Elderly in India,' Sage Publications, New Delhi, 1996.

7

LIVING ARRANGEMENTS OF THE WIDOWED AND CURRENTLY MARRIED WOMEN IN TAMILNADU STATE, INDIA

N. Audinarayana and N. Kavitha

Introduction

In India, the family used to take care of its respective elderly persons and act as the principal source of support and security in old age. Recently, however, on the one hand, the drastic decline in mortality resulted in longer survival of elderly as well as family members (including elderly) and thereby elderly persons have the advantage of more family members to co-reside. On the other hand, lower fertility is reducing the number of relatives and children to the elderly and thus co-residence is becoming difficult. Besides these demographic phenomena, social changes such as industrialization, urbanization, migration and increased female labour participation have disturbed the traditional family household set up. Furthermore, young generations tend to accept the Western values of individualism over the traditional values of familial and filial piety (Martin, 1989).

With these developments, the living arrangements of the elderly have been severely affected by disturbing the multi-generation familial co-residence and compelling them to live by themselves as an elderly couple or alone (if never married/ widowed). Besides this phenomenon, in the recent period, the population of widowed women has started to increase slowly, because of the longer life expectancy of women than men on an average. In the absence of clear social security policies for elderly women they have to face more difficulties than men. Form s social problem perspective, elderly widows living separately is clearly in a disadvantaged position in a comparison to their married counterparts.

Earlier Research

Extensive discussion and research on the general living arrangements of the elderly and of older never married/widowed women has been made in developed countries (Kobrin, 1976; Soldo and Lauriat, 1976; De Vos and Holden, 1988; Thomas and Wister, 1984; Wolf, 1984; Wolf and Soldo, 1988; Burr and Mutchler, 1992; Elman and Uhlenberg, 1995) and to a limited extent in some Asia-Pacific countries (Andrews et al., 1986; De Vos and Holden, 1988; Martin, 1989; Hashimoto, 1991; Population Division, ESCAP, 1992; Da Vanzo and Chan, 1994; Kamo and Zhou, 1994; Siriboon and Knodel, 1994). These studies have documented that advanced age (80+ years), widowhood, urban residence, availability of adult children and/or son(s) and physical disability among the elderly (and among older women in particular) increases significantly the likelihood of co-residence with children. On the other hand, higher educational attainment and economic feasibility (occupational status or self-support capacity, house ownership and income/wealth) among the elderly tend to decreases the propensity to live with their children.

In India, the discipline Gerontology itself is in the infancy stage and thereby studies related to the living arrangements were also very few (NSSO, 1991; Vijaykumar, 1991; Irudaya Rajan, 1995; Audinarayana et al., 1996; Panda, 1997). Most of these looked into only the pattern of living arrangements among the elderly and to a limited extent differentials by age, sex, marital status and place of residence, but not its determinants (except Audinarayana et al. 1996). This paper aims in this direction.

DATA AND METHODS

Data

Data used for this paper were drawn from a study entitled, "Status and Well-being of the Elderly", which was carried out at three districts of Tamilnadu state, India. In all data were collected from

750 elderly (aged 60+ years) — 450 from rural and 300 from urban areas — by interviewing them with the help of a schedule, during July-October 1997. Of these, 516 elderly women — 274 widowed and 242 currently married — who had at least one living child at the time of survey were considered for the analysis.

Analysis

Firstly, with the help of univariate analysis the background characteristics have been discussed, which has been followed by an examination of the pattern of living arrangements of the elderly across the sample elderly women as a whole as well as by their marital status. We then examine the differentials in the pattern of living arrangements across their selected background characteristics through bivariate (cross-tabular) analysis separately among currently married and widowed elderly women. This has been followed by a logistic regression analysis wherein the effects of various determinants of elderly women's living arrangements i.e. in terms of the likelihood of an elderly woman co-residing with her children or not are assessed with the following variables.

Dependent Variable

0 =	Living Alone or only with husband (themselves)
1 =	Living with Children

Explanatory Variables

Place of Residence

0 =	Rural
1 =	Urban

Caste

0 =	Scheduled Castes/Tribes (SC/STs)
1 =	Non-Sc/STs

Current Age of Women

In Completed Years

Literacy Status of Women	
0 =	Illiterate
1 =	Non-Sc/STs

Work Status of Women	
0 =	Non-working
1 =	Working

Monthly Family Income per Adult Member
In Actual Rupees

Number of Living Rooms
In Actual Number

No. of Surviving Sons
In Actual Number

RESULTS

Background Characteristics of Sample Women

Among the elderly sample women, about 60 per cent belong to urban areas and the remaining 40 per cent belong to rural areas, irrespective of their marital status. 64 per cent of widowed and 74 per cent of the currently married women belong to higher caste groups. A large number of currently married elderly women (93%) as against 56 per cent of widowed women are in the age group of 60-69. Most of the sample elderly women, irrespective of their marital status, are illiterates, non-working and belong to lower economic status households. The percent of elderly women residing in large sized houses (two or more living rooms) is more among currently married, whereas majority of the widowed are dwelling in single living room houses. The percent of elderly women who have two living sons and more is slightly higher among currently married than their counterparts (cols. 2-3, Table 2).

Pattern of Living Arrangements

Results provided in Table 1 highlight that among the sample elderly women, as a whole, more than two-thirds (71%) reside with at least one child, 17 per cent live with spouse only and the rest 12 per cent live alone. While 22 per cent of the widowed elderly live alone, 37 per cent of the currently married live with spouse only (strictly speaking these married couples are also living alone i.e., by themselves). Among those living with children, co-residence with married son(s) is the prominent pattern of living arrangement irrespective of their marital status, a typical characteristic of patrilineal society i.e., the cultural norm of living with sons. As expected, the per cent of currently married women living with their unmarried son(s) is comparatively high (19%) than their widowed counterparts (7%). By and large, older women living alone /they are likely to face many hardships in their day-to-day life, because the support from either children or others would be substantially less. On the other hand, those elderly living with children are likely to get all support and care (familial, social, economic, emotional, physical etc.).

Table 1
Patterns of Living Arrangements of Elderly Women

Pattern of Living Arrangements	*Total Women*		*Widowed Women*		*Currently Married Women*	
	%	*No.*	*%*	*No.*	*%*	*No.*
Living Alone	11.6	60	21.9	60	–	–
Living with Spouse (Themselves)	17.4	90	–	–	37.2	90
Living with Children	71.0	319	78.1	214	62.8	152
Living with Unmarried Sons	12.6	65	6.9	19	19.0	46
Living with Unmarried Daughters	2.7	14	3.3	9	2.1	5
Living with Married Sons	40.9	211	48.5	133	32.2	78
Living with Married Daughters	7.8	40	9.9	27	5.4	13
Living with Widowed Daughters	0.6	3	0.7	2	0.4	1
Living with Grand Children	6.4	33	8.8	24	3.4	9

Differentials in the Living Arrangements of the Elderly

The pattern of living arrangements of the elderly people may vary across their socioeconomic and demographic background characteristics. From Table 2 (Cols. 4-5) it is clear that the differentials in living arrangements of the elderly women are highly associated with number of living rooms and per capita family income per adult member among both currently married and widowed groups. Women who have more spacing facilities and who have high per capita family income per adult member are more likely to stay with their children. Number of surviving sons also exhibited a positive association with the living arrangements of the elderly only in the case of widowed women, but is not significantly associated with the living arrangements of the currently married. Work status has a negative association with the living arrangements of the elderly widowed as well as currently married women i.e., working women are less likely to stay with their children as compared to their non-working counterparts. The percentage of women living with children is higher among those residing in urban areas and belonging to lower caste groups than those who reside in rural areas and belonging to higher caste groups, respectively. However, this patter is more conspicuous among the widowed elderly. Current age of women and literacy status do not have any significant association with the living arrangements of the elderly women. These findings, in general, strengthen the fact that the family, which supports the co-residence of elderly women, should be better off in terms of the family income and economic status (measured as number of living rooms) as well as son is the crucial person to look after the elderly women.

Table 2
Background Characteristics and Differentials in Living With Children Among the Widowed and Currently Married Elderly Women

Background characteristics	*Elderly Sample Women*				*Living With Children*			
	%	No.	%	No.	%	No.	%	No.
Place of Residence								
Rural	60.2	165	60.7	147	71.4	118	65.3	96
Urban	39.8	109	39.3	95	88.1	96	58.9	56
Chi-Square Value						10.52		1.00
Significant Level						00.00		N.S
Caste								
Lower Caste Groups	36.5	100	26.4	64	84.0	113	61.5	139
Higher Caste Groups	63.5	174	73.6	173	74.7	101	56.3	9
Chi-Square Value						3.20		0.74
Significant Level						0.07		N.S.

contd.

Background characteristics	*Elderly Sample Women*				*Living With Children*			
	%	*No.*	*%*	*No.*	*%*	*No.*	*%*	*No.*
Current Age								
60-69	55.5	152	63.5	226	74.3	113	61.5	139
70 & above	44.5	122	6.6	16	82.3	101	56.3	9
Chi-Square Value					2.82		0.47	
Significant Level					0.09		N.S.	
Literacy Status								
Illiterate	76.3	209	63.6	154	77.0	161	64.3	99
Literate	23.7	65	36.4	88	81.5	59	60.2	53
Chi-Square Value					0.53		0.39	
Significant Level					N.S.		N.S.	
Work status								
Non-working	75.9	208	70.2	170	84.1	175	68.8	67
Working	24.1	66	29.8	72	59.1	39	48.6	35
Chi-Square Value					18.37		8.85	
Significant Level					0.00		0.00	
Per Capita Monthly Family HH Income (In Rs. per adult member)								
300 & less	40.1	110	36.4	88	62.7	69	50.0	44
301-600	32.5	89	30.6	74	82.0	73	79.7	59
600 & above	27.4	75	33.1	80	96.0	72	61.3	49
Chi-Square Value					30.05		15.33	
Significant Level					0.00		0.00	
No. of Living Room(s)								
One Living Room	42.7	117	28.1	68	59.8	70	60.3	41
Two Living Rooms	26.3	72	36.0	87	88.9	64	54.0	47
Three & More Living Rooms	31.0	85	36.0	87	94.1	80	73.6	64
Chi-Square Value					40.49		7.37	
Significant Level					0.00		0.00	
No. of Surviving Son(s)								
No Surviving Son	15.7	43	6.6	16	55.8	24	68.8	11
One Surviving Son	49.3	135	55.0	133	81.5	110	57.9	77
2 or More Surviving Sons	35.0	96	38.4	33	83.3	80	68.8	64
Chi-Square Value					14.93		3.05	
Significant Level					0.00		N.S.	
TOTAL	100.0	274	100.0	242	78.1	214	62.8	152

Note: Cur. M = Currently Married.
Chi-square values have been calculated for each marital status group of women by their background characteristics. The per cent of women living with children only presented in the table.

Determinants of Living Arrangements of the Elderly

From Table 3, it is evident that controlling for other variables used in the logistic regression model, the effect of per capita monthly family income per adult member on elder's co-residence with children is positive (i.e., higher the monthly family income per adult member, greater will be the likelihood to live with their children) and is statistically found to significant (at 0.001 level) among the widowed and to a certain extent among the currently married women. This is also true in the case of another economic

Table 3
Logistic Regression Analysis of Living Arrangements of the Widowed and Currently Married Elderly Women on their Background Characteristics

Explanatory Variables	*Widowed*		*Currently Married*	
	Beta Coefficient	*Odds Ratio*	*Beta Coefficient*	*Odds Ratio*
Place of Residence (Ref: Rural)				
Urban	1.3012	3.6738*	-0.5326	0.5853*
Caste (Ref: SC/STs)				
Non-SC/STs	-0.7308	0.4815+	-0.3916	0.6760
Current Age	0.0673	1.0696*	0.0096	0.9905
Educational Status (Ref: Illiterates)				
Literates	-0.9709	0.3787+	-0.4758	0.6214
Work Status (Ref: Non-Working)				
Working	-1.8025	0.1649***	-1.0504	0.3498**
Monthly Family Income per Adult Member (Ref: Rs. 300 or less)				
301-600	1.4913	4.4429**	1.4907	4.9070***
601 and above	2.8508	17.3013***	0.4680	1.5968
No. of Living Rooms (Ref: 1 Room)				
2 Rooms	1.6959	5.4518***	-0.2038	0.8156
3+ Rooms	1.8443	6.3237***	0.8240	2.2795+
No. of Surviving Sons (Ref: No Surviving Son)				
1 Surviving Son	1.3900	4.0150**	-0.3777	0.6854
2+ Surviving Son	1.1657	3.2082*	0.1543	1.1669
Constant	-5.1968		1.4589	
N	274		242	
-2 Log Likelihood	180.003		277.006	
Chi-Square	108.032		42.415	
P-Value	0.0000		0.0000	

Note: Beta Coeff. = Beta Coefficient.
+ = p<0.10, * = p< 0.05, ** = p<0.01, and *** = p<0.001.

and privacy variable i.e., number of living rooms in the household. Being engaged in income generating activities and thus being self-supporting themselves results in lower probability of living with children (significantly at a higher level) among both marital status groups of women.

Among the widowed women, those residing in urban areas are more likely to live with one or the other child (significant at .01 level), while this pattern is negative and less significant (at .10 level) in the case of currently married elderly. The effects of the number of surviving son(s) and the current age of women on the likelihood of co-residence with children are positive and significant only in the case of widowed elderly, but their effects are either not clear or negative, and very weak among the currently married elderly.

Elderly women who belong to higher caste groups (non-SC/STs) and literate have exhibited less likelihood to co-reside with children, but at a lesser level of significance (at .10 levels) among the widowed. Though similar pattern exists in the case of currently married elderly, the effects are very weak and insignificant.

Discussion

Like in other Asian societies, here too, majority of the elderly women, particularly widowed, live with their children in general and with married sons in particular. However, the number of elderly living alone (or with spouse) may increase because of the wider acceptance of small family size norm (and since the proportion of couples with sons is likely to decrease) and also because of the persistence of the taboo (culturally) on staying with daughter. Further, the poor are likely to be forced to stay by themselves and thereby turn up as destitute. These in turn lead to less familial support and environment to the elderly, particularly to the widowed.

Monthly family income per adult member and women's occupational status turned out to be the major determinants of living arrangements of the elderly women. Further, there is an increase in the likelihood of co-residence among widowed women if they belong to large houses (no. of living rooms, proxy for economic status and privacy), possess surviving son(s), reside in urban areas and older in age.

In the light of these findings, it may be suggested that the government may provide safety and near family environment either through establishing old age homes or institutions to the aged particularly for widowed or widowers. The recently announced (The Hindu, February 28, 1999: 10) "Annapurna" scheme (i.e. provision of 10 kgs food grains free of cost per month to all indigent senior citizens who are eligible for old age pension but are not receiving it presently and whose children are not residing in the same village) by government of India, is a welcoming sign of food security to elderly. Steps may also be taken to extend monetary support to these elders who are not able to participate in economic activities, and who have no independent source of income.

Acknowledgements

The authors would like to thank the Population Investigation Committee, London School of Economics and Political Science, United Kingdom for providing financial grant to carry out this study. Special thanks are due to Dr. (Ms.) J. Sheela, Research Assistant, Dept. of Population Studies, Bharathiar University, Coimbatore for her appreciated work during the data collection and coding of data.

BIBLIOGRAPHY

1 Andrews, G. R., et al. 1986. Ageing in the Western Pacific: A Four-Country Study. Manila: World Health Organization.

2. Audinarayana, N., et al. 1996. "Living Arrangements of the Elderly Women in Rural Tamil Nadu: Patterns, Differentials and Determinants," paper presented at the International Congress on Aging of International Sociological Association, Trivandrum, India.

3. Burr, J. A. and J.E. Mutchler. 1992. "The Living Arrangements of Unmarried Elderly Hispanic Females," Demography 29: 93-112.

4. Da Vanzo, J. and Angelique Chan. 1994. "Living Arrangements of Older Malaysians: Who Co resides With Their Adult Children," Demography 31, No. 1: 95-113.

5. Da Vos, S., and K. Holden. 1988. "Measures Comparing Living Arrangements of the Elderly: An Assessment," Population and Development Review 14, No.4: 688-704.

6. Elman, Cheryl and Peter Uhlenberg. 1995. "Co-residence in the Early Twentieth Century: Elderly Women in the United States and their Children," Population Studies 49: 501-517.
7. Hashimoto, Akiko. 1991. "Living Arrangements of the Aged in Seven Developing Countries: A Preliminary Analysis," Journal of Cross-Cultural Gerontology 6: 359-381.
8. Irudaya Rajan, S., U.S. Mishra and P.S. Sarma.1995. "Living Arrangements Among the Indian Elderly," Hongkong Journal of Gerontology 9: No.2: 20-28.
9. Kamo, Yoshinori and Min Zhou. 1994. "Living Arrangements of Elderly Chinese and Japanese in the United States," Journal of Marriage and Family 56: 544-558.
10. Kobrin, F.E. 1976. "The Primary Individual and the Family: Changes in Living Arrangements in the United States since 1940," Journal of Marriage and Family 38: 233-239.
11. Martin, G. Linda. 1989. "Living Arrangements of the Elderly in Fiji, Korea, Malaysia and the Philippines," Demography 26, no.4: 627-643.
12. National Sample Survey Organization. 1991. "Socioeconomic Profile of the Aged Persons: NSS 42nd Round (July 1986 - June 1987)," Sarvekshana 15, No.2.
13. Panda, Pradeep Kumar. 1997. Living Arrangements of the Elderly in Rural Orissa. Working Paper No. 277. Trivandrum: Centre for Development Studies.
14. Population Division, ESCAP. 1992. Asia-Pacific Population Journal 7, No.3.
15. Sirboon, Siriwan and Jhon Knodel. 1994. "Thai Elderly Who Do Not Co-reside with their Children," Journal of Cross-Cultural Gerontology 9: 21-38.
16. Soldo, B.J. and Lauriat. 1976. "Living Arrangements Among the Elderly in the United States: a Log-linear Approach," Journal of Comparative Family Studies 7, No.2: 351-366.
17. Thomas, Kausar and Andrew Wister. 1984. "Living Arrangements of Older Women: the Ehnic Dimension," Journal of Marriage and Family 46: 301-311.
18. Vijayakumar, S. 1991. Family Life and Socio-economic Problems of the Aged. Delhi: Ashish Publishing House.
19. Wolf, D.A. 1984. Kin Availability and the Living Arrangements of the Older Women," Social Science Research 13: 72-89.
20. Wolf, D.A. and B.J. Soldo. 1988. "Household Composition Choices of Older Unmarried Women," Demography 25: 387-403.

8

TRANSITION, TRANFORMATION, AND RE-SOCIALISATION: A BIOGRAPHICAL APPROACH TO THE ELDERLY QUESTION[1]

Ganesha Somayaji

Introduction

An important aspect of demographic transition in the new millennium is the rapid increase in the population of the elderly. This is a matter of great concern in the over populous country like India. Many consider the transition as a burden and strike an alarm: "The population aged 60+ is increasing rapidly in our country from 56 million in 1991 to 70 million in 1998 and is expected to be 177 million by 2025. This aging population presents a burden on the socio-economic and health infrastructure of our society..."(Sandhu 1999: 15). Whether this ageing population is really a burden? Are we prepared to shoulder this burden as a challenge? How shall we respond to this challenge? These questions are addressed to all those who are anxious of improving the quality of life of the increasing elderly population of various categories – literate and illiterate, rural and urban, women and men, affluent and the poor and so on. The questions solicit answers from several levels of human experiences ¾ the individual, the familial, the societal and the governmental.

A number of recent studies on the conditions of the elderly in India, basing themselves on the quantitative data gathered from the macro-national level surveys and qualitative data from case studies, made certain attempts to provide an integrated perspective to the question of elderly in India (Dandekar 1996; Rajan et al. 1999; Joshi 1999; Durairaj and Rangasamy 1999). However, in their ultimate analysis they incline more towards recommending refining the governmental policies and programmes aimed at preparing the entire Indian society to face the challenge of increasing population of the elderly.

Dandekar (1996), for example argues that the thrust of the governmental policies and programmes should be directed at providing old-age pensions for the rural old for two important reasons: (a) the rural old are well-integrated with their social milieu and (b) the pension schemes are a cheaper alternative. For the problems afflicting the urban old she visualises old-age homes as offering a viable solution. The governmental and non-governmental organisations may take lead in institutionalising the urban old so as to redeem them of the problems of poverty, housing shortage and intergenerational conflicts. In a similar style, Rajan et al. (1999) provide a comprehensive understanding of the socio-economic and demographic dynamics of India's elderly and chalk out elaborate policy prescriptions for improving the quality of life of India's senior citizens.

These studies dream of managing the elderly boom in India with the help of the policies and programmes of governments and philanthropic activities of non-governmental organisations. However, our experiences with the governmental policies and programmes aimed at ameliorating the conditions of such target groups as children, women, and tribe offer telling stories of mismanagement and dysfunctions. Given the diversities and inequalities of various types found in our country we may very well doubt the efficacy of any holistic engineering enterprise.

In this context it is essential to recall the fact reiterated time and again by social gerontologists that the demographic transition coupled with social transformation restructure the social worlds of the elderly. This ubiquitous process of formation of the social worlds varies in its existential contents for individuals and families as members of different social categories. The influence of governmental policies and measures too vary for these categories. Therefore, the external interventions mentioned above are not sufficient to improve the quality of life. As rightly observed by Rao and Parthasarathy (1999) certain preparations are required not only on the part of intervening agencies but also by the immediate social milieu of the elderly and the elderly personalities *per se*. Keeping this in view, an attempt is made in this paper to demonstrate the dimensions of 'the elderly question' with the help of a biographical approach.

In order to assess the elderly situation we have to peep into the multiple biographies — of the young and old, of the families, of the social categories and of the communities. I will further sharpen this approach by adding autobiographical touch to the issue under consideration by reconstructing the social worlds of the elderly of my own household, village and caste.

Brahmin Elderly of a Locality in Transition

The locality under consideration is Chitrapadi *Honda*.[2] It is a part of Chitrapadi village, which in turn is one of the wards of Saligrama Town Panchayat of Udupi District. It is situated 25 kms. North of Udupi Town on the National Highway 17. The *jati* composition of the households of this multi-*jati* locality and the actual elderly population are given in table one.

Table 1
The Elderly Population of the Locality

Caste	*Household with Elderly*	*House hold without Elderly*	*Total*
Brahmin	19 (36)	07	26
Vishwakarma	06 (07)	05	11
Ganiga	03 (03)	03	06
Nairi	01 (01)	02	03
Moger	03 (04)	01	04
Poojari	–	02	02
Total	32 (51)	20	52

Note: Figures in parentheses denote the actual number of Elderly.

Traditionally, Brahmins have been the dominant *jati* both in terms of numerical strength and land ownership of the locality. But the situation is now changing. Though the whole locality is experiencing demographic transition and social transformation, in the case of Brahmins the change is very drastic and apparent. Some highlights of their experiences are given below.

1. Each household has at one member working in distant cities—Bangalore is a major destination.

2. Literacy and high educational level and entry to professions like teaching and engineering.
3. Land loss due to land legislation.
4. Sale of land to non-Brahmins leading to the increasing share of out-migrants in household expenditure.
5. Increasing out-migration and growing number of households managed by the elderly.

Among the non-Brahmins of the locality the adults manage almost all households. This is due to the new found land ownership, low educational level hindering mobility, and continuation of hereditary occupations and availability of semi-skilled jobs within and around the locality. The non-Brahmin elderly are not included in the scope of this paper.

Social Worlds of the Elderly

The external and internal elements together formulate and reformulate the social worlds of the members of any age-cohort. The external elements are the living conditions and the internal elements are the social-psychological states and the personality systems. If the former refers to the objective social conditions the latter decide the degree of involvement in and integration into society. The latter may also be referred to as good adjustment or re-socialisation. Transition from membership in one age-cohort to the other and transformation taking place in the living conditions change the nature of the social world.

In the case of the elderly matters of retirement, widowhood, declining economic resources and residential relocation — all affect the quality of life (Unruh 1983: 47). We may take retirement as a point of reference. It offers both positive and problematic alternatives. On the one hand it marks a relief from stresses of job. At this stage may arise opportunities to develop new interests and activities with room for wider range of choices than those the individual has enjoyed at any earlier point in his life. On the other hand, retirement generally results in loss of routine with regard to utilisation of one's working hours, reduction in income, loss of status as a contributor to the economy and broken contacts with the customary associates (Rao and Parthasarathy 1999: 16). Changing social roles and subsequent re-socialisation, level of economic security, pass time activities, health conditions and health security – all contribute to the formation of the social worlds of the elderly.[3] Some of these may now be taken for careful consideration.

Literacy

Literacy and education contribute to the well being of the elderly in various respects. Education is functional in several ways for those in the late life. Firstly, it provides economic stability through employment for regular pay before retirement and pension and other benefits during retirement. Secondly, it enables smoother adaptability of the elderly towards the socio-economic transition in the society. Thirdly, longevity also has a strong association with education; literacy levels and life expectancy at births is highly correlated (Rajan et al. 1999: 33). This is due to the health consciousness of the educated person. Fourthly, the reading habits associated with education and other activities related to this help the literate elderly in swimming across the vast sea of leisure available in later life. And finally, the educated elderly are the source of information and may play advisory role in their neighbourhood that increases their self-respect and own level of confidence.

Out of 36 elderly observed, only two are illiterate who are women and 80+ in their age. Four men are highly educated and retired as teachers. The total of ten households with elderly subscribes to one or the other newspapers and five of them regularly purchase Kannada magazines. Mostly the men spend some time daily in reading and women are busy in attending to regular household chores. Some women are found reading religious literature. The four retired are consulted for advice by the Brahmins and non-Brahmins alike in various matters: children's education, filling of various types of forms, seeking governmental assistance during various occasions of crop failures, and reading and writing letters.

Financial Security and Work Participation

The financial situation of the aged is closely associated with the socio-economic environment in which they reside. In general the economic status of a person is dependent on her or his past work status, level of education and the present activity status (Rajan et al. 1999: 217).

In the locality under observation, except for the two women and one 80+ aged and four who lost/sold land, all others are actively engaged in agricultural work, actual or supervisory. However, no one is landlord here. Income from agriculture is to be supplemented by rendering priestly services or pensions or monthly remittances from the out-migrants. Elderly women participate in several works related to cultivation: weeding, thrashing and cleaning the grain. Most of the households maintain cows and the women elderly engage in such tasks as cleaning the cowshed and milking.

Apart from cultivation, as noted earlier, there are certain supplementary sources of income. The *vaidika* elderly work as priests whenever they are invited. Some elderly men from the *grihasta* households work as professional cooks. Very recently the premises of the Shiva temple of the locality has been started to be used to render services relating to the performance of *sanskaras* and *pujas* of several types. The services are extended to the non-Brahmins also. Due to this development many elderly get regular employment.

Two women who lost all of their nearest relatives live with their distant relatives and are in receipt of government pension for the elderly. Some even get regular interests over fixed deposits in nationalised banks. On the whole we may state that the elderly in this locality are somehow capable of fulfilling their necessities and comforts. Another interesting observation is that all the capable elderly are actively engaged in one or the other type of work. They may not be as productive as they were in their yesteryears; their very engagement we may discern as providing them the satisfaction of being alive.

Health Conditions

Ageing is associated with fatigue and a decline in functional capacity of the organs of the body due to physiological transformation. The elderly are one of the most high-risk groups in terms of health (Jayakumar 1992: 3). In the locality, except for one pensioner, one 80+ elderly and two 70+ all others are quite healthy. Very rarely they visit the doctor.

The problems of the three exceptional cases are very severe. Two of them have problems with their legs and can move only within their houses. The two 70+ suffer from kidney problems. All of them are men. The children of all of these elderly stay in cities and they are being cared by their wives who are aged. This is an all India phenomenon. Census 1991 reposts that about 44 per cent of the elderly women and 81 per cent of the elderly men were living with their spouses. While men are likely to be cared for by their spouses the same cannot be said for women (Karkal 1999:WS-56).

The comparative better standard of health of the elderly of this locality may be due to their continuous engagement in one or the other type of work even in this stage, dietary practises (consumption of vegetables, milk and milk–products) and the absence of bad habits. Contrarily, the absence of these conditions adversely affects the health of the non-Brahmin elderly of the locality.

Studies conducted elsewhere in the country also reiterate that many aged are unable to arrange balanced diet and ensure for themselves adequate amount of proteins, vitamins and minerals. The consequences have been wide spread physical deterioration and ailments of various types (Bhatia 1983: 143). However, the elderly of the locality under observation are not facing health problems that emerge as a result of dietary imbalances. Even then, some are advised by their doctors to control their dietary habits. It may be noted that those who are presently in the young-old stage may encounter health problems associated with old-old stage later on. How will they be taken care of in future depends on the living arrangements.

Living Arrangements

The question of living arrangements relates to the familial circumstances of the elderly: Do they live with their children? Or do they live independently? Whether they are living with their spouses? Or are they widowed?

Usually, the living arrangement is understood in terms of several conditions. Some of them are as follows.

1. The family type in which the elderly live.
2. The authority, which the elderly enjoy.
3. The place they stay and the people with whom they stay.
4. The type of relationships they keep with their kith and kin.
5. The extent to which they can re-socialise to the changing environment (Dandekar 1996:38 and Rajan et al. 1999:39).

The quality of life of the elderly depends on the type of living arrangements. Jayashree (1999), for example, in her study of elderly in the early phase of old-age found out that co-residence with relatives, financial independence, continued emotional and material support to children and continued exercise of power in family affairs enhance the quality of life. Thus in the early phase of old-age, intensity of problem associated with both ageing and retirement are low. Of course she admits that this may not hold true for the elderly in the old-old stage.

Table 2
Living Arrangements

Living arrangements	*Men*	*Women*	*Total*
Staying with children	05	08	13
Staying with others	–	02	02
Staying with only spouse	09	09	18
Staying single	–	03	03
Total	14	22	36

Table 2 gives a picture of living arrangement of the elderly in the locality.

The whole locality is greying; in twelve households only the elderly stay. The children and other relatives are occasional visitors. Out of them three stay single because of the death of their spouses. Apart from the nine elderly couple who stay together for themselves three more couple are living with their children in the locality. All others have lost their spouses. The different living arrangements have differential implications for the elderly who experience them. Their problems of re-socialisation vary in accordance with living arrangements. Those who are staying with children and other relatives have to adjust with mainly loss of authority, dependence on children, generation gap and quarrels. In one household partition has taken place recently and the widowed mother has to move from one son to the other after her successive quarrels with the sons and the daughters-in-law. In this living arrangement there are certain benefits too. Absence of loneliness and company of the children are some of them. They are also assured that when they reach the 'old-old' stage they need not move to the far away places. The elderly in this locality are very much interested in spending their last days here only.

The elderly couples that stay together are far better placed than those who stay single are. All of them have regular sources of income either in terms of pension or remittances from the relatives who work in the cities. They are relatively less isolated. The problems of generation gap are absent. However, they are more worried of their future when they reach the 'old-old' stage.

A few couples have the problem of quarrel with each other. Even the elderly who stays with some of her distant relatives faces the problem of personal adjustment and always quarrels with them. In a way, it may be said that the entire locality is characterised by frequent quarrels and loud exchange of bad words. However, the misunderstandings are of very short duration. Reconciliation takes place many times without the intervention of a third party. One reason for frequent quarrels and their dissolution may be geographical propinquity. The whole locality is spread across not more than a square k.m. Apart from this there is a social responsibility. Each household arranges dinners during ceremonial celebrations throughout the year. The whole locality participates in them. Reconciliation takes place on such occasions. During such dinners even the out-station relatives of the concerned households come down to the locality. On their arrival the personality clashes within the household too are resolved to some extent. However, it must be noted that just like quarrel the phase of resolution too is short lived. Thus quarrel is a perennial source of tension for the elderly of this locality.

As has been noted earlier, the number of households managed by the elderly by themselves is increasing and this is a matter of great concern for the residents of the locality. Two houses of the locality have already been locked, the land sold and the sick parents have been taken to Bangalore. The fear that looms large in the minds of many elderly is that whether such things happen in their case too?

An important problem being faced by the elderly who manage themselves is that of looking after the fields. The growing scarcity of manual labour coupled with declining physical strength is the source of much stress. Because of their emotional attachment to the ancestral land they find it very agonising even to think of selling it. Thus they are caught in between the children who stay away and the land where they have been living since their birth.

As for the type of house is concerned the elderly of the locality do not have any problem since all houses are tiled. Most houses have coconut groves surrounding their houses. They have their own wells and lavatories build outside the house. Only one house has go toilet facilities within the house. The absence of toilets within the house is creating a lot of inconveniences to some of the elderly. In near future this may develop to be a severe problem.

Leisure and Free Time Activities

Leisure management constitutes an important component of the living conditions of the elderly. Its nature differs for the elderly of different categories. The educated elderly spend their time in reading newspapers and books. Most of the women are busy in attending to household chores or works in eh fields. Watching television is a pass time activity for all. Visiting temples and reading religious books and performing puja are popular among many. Most of the elderly men who are physically fit spend their evenings in the near by Pete where they engage in hours-long conversations with their friends from neighbouring villages. Most of them have regular siesta in the afternoon. Participating ceremonial dinners in the household of the neighbourhood is another regular time-pass. Thus it may be noted that the leisure time activities of eh elderly in locality don't have any financial implication. Leisure management is not at all a problem for them.

Conclusion

A salient point emerges from the above reconstruction of the social worlds of the elderly in the micro setting: the category elderly comprises multiple sub-categories such as young-old and old-old, elderly women and men. Each sub-category and the persons constituting the sub-category have lived in experiences specific to them. We can only make certain crude generalisations.

The elderly under consideration do not suffer from economic and housing problems. The health standards of the young-old are comparatively better. The poor elderly are provided with old-age pensions. They have also found out for themselves pass-time activities having limited financial implications. This does not mean that they do not have any problems. Frequent quarrels, out-migration of young and adult members and non-availability of workers to carry out agricultural work are some of the problems.

The factors of personality and social transformation are at the root of these problems. Quarrels, attachment to land, deteriorating health, and pass-time activities are of the former category. Land alienation, improving educational standards of the family members and out-migration belong to the second category. Both of these aspects are influencing the quality of life of the elderly.

The problems of general nature, such as those relating to finance or health, demand interventions from both state and the NGOs in the form of providing such assistance as old-age pensions and free health check-up and medical aid. Other problems that arise due to social transformation and consequent requirement of re-socialisation need to be attended on personal and interpersonal levels. Reconstructions of the biographies of the elderly under consideration are important devices for both interpretative understanding of their situation and initiating interventions. Personal level understanding and interpretation includes among other things planning for enduring financial security in the late life, participating in work activities as long as the body co-operates, leading a bad-habit free life throughout, pursuing hobbies and avoiding quarrels add up to the own level of confidence. On the interpersonal level both the elderly and their family members need to reiterate for themselves the existential regularity that nobody is indispensable for this world and that we are indispensable only for ourselves.

For all said and done, proper preparation is required at all levels by all categories of individuals. Rao and Parthasarathy (1999: 22) have neatly encapsulated the biographical dimension of the elderly question.

"...Children and adolescents should be given as much opportunities as possible to look after the elderly members of the family. In early adulthood onwards one needs to plan for long-term savings, building house, education and marriage of sons and daughters. It is also important to develop healthy attitude towards old age and positive out look on life and death simultaneously."

NOTES

1. This is revised version of my presentations at two national seminars. (1) 'Issues and Problems of the Aged' organised by the Mangalore Sociology Association on December 4-5, 1999 at St. Aloysius College

Mangalore. (2) 'Problems of the Aged in India: Challenges and Remedies' organised by the Department of Sociology, Kuvempu University, Karnataka on December 28-29, 2000.

2. The Chitrapadi village is divided into two parts on the basis of the terrain: *Honda* and *Bettu*. *Honda* is the low-lying area and *bettu* is the highland.
3. Ashish Bose has developed a statistical and anthropological method to be employed in the study of the living conditions of eh elderly. Designated as HO-FIT this method is based on his study of the elderly in Delhi sponsored by the United Nations Population Fund. Each letter in HO-FIT stands for particular measurement. 'H' is for health security, 'O' for own level of confidence, 'F' for family security, 'I' for income security and 'T' for Transcendental support. He feels that data for all the five elements is required to assess the condition of the elderly (reported by Rajkumari 1999).

REFERENCES

Bhatia, H.S. (1983), *Aging and Society*. Udaipur: Aryan Book Centre.

Dandekar, Kumudini (1996), *The Elderly in India*. New Delhi: Sage.

Durairaj, N. and Rengasamy, Kala, Rani (1999), 'The Aged: Need Love and Protection', *Social Welfare*, 46 (7): 6-7.

Jayakumar, Stanley (1992), 'Health of the Elderly', *Social Welfare*, 34 (7): 3-8.

Jayashree (1999), Living Arrangements Enhance Quality of Life, Social Welfare, Vol. 46, No.7.

Joshi, Uma. (1999), 'Creating Social Sensibilities for the Aged', *Social Welfare*, 46 (7):3-5.

Karkal, Malini (1999), 'Aging and Women in India', in *Economic and Political Weekly*, 34 (44): WS54-WS56.

Rao, V.N. and Parthasarathy, R. (1999), 'Coping with Retired Life Needs New Attitude', Social Welfare, 46 (7): 16, 17 and 22.

Rajan, Irudya, S. U.S. Mishra and Sankara Sarma P. (1999), *India's Elderly: Burden or Challenge*. New Delhi: Sage.

Rajkumari, Anuradha (1999), 'Pursue a Hobby to be Happy in Old Age', in *The Navhind Times*, October 8, 1999.

Sandhu, S.S. (1999), 'Foreword', in Irudya Rajan S, U.S. Mishra and Sankara Sarma P: *India's Elderly: Burden or Challenge*. New Delhi: Sage.

Unruh, David, R. (1983), *Invisible Lives: Social Worlds of the Aged*. New Delhi: Sage.

9

SOCIAL CONSTRUCTION OF AGEING: AN EMPIRICAL STUDY OF THE PERCEPTION OF THE URBAN ELDERLY

Vighnesh N. Bhat

Introduction

The approach to the Xth Plan Proposal makes several planned propositions to the betterment of the elderly population in India in the coming years. More financial assistance to NGOs, strengthening the hands of Panchayat Raj institutions, encouraging Self Help Groups, more research in geriatrics and gerontology etc. are thought of as possible ways to minimise the future damage to Indian society in terms of treating its 'senior citizenry.' Along with legislative measures to protect the rights and privileges of the aged in our society, means to strengthen traditional social institutions and social bonds are also in the making. India has started realising the importance of addressing itself to the question of the elderly population and its problems in the context of national development[1]. Understanding the elderly population — both conceptually and in pragmatic terms — has become an important consideration for the social scientists in India today as it is true elsewhere as well.

Traditionally, Indian culture always had been tolerant and diverse culture at all possible planes. Indian-ness of this society manifested, and continues to pageant, in its cultural composition of diverse ethnic practices. There have been certain ideas and practices that are common to disparate groups over a long time, however. Respect for the elderly members of the collectivity is one such manifestation prevalent in our society at all levels and in all regions which has run into rough weather in recent years. This fact, having significant sociological overtone, needs to be carefully looked into while one analyses the problems of the elderly in India as the country is fast heading toward the eventuality of greying in significant number

Age dynamics are essentially biological phenomena but they also have a significant psycho social dimension. It is now commonly accepted that growing old — earlier held as a natural biological process — is associated with serious cultural issues beyond its biological dimension. Ageing was not a serious problem in traditional India because of its social structural realities then. The life expectancy in our country was rather low until recently due to health hazards and other wrath of nature that kept the 'aged population' a tiny group. Thus it was not difficult for the social system to accommodate its senior members with some degree of esteem. In fact, in traditional India, as well known, the elderly members were considered as the reservoir of wisdom and intelligence for the benefit of future generations. It may be noted that the great sages of earlier times were portrayed as aged and patriarchal in nature. In a society of this nature, the older members did not find it difficult to step away from the responsibilities of the joint-family and relegate themselves to *vanaprastha* honourably. We are witnessing a different scenario today. What is true for the rest of the world is equally true for our society that necessitates hard soul searching.

Needless to stress the fact that global society is greying very rapidly. An average man in the world today lives for over 65 years. In Japan, which has the highest human life expectancy on earth today, male life expectancy is 76 years and female life expectancy is 83 years (Srivastava 2000)[2]. Enhanced nutritional endowment advances in the medical field, better information and communication, and the like have resulted in an impressive increase in average human longevity. The problems related to 'ageing' and of 'old age' become particularly crucial to the Third World. It is estimated that over 50 per cent of the total 258 million individuals aged over 65 years were found in the developing world in late 1980s (Sahayam 1988)[3]. In fact, three four countries projected to have the largest number of old people in the year 2025 are China,

India and Indonesia (Siegal & Hoover 1982)[4]. The average life expectancy in India was 62 years as per the 1991 Census; this was an increase of over 12 years between 1970 and 1990. While exact statistics are not readily available for the recent years, there is little doubt that life expectancy has gone up further. As a result of this increase, India's elderly population aged above 60 has been estimated at 60 million during mid-90s. The government figures project this number to rise to 76 million by the end of this year. In other words, by the year 2001, 7.7 per cent of the total Indian population will be above 60 and it will go up by another 1.9 per cent by the year 2016[5].

As the population increases owing to the process of modernisation and resultant growth in the quality and quantity of public health measures, we are confronted with the serious problem of emplacement of our 'senior citizens' with dignity once accorded to them by our society. Work rectitude of industrialisation forces the employed couple to withdraw from joint families and to give up the burden of caring for their elderly parents within the family. This results in psycho-social difficulties of varied dimensions. Equally difficult is the dignified separate living of the aged people from the families of offspring. Mounting economic, health and psychological problems of the elderly population frequently makes this group highly vulnerable to varied kinds of discrimination and resultant exploitation. In sociological literature this process of discrimination is termed 'ageism' in the echelon of 'sexism', 'racism' and the like.

Conceptual Frame

According to Atchley (Atchley 1978)[6] problems of the elderly are heightened because of three major socio-economic reasons: (1) labelling the aged as fragile and incapable, (2) the idea that work is the measure of any worthwhile life, and (3) economic deprivation often leading to cultural isolation and psychological depression. Each of these factors reinforces the other two. In the modern world where life has become expeditious and swift, the aged people find it increasingly difficult to cope up with the speed and flow of information. Further, as the unemployment rates sore, especially in the developing nations with the prolonging of life expectancy due to improved health care, death no longer creates openings for the labour force. Eventually a social substitute for death (and therefore new openings) as a means of exit is instituted in the form of retirement of the old. Voluntary retirement schemes amply demonstrate such a pressure.

Old age is a cultural construct[7]. Biologists and health professionals speak of chronological/biological age whereas psychologists speak of mental age. Sociologically speaking, every member in a given society is expected to play a particular role with defined social position conferred on him/her. This helps society to spread out activities relevant to one's sex, age or other such variable. Respect accorded to a particular activity performed by an age group makes that group as high or low. In modern societies during the long period of adulthood, people are required to conform to roles and behavioural standards that are accorded to them by their socio-cultural structure based on achievement. When the individual retires, he loses his achieved role-status and the behavioural-standards that accompany that role-status. As there is a general absence of this new role-model of 'the aged', the elderly are put into the pigeon holes of age-specific behavioural specifications rather than their earlier achieved status. Their world grows smaller and smaller as they leave work, friends and family members die, and as their mobility decreases. Popular belief that the aged population is senile, lacking in individuality, unproductive, conservative, and resistant to change is purely a cultural construct and often does not stand to concrete empirical proof.

Death is another construct very closely associated with old age. The aged people are culturally made to accept death although most of them fear dying as much as the younger ones. A double standard of the conception of death prevails in Indian society. When a child or a young person dies, people grieve openly cursing the nature for pricking the budding talent at such a potential/productive age. The death of an older person, on the other hand, elicits a very different community response. Often even the family members view this as natural and not inappropriate. This culturally constructed perception of death by the younger generations brings in a sense of hollowness and vacuum among the elderly and make them all the more miserable.

Work and work ethic are considered as the principal good in modern society. It is assumed that without work you are without a role and without status. The financial benefits from work are held as the most important payoff. Hence the younger population craves for jobs. With large-scale unemployment and underemployment, the developing nations often favour a reduction in retirement age of those in service. People after attaining certain age and service are encouraged to opt out of work voluntarily. This is viewed as a possible solution to the ever-increasing frustration of the unemployed youth. On another axis, retirement from work is taken as the beginning of old age. That is why, retired people are considered as 'aged' and fragile. While a majority of them are still fit to work for several more years due to increased longevity and better quality of life, they are dubbed as inefficient and weak. This clearly manifests in the stereotype image of 'senior citizens' with the stigma attached to this role.

After Berger and Luckman (Berger & Luckman 1971)[8], we know that reality is socially constructed. The sociology of knowledge helps us to analyse the process through which old age is socially constructed and made use of. Old age is not simply a matter of accumulated years or decrease in physical abilities: it is a set of social expectation and commonly held beliefs, instead. This often results in the perception that the elderly are a major obstacle for the young. To add to it, old people are regarded as having declining intellectual capabilities. This negative ideology, which often results in the discriminatory practice of ageism, is characterised by several stigmatic beliefs. Some important ones may be listed as the follows:

1. aged people are generally sickly and unhealthy;
2. they often suffer from senility;
3. most elderly persons develop rigid and inflexible personality;
4. aged people, in general, are depressed, dejected and keep themselves isolated;
5. elderly population is generally unproductive and uninteresting;
6. elderly people despise erotic issues.

In India, as in several other societies, there is an increasing tend towards treating the old people as a separate group and according them special privileges. This is reflected in giving them old-age pension (varying from Rs.30 to 250 in different States), bus passes, rail and air travel concessions, etc. This mode of treating the elderly population as a separate and helpless category is nearly instrumental in aggravating the problem of ageism. Such practices eventuate in a vicious cycle of societal expectations, and individual's role-play, resulting in a negative 'self-fulfilling prophecy'. Older people are forced by the society to act the role of the *elderly*, to give up working, withdraw from social activities, and be depended on others, and so on. The elderly population in India today acts in the manner socially expected of this group, resulting in *social construction of old age* in which society sets this group apart.

Keeping the theoretical perspective of social construction of old age in India today, the present paper tries to understand the problem in a micro situation. Main areas of concentration for this study were:

(i) social, family and interpersonal relationship;
(ii) economic conditions;
(iii) problems associated with health;
(iv) family and social-psychological opinions; and
(v) gender discrimination in varied walks of life.

Objectives of the Study

The study was intended to understand the problems and factors associated with the construction of typical concept of 'old-age' in an urban setting. The aim of the research work is to initiate a larger and more comprehensive study in this area of vital importance with special emphasis on gerontological issues.

Study Area

The present paper does not permit a detailed cultural and civil portrayal of the study area due to paucity of space, only a brief outline of the region is given in this paper.

Shimoga District is situated in the western part of the State of Karnataka and, is surrounded by the Districts of Dharwad in the north, Chickmagalur and Udupi in the south, Davanagere in the east, and Uttara Kannada in the west in between 13 56 norths and 75 38 east latitude and longitude respectively. There are two important rivers flowing through the District — river Tunga and river Bhadra. The District comprises of seven Taluks with a thick forest cover and fertile soil. According to 1991 Census, the total area of the District is about 10,553 sq. kms with a total population of over 1.9 million, distributed in about 2,000 villages and towns. Rate of literacy in 1991 was 61. 53 percent Bhadravati city is just about 18 kilometers from Shimoga, the District headquarters. Shimoga city is considered as a fast-growing but still 'conservative' urban area. The general impression of this town as illustrated in popular images and literature is one of traditional and conservative outlook toward life in general. Religious rites and cultural programmes crowd the town round the year. People in general are conscious of their castes, and hence, highly volatile with regard to acceptance or rejection of community values. Shimoga city is well-known for its educational activities and musical talent.

Sample

150[9] elderly citizens (75 men and 75 women) of Shimoga city constitute the study sample. Vidyanagar, Vinobhanagar and Gandhi Bazar areas were selected for the purpose of investigation and analysis. Here, the term 'elderly population' was conceived to constitute all those citizens of Shimoga city who have attained the age of sixty or above, and who are considered as normal sane human beings. The sample has been further sub-divided into three age-cohorts, namely:

(a) those elders between the age-group 61 - 70;
(b) those between 71 - 80;
(c) those who are 80+.

While *caste* and *class* were not explicitly considered as *variables* in this small-sample study, the randomness of the selection process has led to a fairly representative sample allowing some general observations on these variables as well.

METHODOLOGY

Data Collection

Data collection was done with the help of individual interviews of the senior citizens by the researchers at respondents' convenient time and space. An interview schedule, pre-tested for its relative validity and reliability, was used for this purpose. Collected data were codified, arranged and analysed in the sociological-methodological frame to present them in tabular form. The tables were analysed to arrive at broad inferences and some general conclusions. While tables are omitted due to the compressed space and confined compass of this write-up, end results are presented in the summary form below. Further, this being a qualitative sociological study, no statistical tool has been used to validate the interview data. Qualitative support to the study data comes from interviewer's observation in the field during and after the interviews. Information is analysed with sociological conceptual frame to arrive at tentative conclusions.

Results

1. Marital Status has the greatest impact on living arrangements of the elderly population. This is not unexpected as it goes well with common-sense observation as well. A number of studies in the Indian societal context have confirmed this result (Easwaramoorthy 1991)[10]. This is also an expected outcome because in the Indian social context, family still plays a major role in deciding individual's life ambitions and person's routine activities are closely tied with those of life-partner.
2. Percentage of the elderly living alone was 8 percent (12 individual respondents) for the urban area of Shimoga. This result is also in tune with a few earlier national level studies conducted in rural and urban areas[11]. This result is also supported by general observation and commonsensical insight. While the proportion of parents living independently away from their offspring is still not alarmingly high, this indicates a trend toward unattached parent-child relationship at old age.
3. The available literature on Indian old age problems establishes that the risk factor for mental morbidity in the ageing population stands comparatively higher than for the general population, estimated at 120 and 70 per million. The main risk factors are loss of fortune, fall in self-esteem, sense of helplessness, poor education, substandard health, social and gender discrimination, financial debt and status as a widowed person (Joshi & Sengupta 2000)[12]. In the present study, it was found that the health status of the elderly

population in general is much worse than what is generally expected. Chronic diseases are quite common among them. About 11 percent suffer from communicable diseases. They do not get adequate medical facilities in spite of the fact that Shimoga city has relatively a large number of hospitals, dispensaries and clinics.

4. One possible way of bringing the elderly population into the mainstream of society is through furthering an ideological revolution at the level of family. The family as an institution can play an exemplary role in fighting ageism, and in the realisation of many aspects which are now enshrined in the proposed National Policy for the Older People. In the present research study however, family in general, as a social and economic unit has been less than encouraging to all its senior elders. Elderly members were often ignored as *old-fashioned* and irrelevant to the present way of thinking and living.
5. The present empirical study once again proved the earlier research findings that interpersonal relationships between the old and the young mainly depended upon the family background of the aged. Quality of relationship was also influenced by economic status and health status of the elderly. While the percentages of the negative correlation between sound financial position of the elderly members and negative treatment by the their younger counterparts are not very high and may not be *statistically significant*, they sound a warning bell to the future things to come in the Indian family set up that cannot be ignored.
6. One of the issues that have come up repeatedly was the fear of death and after-death rites among several elderly respondents. The concept of death is not taken philosophically as *an inevitable thing to happen in human life* in the sense often portrayed in Indian axioms. An overwhelming 76 percent (114 respondents) expressed their manifest or latent fear regarding death while they confessed that the idea of death often is a source of anxiety.
7. Non-acceptance of novelty is also found to be one of the critical reasons for the problems of the elderly. Many of them (100 respondents or 66.7 percent) have attributed their rigid socialisation as the reason for their difficult in accepting the

present pervasive and permissive practices. The special area of difficulty was the gender relationship in the family and man-woman relationship in public life.

Broad conclusions of this study may be stated in the following words. The aged can maintain their status and good interpersonal relationships if (a) their spouses are alive, (b) they are physically good, (c) they own some property and/or valuables, and (d) they can adjust to changing family conditions and values.

History of India in recent centuries tells us that the process of modernisation, couched with Western living arrangements and lifestyle, has presented to us a change from life-form in which chronological age was much less important to replace it by an increasingly age-relevant life-form. Independent India, with its industrial capitalistic development model, has brought in increased awareness of age as a basis of social distinctions and greater signification of age-groups[13]. While it is being clearly acknowledged now that age and age-related aspects of the social actor are key aspects of social stratification system, theories of ageing are relatively less developed. The political economy approach to the process and consequences of ageing, with its emphasis on the social construction of the 'elderly' groups seems to have logically into a post-modernist approach to the 'deconstruction' of the prevailing attitude of the society towards the aged. Concepts like 'age elite', 'age warfare' and the like are the indications to the things to come in the near future. This view has enough to offer to the Indian scholars in the area of cultural gerontology.

Let us be prepared for a changed scenario. As demonstrated by Rajan and others[14], the number of elderly in India is expected to increase sharply from 55 million in 1191 to 135 million in 2021. Such a prospective demographic imbalance in the Indian population in the coming decade or two certainly would pose serious problems in terms of socio-cultural adjustments and gaps in the adaptation process. With the declining position of joint families due mainly to industrialisation and urbanisation, institutional arrangements for the elderly population seems to become imperative in the coming years. Problems of ill-health, poverty and information illiteracy and the resultant innocence about the changing world may put this needy section into a state of absolute despair and hopelessness unless the society develops a more positive, accommodative and supportive attitude towards the aged. This becomes all the more serious in urban India with its coming crisis in normative basics and scarcity of necessities.

Freud, in his well known work *Civilisation and its Discontents* (1961)[15], has said the following paragraph: (As we grow old), we are threatened with suffering from three directions: from our own body, from the external world, and finally from our relations with other human beings. The suffering which comes from this last source is perhaps more painful to us than any other. This is all the more convincing when even a cursory glance at the rural Indian elders (both the young-old and the old-old) provides enough evidences to this effect. Not many in the family, nor in the community prefer to give a helping hand to this highly vulnerable section of our society to make them spend their last years with some sense of gratification, self-pride and contentment. While this seems to be universally true, rural India seems to be facing a stiff challenge and a major endeavour. Quality ageing is a social construct and its facilitation and enhancement depend considerably on how others perceive the elderly population in terms of their mental agility, physiological agility and emotional disposition. There is a lot that needs to be done by the younger groups in a collective way.

NOTES AND REFERENCES

1. For some general observations on this issue, refer to the Editorial, *News Letter*, Association of Gerontology, Varnish, June 2002, pp.1-3.
2. Refer Srivastava, V.K., 'Ageism' in *Seminar* — 488, April 2000, pp. 21-25 for comparative life expectancy statistics of some selected countries.
3. See Sahayam, M. D., 'Aged Females: the Most Deprived Among the Deprived', *Indian Journal of Social Work*, XLIX, 3, 1988, p. 261.
4. See Siegal, J.S. and Hoover, S. L., 'Demographic Aspects of the Health of the Elderly to the Year 2000 and Beyond', *World Health Statistical Quarterly*, 35, 1982, pp. 132-202.
5. See the advertisement inserted by the Ministry of Social Justice and Empowerment, Government of India, in the national dailies, 1 October 1999.
6. Atchley, R. C., 'Ageing as a Social Problem: An Overview' in M.M. Seltzer, et. al (Eds.) *Social Problems of the Ageing*, Wadsworth, Belmont, 1978.

7. For an interesting discussion on the pragmatic construction of the 'old' in the present Western normative context, refer M. Poole, *Constructing the 'New Old: Gender. Ageing and the Magazines,* a paper presented in RC 11, Sociology of Ageing, Brisbane, XV World Congress of Sociology, July 2002.
8. Berger P. L. and Luckman T., *The Social Construction of Reality,* Penguin, Harmondsworth, 1971.
9. The term 'elderly' here means persons who have attained the chronological age 60+ years. While respondents' oral statements were taken as proofs of their stated age, observations, in no case, were contrary to these proclamations, lending high reliability to the study sample.
10. See, for instance, study conducted by Easwaramoorthy, M. "A Study on Adjustment in Relation to Marital Status Among the Rural Aged" in Indira Jai Prakash (Ed) Quality Aging, Association of Gerontology, 1991, pp. 129 - 134.
11. This result is in tune with a nation-wide survey conducted by National Sample Survey Organisation of India. For details, see *Sarvekshana,* New Delhi, 15 (1-2), 1991.
12. Refer Joshi, P. C. and Sengupta, S. N. 'Health Issues', *Seminar,* 488, April 2000, pp. 40-43.
13. For a critical discussion of this statement, read Bradley, H. *Fractured Identities: Changing Patterns of Inequality,* Oxford, Blackwell Publishers, 1996, pp. 176-9.
14. Rajan, I. S. U. S. Mishra and P. S. Sharma, Ageing in India: Retrospect and Prospect, *Indian Social Science Review,* 2, 1, 2000, pp. 1-47.
15. Freud, Sigmond, 'Civilisation and its Discontents,' New York, Norton, 1961.

10

AGEING WOMEN FROM LOW SOCIO-ECONOMIC STATUS—A STUDY

Anupama Shah and Uma Joshi

Introduction

Recently, the aged and their problems have become the subject of study for social scientists. In many developing countries, gerontology has been studied since long time. However, the serious thought that old age is a critical phase of life as much as childhood or adolescence and hence requires special consideration, is of fairly recent origin.

Period of Old Age

Old age is the closing period of the life span. It is considered as the second childhood because both children and old persons have to depend on others for many of their requirements.

Old age is a relative term, which does not depend entirely upon years, but upon temperament and health. The changes in the early part of the life span are evolutional. They lead to maturity of structure and functioning. In the later stage of the life span, they are mainly devolution showing a regression to early stage. These changes are referred to as 'ageing'.

Population experts predict that in the years to come, the greatest increase in the elderly persons will be found among women over the age of 65 years and both men and women over 75 years. India also, therefore is greying rapidly. Longevity is up from 54 years in 1980 to 62 years at present.

The concern and care of the aged have attracted global attention of the scientists and administrators. As per the decision of the

United Nations Organisation, the year 1982 was observed as the 'International Year for the Aged'.

Problems of the Aged

The major problems of old age could be devaluation in status and income, deteriorating health, retirement, dependency, fear of death and shock of growing old. Old age should be tranquil as childhood should be playful. However, nobody prefers to have old age for longer time, as aged people are looked upon as useless, non-productive, rigid and burdensome. This leads to various problems like cultural rejection, self-rejection, anxiety and panic, psycho-physiological exhaustion, isolation and unrealistic preoccupation. Thus, old age changes the perception of things and attitude of the aged regarding others also changes.

More women are now entering the work force and are less available to take care of the aged. With the rise of nuclear families, the control of the aged over the grown up children and the family property is declining. This adds to the insecurity among the elders. The feeling for the elders, one that of respect, love and support by the young ones is being replaced by that of a burdensome attitude and neglect.

Many studies have reported the problems and the effect of the greying crisis in the society on the whole. Birren (1959), Tibbitts and Donahue (1962), Townsend (1971), Desai (1972), have emphasised that in a developing country like India, the increasing number of the aged persons will prove to be a serious problem in the near future. Their problems are mainly economic and social (Sharma, 1965), Mohan (1983), emphasised that modernisation, urbanisation and industrialisation have helped in increasing the life span of the people. But these same aspects have also created many problems for the aged in terms of alienation, dependence, gerontology, sexual aberration and certain socio-psychological syndromes. Chandra (1970) reported that for the millions in the developing countries like India, longevity without social security schemes means a drag of physical, social and psychological burden and a form of living under strain.

The position of women in the urban areas in India is very pathetic and in case of aged women, it seems hopeless. Not only women outlive men in India, as all over the world, non-acceptability of widow remarriage, illiteracy and low economic independence add to their woes.

It is important to study the satisfactions and problems of poor urban ageing women to understand the total issue of ageing in India.

Need for Research on Ageing Women

Leonard (1981-82) had reported that marital status, occupational prestige, years of formal education, race, annual income and specific life satisfaction measures are significantly related to successful ageing.

The socio-psychological problems of the aged and their management vary from society to society and also in different period of the same society. Indian cultural and democratic set up demands a special treatment to the issue by the social scientists and the present research is a step in that direction.

The socio-psychological problems of the aged and their management vary from society to society and also in different periods of the same society. Indian cultural and democratic set up demands a special treatment to the issue by the social scientists and the present research is a step in that direction.

The democratic national constitution in India favours the concept of equality. More knowledge, therefore, is required regarding the problems of aging, poor, urban women in specific areas namely, health, economic security, social status, personal worth and psycho-emotional security.

Home scientists have been involved in adult education. They often work with adults. Less attention, however, has been given to the aging and aged people's group. Home science cannot create a quality environment without continued research, the results of which can be fruitfully utilised for planning extension programmes and social welfare services for the aged females. There are a few residential homes for the aged in the urban settings. However, more social welfare services are need for the aged. So an accurate assessment of existing services will help in planning more and better services for improving the quality of life for the aged poor women. So an investigation into the satisfactions and problems of the urban, poor aging women, the perceptions of their family members and the assessment of the status of social welfare services available to them is justified.

The present study was undertaken to study the ageing women belonging to low socio-economic status regarding their problems and satisfactions, perceptions of their family members regarding health, economic, security worth, status and psycho-emotional security and the social welfare services available for them in Baroda city.

Objectives of the Study

1. To study the ageing women belonging to the low socio-economic status from the city of Baroda, Gujarat regarding their socio-personal characteristics namely,
    - age,
    - level of education,
    - religion,
    - marital status,
    - type of family,
    - house and vehicle,
    - gainful work and economic dependence,
    - social and religion participation,
    - Familial roles.
2. To study the problems and satisfactions of the poor urban ageing women with reference to the selected aspects, namely,
    - health,
    - status,
    - personal worth in the family,
    - Psycho-emotional security.
3. To study the problems and satisfactions of poor urban ageing women in relation to the following variables with selected aspects, namely,
    - age,
    - religion,
    - marital status,
    - occupational status,
    - type of family,
    - Per capita income of the family.

4. To study the perceptions of the family members regarding the ageing women in their family with respect tot he selected aspects, namely,
    - health,
    - economic dependency,
    - worth,
    - status, and
    - Psycho-emotional security.
5. To compare the problems and satisfactions of the poor urban ageing women with their perceptions of their family members regarding the selected aspects, namely,
    - health,
    - economic dependency,
    - status,
    - personal worth in the family,
    - Psycho-emotional security.
6. To study the agencies for the ageing people in the city of Baroda and Ahmedabad with respect to their
    - type,
    - objectives,
    - facilities available,
    - financial status,
    - future plans, and
    - publicity measures taken for promoting the agency.
7. To offer suggestions regarding the welfare of the poor urban ageing women, to aid the national policy on ageing.

METHODOLOGY

Selection of the Sample Ageing Women

Universe of the Study: Urban ageing women, who belonged to the low socio-economic status, formed the universe of the study. The population of the study consisted of the women whose - recorded or estimated age was 55 years or above from the State of Gujarat, 1992. The list of low socio-economic status housing areas was taken from the Urban Community Development Office, Baroda. Dr. K.G.

Desai's standardised socio-economic scale for urban areas in Gujarat was used for measuring the socio-economic status and purposively selecting 200 aging women from Baroda city according to the variables included in the study. No formal document to show the age of the women was available. Hence, age estimation was done by the aging women themselves and/or through their family members. They were aided by recall of important historical events such as floods, famines, war, independence struggle and also personal events like birth of children or marriage.

Family Members

Universe of the Study: The family members of the urban ageing women, who belonged to the low socio-economic status, formed the universe of the study.

One male member (son or son-in-law) and one female member (daughter or daughter-in-law) were selected randomly from the families of ageing women included in the study. They each formed 25 percent of the selected ageing women's sample.

Agencies

The government and voluntary agencies offering social welfare services to the aged women and men in the city of Baroda, were identified from the voluntary organisations' directory, Charity Commissioner's Office and by contacting different religious organisations. Information was collected from all the seven organisations functioning during the period of data collection.

The number of organisations offering social welfare services to the ageing women and men in Baroda city were few. Hence, data were also collected from some organisations working for the aged in the city of Ahmedabad.

The institutions were identified from the office of the Gujarat State Social Welfare Advisory Board and from the Department of Social Defence Gujarat State. Information was collected from the three organisations functioning during the period of data collection.

DESCRIPTION OF THE TOOLS

Ageing Women

A structured questionnaire cum checklist to be filled personally by the investigators was prepared. For each question regarding background information, maximum possible responses were worked out for ease in data collection.

Family Members

For measuring the satisfactions and problems of ageing women as perceived by their family members, an interview schedule consisting of structured items and two-point response system was used.

Social Service Agencies

A structured questionnaire was prepared to find out the number and type of services offered the number of beneficiaries and the extent of help extended to the aging women and men by the government and voluntary agencies in the city of Ahmedabad and Baroda. All the tools were translated in Gujarati.

Pre-testing of the Tools

Pre-testing of the tools was done to find out if the ageing women could understand the questions and respond with ease to the items listed, time taken for responding to the questionnaire and clarity of the items. Five ageing women and their family members (male or female) from five low socio-economic slum pockets of Baroda were selected for this purpose. Necessary changes based on the results of pre-testing were made in the questionnaire.

Collection of Data

The investigators went to the already identified low socio-economic housing areas in the city of Baroda. They first collected and scored information regarding each ageing women in relation to her caste group, vocation, level of education, total monthly income, type of residence and type of vehicle used, by using the K.G. Desai standardised socio-economic scale for urban areas in Gujarat. This was essential to identify the ageing women belonging to the low (0-10 score range) or low middle (11-15 score range) socio-economic groups. The ageing women, who were identified from these low socio-economic groups and the male and female family members of some of the families of ageing women, were then interviewed personally by the research investigators.

The total time taken to fill the questionnaire with each aging women was approximately 60 to 90 minutes, 20 to 25 minutes with each family member and about 30 minutes for an agency.

Problems Faced During Data Collection

1. Difficulty in availability of both the male and female family members at the time of data collection.
2. Lack of readiness to respond to certain questions like income of the family, relationship with daughter-in-law.
3. Excessive time consumed with some of the respondents as they wanted to express their feelings.

Plan for Scoring and Categorisation Variables

The variables for the study were selected and categorised as follows:

	Variables	*Categorisation*
1.	Age	55 to 59 years, 60 to 70 years 71 years and above
2.	Religion	Hindu, Muslim
3.	Marital Status	Widowed, With husband
4.	Occupational status	Gainfully employed, Not employed
5.	Type of family	Alone, With husband, With one son/ daughter, With more than one son/ daughter
6.	Per Capita Income	Less than Rs. 100/-, Rs. 101/- to Rs. 200/-, Rs. 201/- and above.

For the other aspects namely, level of education, house and vehicle, gainful work and economic dependence, social and religious participation and familial roles, the categories that are given in the questionnaire were used.

Sample—Ageing Women

The problems and satisfactions of the poor urban ageing women were studied in relation to selected aspects namely - number of health problems, feeling of personal worth, status and psycho-emotional security. The plan for scoring and categorisation of these aspects was as follows.

Health

There were 19 problems relating to health. The ageing women were categorised according to the number of problems experienced by them.

Number of Problems	*Category*
14 to 19	Too many
7 to 13	Many
0 to 6	Few

Personal Worth, Status and Psycho-emotional Security: There were 12 statements each in the aspect of personal worth status and psycho-emotional security. Scoring of the positive and negative statements was done as follows:

Type of Statement	*Score for type of answer*	
	Yes	*No*
Positive	1	0
Negative	0	1

Categorisation of the ageing women according to their feeling of personal worth, status and psycho-emotional security in their family was based on the score ranges as follows:

Personal Worth	Score Range	Categorisation
	9-12	Considered worthy
	6 - 8	Somewhat worthy
	0 - 5	Worthless
Status	Score Range	Categorisation
	9 to 12	High
	6 to 8	Middle
	0 to 5	Low
Psycho-emotional Security	Score Range	Categorisation
	9 to 12	Secured
	6 to 8	Somewhat secured
	0 to 5	Not secured

Intensity indices were calculated to know the extent of feelings for each item related to personal worth, status and psycho-emotional security as reported by the aging women and their family members. The formula for calculating intensity index for a feeling was as follows:

$$\textit{Intensity Index} = \frac{\textit{Summated score of all The respondents for that feeling}}{\textit{Total number of respondents}}$$

Sample—Family Members

The perceptions of the male and female family members were studied with respect to the health, economic dependency, worth, status and psycho-emotional security of the ageing women in their family.

Health

There were four items with three responses in each, relating to the perceptions of the family members regarding the health of the ageing women in their family. Scores were allotted for the respondents of the family members as follows:

Score	*Response depicting*
1	Constant Care
2	Occasional Care
3	No Care

Categorisation of the ageing women according to the perceptions of their family members regarding their health was done as shown:

Score Range	*Categorisation*
1 - 4	Too problematic
5 - 8	Problematic
9 - 12	Not problematic

Economic Dependency

There were seven items with three responses in each, relating to the extent of economic dependency of the aging women on their family members. The responses of the family members were scored as follows:

Score	*Response depicting economic independence*
1	Highly
2	Partially
3	Not at all

Score Range	Categorisation
15 - 21	Independent
8 - 14	Partially dependent
1 - 7	Totally dependent

Worth, Status and Psycho-emotional Security

There were eleven items in the aspect of worth and status and ten items in the aspect of psycho-emotional security of the ageing women as perceived by their family members. Scoring of the positive and negative statements was done as follows:

Type of Statement	Score allotted for the type of answer	
	Yes	No
Positive	1	0
Negative	0	1

Categorisation of the ageing women according to the perceptions of family members regarding worth and status of psycho-emotional security in their family was done as follows:

Worth	Score Range	Category
	9-11	Excellent
	6 - 8	Good
	0 - 5	Poor
Status	*Score Range*	*Categorisation*
	9 to 11	High
	6 to 8	Middle
	0 to 5	Low
Psycho-emotional Security	Score Range	Categorisation
	9 to 10	Secured
	6 to 8	Somewhat secured
	0 to 5	Not secured

Plan for Statistical Analysis

Sl. No.	Items	Statistical Measures
1.	Background information regarding the ageing women	Percentage
2.	Problems and satisfactions of the ageing women in relation to selected variables and aspects of aging	Chi-Square

Sl. No.	*Items*	*Statistical Measures*
3.	Item wise distribution of aging women in relation to their feelings of personal worth, status and psycho-emotional security	Intensity Index
4.	Perceptions of the family members regarding selected aspects of ageing	Percentage
5.	Item wise distribution of family members according to their perceptions regarding worth, status and psycho-emotional security of the ageing women	Intensity Index
6.	Information regarding the social welfare agencies serving the aged	Percentage

Formula of Chi Square

$$Y^2\Sigma \ \frac{(0-E)^2}{E}$$

Where, O = refers to observed frequencies

E = refers to the expected frequencies

Source: Gupta, S.P. Statistical Methods, New Delhi, S. Chand and Sons, 1989; A-4.2.

FINDINGS

Major Findings based on Reports of Ageing Women

Background Information

Majority of the ageing women

- were from the low socio-economic status groups,
- were in the age group of 60 to 70 years,
- were illiterate,
- were Hindus,
- from the Hindu community were Rajputs by caste and Shaikhs from the Muslim community,
- were widowed,
- lived in a home with one or two rooms with shared bathrooms,
- were from families with monthly per capita income between Rs. 100 to Rs. 200,

- were gainfully employed in the past, but were not employed at the time of data collection,
- reported weakness due to ill-health as the main reason for discontinuing their work,
- did not know any of the activities related to cottage industries,
- had one gainfully employed son but had no gainfully employed daughters-in-law,
- were partially dependent on other family members for economic reasons,
- reported that the monthly allowances given by their son(s)/daughter(s) were the main source of income for them,
- did not receive monetary help from he government, their workplaces, moneylenders or as donations, but they borrowed money from friends and neighbours,
- spent their leisure time in the back or front space of their house,
- reported that talking with women in the neighbourhood and visiting friends and relatives were the main social activities in which they participated,
- reported that they spent their mornings by visiting places of worship, attending Mahila Mandal activities in the afternoon and watching television or cinema at night,
- reported that they talked with women in the neighbourhood in their free time, attended mass bhajans and prayers at the time of festivals and watched television or cinema everyday,
- carried out various household activities like cutting vegetables, cleaning grains and looking after the sick or all members of the family and not for themselves only,
- reported fatigue, pain in the joints and poor vision as their health problems,
- took medicines from a private doctor.

Little more than fifty percent of the ageing women

- stayed either with one son or daughter,
- had six to ten members in their family,
- reported that their family possessed a cycle,
- reported that their monthly allowance was sufficient for their own social expenses,
- took decisions for the type of treatment, expenditure and food for the sick people in the family.

One third or little more percent of the ageing women

- had 21 to 40 sq. feet space per person in their house,
- reported that their family's total monthly income ranged between Rs. 501 to Rs. 2,000,
- who were gainfully employed at the time of data collection, reported that the place of their work was within walking distance (5 to 10 minutes) from their home,
- had one or two persons gainfully employed in the family.

Very small, that is, the three to eighteen percent of the ageing women reported that they owned individual property, in the form of land, house, utensils, and ornaments.

Higher percentage of the age group III (71 years and above) were

- widows,
- not gainfully employed,
- from families, having less per capita income,
- living alone.

From Muslim women, higher percentage belonged to age group III, while among Hindu women; higher percent belonged to age group I (55 to 59 years).

Detailed Findings Based on Reports of Ageing Women

- The ageing women included in the study, were from low middle and low socio-economic status groups,
- The age of the ageing women ranged from 55 years to 71 years and above,
- The level of education of ageing women ranged from illiterate to 7th grade,

- Both Hindus and Muslims ageing women were taken from the study.
- The Hindu ageing women represented various castes namely, Rajput, Maratha, Harijan, Solanki, Fulmali, Vankar, Brahmin, Valand, Kayastha, Khatri, Patel, Rabari, Shoemaker (Mochi), Koli, Parmar, Thakarada, Vaghari, Baniya, Barot, Bhoi, Black-smith, Bramhbhatt, Chaudhari, Garasiya, Ghanchi, Lohana, Machi, Mahavar, Makawana, Prajapati, Rathod, Rawal, Rohit and Vasawa.
- The Muslim ageing women represented sects namely, Shaikh, Tai, Pathan, Garasiya, Rathod, Barber, Patel, Vohra, Bahelim, Diwan, Mansuri, Memon, Milkman, Qureshi, Raj, Rana and Vaghela.
- The ageing women stayed in any one of the arrangements:
  - Alone
  - With husband
  - With one son or daughter
  - With more than one son or daughter
- The ageing women had family members ranging from 1 to 11 and above.
- The ageing women lived in a home with one or two rooms without bathroom or independent room with bathroom or hut.
- The space available to the ageing women's families ranged from 1 to 144 sq. ft. space per person.
- The vehicles possessed by the family members of the ageing women were cycle, moped, scooter and rickshaw. Forty percent of the family members had no vehicle.
- The ageing women reported that their family's total monthly income ranged from less than Rs. 300/- to Rs. 2,000/-.
- The per capita income of the families ranged from less than Rs. 100/- to Rs. 201/- and above.
- The number of gainfully employed persons in the ageing women's family ranged from four to one and very less per cent that is 3.50 percent were not gainfully employed.

- In the ageing women's families, following were gainfully employed,
  - Husband
  - One to four sons
  - One to two daughters-in-law.
- The ageing women had family members who were serving (in shops and offices), having their business, and working as labourers. Pension of their husbands as well as their own pension was one of the sources of income for the aging women.
- The ageing women reported that they had worked up to the age ranged from 25 to 68 years. Some did not remember while some were still continuing to be gainfully employed.
- One fifth of the ageing women who were gainfully employed at the time of data collected reported a variety of work in which they were employed such as :
  - Maid servant
  - Small shop owner
  - Vegetable vendor
  - Cottage industry worker
  - Sweeper
  - Cook
  - Rag picker
  - Ayah
  - Dai
  - Labourer.
- Many reasons were reported by the aging women for discontinuing the employment such as:
  - weakness,
  - difficulties in seeing,
  - difficulties in walking
  - difficulties in hearing
  - social taboos

- household work
- unavailability of work
- ill health of husband
- younger generation working, and
- no need of supplementary income.

- The duration of work for the ageing women ranged from one to twelve hours per day.
- The gainfully employed ageing women reported that the time spent to reach the place of their work ranged between 5 minutes to 45 minutes; some ageing women reported that they had to go for their work by bus while some worked at home only.
- Ageing women reported that the sources of monthly income were:
  - allowance given by their son/daughter
  - their own gainful employment
  - husband's pension
  - husband's pay
  - bank interest
  - agricultural produce
  - their own pension
  - begging
  - government allowance, and
  - money from sale of milk.

Their monthly allowance ranged from Rs. 25/- to Rs. 40/- and above and some were given monetary help only when required.

- The percentage of the ageing women reporting that their monthly allowance was sufficient for their social expenses, clothes, food, medicine and house rent ranged from 54 to 17, in the decreasing order.
- The percentage of the ageing women reporting of individual property like utensils, furniture, house, ornaments and land ranged from 12 to 3 in decreasing order while the percentages for the ageing women holding the above mentioned property jointly with their

family members ranged from 70 to 9.

- The families of the ageing women approached many sources for monetary help during emergency, they were:
  - Donation
  - Government
  - Moneylender
  - Employer
  - Son/daughter
  - Relatives
  - Friends, and
  - Neighbours.
- The social, cultural and religious activities participated by ageing women were:
  - talking with women in the neighbourhood
  - visiting friends and relatives
  - attending mass bhajans and prayers
  - visiting places of worship
  - watching television and cinema
  - attending activities of mahila mandal
- The time for these activities was afternoon as well as night.
- The duration of the ageing women's participation in social, cultural and religious activities varied, they visited relatives, friends and places of worship on some occasions and festivals while they were talking with neighbouring women and watching television every day.
- The ageing women took part in decision making regarding different activities at home like:
  - treatment during illness in the family
  - special occasion's expenditure
  - daily / weekly family expenditure
  - household chores
  - children/grand children's education
  - children's employment.

- The ageing women reported that they participated in different activities at home namely:
  - cutting/peeling vegetable
  - care of sick children/persons
  - cleaning grains
  - making bed
  - cleaning utensils
  - sweeping the floor
  - washing the clothes
  - grinding
  - cooking
  - shopping (grocery/vegetable)
  - feeding small children
  - playing with small child, telling stories, taking for a walk
  - putting a small child to sleep
  - getting the flour made from the flour mill
  - giving religious education to children
  - looking after animals
  - collecting cow-dung.

The above mentioned activities were carried out by the ageing women for all the members of the family and not just for herself or her husband only.

- The ageing women suffered from various health problems; they were:
  - Fatigue
  - Pain in joints
  - Poor vision
  - Dental difficulties
  - Dizziness
  - Pain in back
  - Pain in chest
  - Operations

- Digestive troubles
- Tremors
- Breathlessness
- Poor hearing
- Fracture
- Profuse bleeding

The above-mentioned health problems ranged from 83 to 3.50 percentage in decreasing order.

- Due to ill health, the ageing women faced difficulties such as climbing staircase, rickshaw, bus and train, walking, doing manual work and carrying out daily routine activities, which ranged from 68 to 8 percentages.

Overall, majority of the ageing women reported:

- many health problems,
- that they considered themselves to be somewhat worthy members in the family,
- that their status in their family was high,
- that they felt secured psycho-emotionally.

Item Wise Perceptions of Ageing Women

Findings regarding the item wise feelings of personal worth, status and psycho-emotional security of the ageing women are presented here.

Item Wise Feelings of Ageing Women Personal Worth

High percentage of the ageing women considered themselves to be most worthy as revealed through the items which showed that their family members could go out at any time due to their physical presence in the house, they did not have to forego their pleasures nor were they embarrassed by the old ways of doing things by the ageing women in their family.

Whereas, low percentage of the ageing women felt less worthy as mentioned through the items which showed that they had no aim in life except eating, that old used clothes and left over food were sufficient for them and that life should not be longer any more.

Status

High percentage of the ageing women felt that their status in their family was high as revealed through the items which showed that they were given superior quality food along with other family members, they were allowed to use bathroom / toilet first or whenever they wanted and were addressed with respectable words such as 'maji', 'bai', 'sasuma', etc.

Psycho-Emotional Security

High percentage of the ageing women felt most secured psycho-emotionally as revealed through the items which showed that they did not feel that they were a nuisance in their family because of their sickness, weakness or old age talks, they enjoyed the company of other people and their family members wished them to live longer.

Whereas low percentage of the ageing women felt less secured psycho-emotionally as revealed through the items which showed that they felt scared to go out alone, they did not have good company of other women of their age and because they got irritated easily.

COMPARATIVE ITEM WISE PICTURE OF AGEING WOMEN AND FAMILY MEMBERS

Personal Worth

Ageing women and both their male and female family members reported the worth of the ageing women through different items. On the whole higher number of the family members indicated worth of the ageing women through all the items compared to the ageing women who did not report their own worth through many items.

Status of Ageing Women

Both the family members and the ageing women reported items showing high and low psycho-emotional security; while the items for the former were different they were same for the latter.

On the whole, for personal worth, status and psycho-emotional security, the higher number of family members (than the ageing women themselves) and more female than male members reported positive feeling through the individual items.

Variable Wise Findings

Significant differences were found in the number of health problems, feeling of personal worth, status and psycho-emotional security reported by the ageing women according to the variables of the study. They are as follows:

Variable	*Aspect*	
Age	-	Number of health problems,
	-	Personal worth,
	-	Status,
	-	Psycho-emotional security.
Marital Status	-	Number of health problems,
	-	Personal worth,
	-	Status,
	-	Psycho-emotional security.
Religion	-	Number of health problems.
Per Capita Income	-	Personal worth

Higher percent of the ageing women in the youngest age group (55-59 years) as compared to the aging women in the older age groups, reported:

- fewer health problems,
- that they considered themselves to be worthy members in their family,
- that their status in the family was high, and
- that they felt secured psycho-emotionally.

Higher percent of the ageing women living with husband, as compared to the widowed ageing women, reported:

- fewer health problems,
- that they were considered worthy in their family,
- that their status in the family was high,
- that they felt psycho-emotionally secure in their family.

Higher percent of the ageing women from families with per capita income of Rs. 201/- and above reported that they were considered worthy members in the family rather than the ageing women from families of other lower per capita income groups.

Findings Based on the Reports of the Family Members

Overall majority of the family members perceived:

- the health of the ageing women in their family as not problematic,
- the ageing women as economically totally dependent on the family,
- the worth of the ageing women in their family as excellent,
- the status of the ageing women in their family to be high,
- the ageing women in their family as feeling secured or somewhat secured psycho-emotionally.

Majority of the family members of the ageing women in the age group of:

- 71 years and above than the other younger age groups perceived the health of the ageing women in their family as not problematic.
- 55 to 59 years as compared to the other older age groups reported that the aging women were economically totally dependent on them, their worth in the family was excellent and their status in the family was high.

Comparatively, higher percent of the:

- female than the male family members perceived the health of the ageing women in their family as not problematic and their status in the family as high,
- male than the female family members reported that the ageing women in their family felt somewhat secured psycho-emotionally and their worth in the family was high.

Equal percentage of both the male and female family members reported that the aging women in their family were economically totally dependent on them.

1. Comparatively, higher percent of the female than the male family members of the aging women of the youngest age group, reported the health of the ageing women in their family as 'not problematic' and their status in the family as 'high'.
2. Comparatively, higher percent of the male than the female family members of ageing women in the youngest age group

reported that the ageing women in their family felt psycho-emotionally secured.

3. Comparatively, higher percent of the male than the female family members of ageing women in the oldest age group perceived the worth of the ageing women in their family as excellent.
4. Comparatively, higher percent of the female than the male family members of ageing women in the oldest age group reported that the ageing women in their family were economically totally dependent on them.

Social Welfare Agencies

Majority of the social welfare agencies:

- had both males and females as their beneficiaries,
- functioned mainly to provide happiness to the aged,
- had aged people from families with monthly income below Rs. 3,000/-,
- took fees from the families of the aged people,
- received financial help through donations,
- provided the facility of a visiting doctor, a library and food,
- possessed their own building,
- were of residential type,
- had plans for more rooms to accommodate greater number of aged people,
- had problem of space,
- had variety of plans for future expansion of their activities,
- publicised their activities through advertisements in the newspapers.

DISCUSSION

Living Conditions of the Ageing Women

Majority of the ageing women from low socio-economic status really presented a very sad picture about their life. Many depended economically, entirely on their children or were left to live by themselves in a sad condition. They had to prove their usefulness in their homes by still doing household work and looking after sick family members even when they themselves were suffering from a variety of physical ailments. The status of poor old women is not likely to improve in the immediate future, since the factors (less income, inadequate housing, poor medical care and nutrition) that affect health conditions will not change much among the poor women. The poor old women must have suffered in silence as the free public hospitals are not within everybody's access and private doctors are too expensive.

Majority had been employed in the unorganised sector mostly as servants in their younger years. This had left them with poor salaries in past and absolutely no independent income of their own in form of pension/provident fund or bank interest. Cottage industries can provide income through self employment and respectability to those aged who are still physically fit.

Majority considered their allowance from family members enough just for social expenses which are a must in the lower classes. This must have been done at the expense of their comforts and needs. Poor old women need to be helped in kind - food, clothes, footwear, medicine and free public transport.

Factors Responsible for Problems of Aged

The old women's presence proved useful in the homes. In spite of their low physical and materialistic status and near non-existent recreational life, both they and their family members considered them worthy and of high social status in their homes and neighbourhood. However, some strains were noted in this study also. It suggests that the family is and will continue to be the most important source of support for the elderly in India but will decline in the future due to increased number of frail and impaired elderly as well as increased industrialisation and urbanisation resulting into changing family structure and gainfully employed female members. The plight of poor old women seemed to be worsening because of added problem of widowhood, which ushers in new problems of lowered status and lessened financial support.

Age and Associated Problems

Age definitely seemed associated with increased number of health problems and decreased sense of worth, status and psycho-emotional security. The family members found the physical presence of the old women very beneficial as long as they did the household work and looked after the house when they were out. But the question is raised - will they still be loved and looked after when they no longer will be proved useful with advancement in age? Though not substantial, somewhat higher percentage of the women from the oldest age group (71 years and above) were living alone compared to women from the younger age groups. They expressed decreased psycho-emotional security.

Ageing Women and Family Members

There were discrepancies in the reports of family members and the ageing women about the worth and status of the ageing women, the former being higher and the latter being low. This finding can be checked through further research to ascertain whether an actual gap is existing between the treatment and the reports by the family members or is it the illusion on part of the aging women. In either case, a better dialogue and interaction seem to be required to overcome either an actual gap or a feeling of gap in the perceptions of the ageing women and their family members.

The male family members and the younger family members compared to their counterparts considered the ageing women as more problematic health wise and less worthy. More females than males were aware of the negative feelings of the ageing women. Can the males and the younger generations be given education to sensitize them to the problems of the old women and the useful roles previously played by them in the welfare and the development of the family?

Homes and Day Centres for Elderly

Since all along, the family has been expected to undertake the responsibility of looking after the aged in our traditional country, it was natural not to find a great many homes and day centres for the elderly. Just 7 were located for the city of Baroda with a population of 11 lakhs and majority were established in the last two decades only and were managed by the voluntary organizations and trusts. Facilities and activities for the aged in these homes and the day centres were also few, since majority depended on donations in cash and kind.

The homes and day centres for the aged, especially for the poor old women need greater acceptance and support. Due to lessened income, poor health, enforced isolation, retirement and widowhood, many older women simply cannot be autonomous and can get organised to make decisions about their lives or to plan ahead. The aged are too old to fight any battle even though the law may be on their side. Article 41 of our Constitution and Section 125 of the Code of Criminal Procedure 1973 refer to the laws related to the welfare of the aged. Going the way of the west with homes for the elderly may not be the best answer, but at least the crisis of sever neglect of the aged can be avoided through them.

Future Actions for the Aged

Considering the increasing number of aged, specially widows, and their near total economic dependence and diminishing psycho-emotional security plans for both homes and day centres for them to be taken up in a big way. Funds for these agencies be given priority both by the society and the government.

Future actions can include two types of programmes — those generating awareness among young (such as rallies, poster competitions and symposium), and those which actually bring benefits and enjoyment to aged, (such as cultural and entertainment shows, sticker sales, games and get-together).

More organised moves need to be made to meet the demands of the elderly such as separate counters at railway platforms, post offices and banks and 50 percent concession in rail-fare for short distances also. It is strongly felt that the care of aging women, who have led useful lives in their younger years, cannot just be left to the families alone any longer. More involvement of the nation and the society is needed in terms of finance and services. The rich and the privileged classes may be able to arrange for their welfare but the poor and down trodden, more so the women, really need all our help in their declining years.

Recommendations

(A) Recommendations for the Care and Welfare of the Ageing Persons

- Special attention is suggested for elderly women than men as more women outlive men as widows.

- The need for psycho-emotional security is given top priority in the care of elderly persons.
- Free or subsidised Medicare for commonly reported ailments in the residential areas through an arrangement with government or private hospitals or mobile units be provided.
- Medicare can include checkups, medicine, surgery and help in kind such as spectacles, dentures and wheel chairs.
- Geriatric wards and reservation of some week days for the elderly can be provided for faster medical checkups.
- Some old age security schemes providing financial support be worked out. The amount of financial support can vary according to the needs of the poor.
- Local voluntary agencies can be involved in the scrutiny of the cases for financial support for speedy service.
- The economic help to a large extent can be in the form of kind (clothes, footwear, and medicine, free and public transport) to benefit the poor elderly themselves and not their family members.
- The poor able ageing women can be taught some cottage industries to help them to have independent income and also to feel psychologically independent.
- Arrangement for supplying raw materials to the ageing women and purchase of the final products from them at a reasonable rate can be made, both, to facilitate the work as well as to prevent the exploitation of the poor old women.
- Both the formal and non-formal programmes can be organised to develop traditional respect for the elderly and the awareness about their problems among the younger generation.
- The need for the above programmes be recognised, specially in the face of very fast industrialisation, urbanisation and modernisation in the Indian society.
- Since the female family members were already aware about the needs of the poor elderly women, the male family members be sensitised about the needs of the ageing women.

- The younger generations (children and grand children) can be encouraged to accord high status to treat elderly with respect and to look after their physically handicapped since their presence actually helped the families by facilitating household work and going out of the family members for social and work purposes.
- A positive concept be developed among the young regarding the social and recreational needs of the poor ageing women. This can be achieved both by the educational and publicity programmes.
- The families should be encouraged to keep the elderly women with them as the first option as the ageing persons will feel comfortable and happy in the familiar surroundings.
- Both, the family care and the organised help, to be encouraged for the aged.
- The help of old age homes can be availed selectively in cases of the poor women with absolute non-availability or inability of the family members to look after them.
- More day centres than the full time homes for the aged be ,promoted to help the poor women, both, to keep the link with their families and to avail the necessary help and care at the same time.
- Government and voluntary agencies can consider setting up of homes and day centres for the aged seriously and positively.
- Facilities can be increased in the old age homes and day centres to help the aged feel comfortable and "cared for".
- To help the aged feel happy ad useful, besides the physical facilities, social, recreational and work activities also can be provided at these homes and centres.
- The free social and recreational programmes for the elderly be organised by the schools, performing arts department, extension departments and cultural organisation.
- More integrated approach be adopted in setting up the old age homes and day centres to serve the old effectively by covering many aspects of old age care.

- These homes and centres for he aged can be free or subsidised to accommodate the poor women.
- They can be single sex or combined for both the sexes.
- Since various types of the personnel are required to run the homes for the elderly, employment opportunities for the younger and older generations be created by setting up the old age homes.
- Change in the traditional societal belief regarding the sole responsibility of sons in looking after their mothers be accepted. More daughters be encouraged to look after their mothers.
- More women be encouraged and helped to have higher, economic status to have substantial say in the care of their old mothers.
- Various fund raising activities be taken up for providing the facilities to the aged.
- The society be encouraged to donate generously for the welfare of the old, both in kind and cash.
- Low socio-economic sections can be persuaded not to engage into unnecessary heavy social expenses but to spend money for their real personal comforts and needs.
- Anti poverty programmes be given serious encouragement to help the poor women to decrease their economic plight.
- There is a need to cover unorganised sector also with insurance and other old age security scheme to provide protection to poor old women.
- Population control programmes be made effective to encourage people to actually have small size families to limit their expenses so that, in turn, the families can spend for their elderly.

(B) *Recommendations for Further Study*

Further research can be conducted on the following topics:

- Problems and satisfactions of ageing women belonging to middle and high socio-economic status.
- Problems and satisfactions of ageing women in rural areas.

- The problems of ageing women in relation to variables other than studied in this study.
- Roles of ageing women within the family in relation to the variables such as type of family, age and economic status.
- Fears of ageing women in relation to variables such as their personality, economic status, family structure, etc.
- Priority needs of the ageing persons.
- Personality characteristics of ageing women.
- Longitudinal studies of ageing characteristics and problems in various areas such as physical, social, psychological and emotional.
- Ways of coping with ageing adopted by the ageing persons in relation to the variables such as health, status, socio-economic status.
- Comparison of problems and satisfactions of working and non-working ageing men and women.
- Adjustment problems of ageing women who were employed or unemployed in the past.
- Comparison of the perceptions of male and female family members regarding the ageing women/men.
- Attitudes of family members (children, youth and adults) towards ageing persons.
- Comparison of the retirement plans of ageing men and women just before their retirement.
- Leisure time activities of ageing persons/ retired people.
- Existing patterns or ways of coping with retirement.
- Family support patterns followed for ageing family members.
- Cultural variations in the treatment of the ageing persons.
- Ways to prolong the useful roles played by the ageing persons in the family and the society.
- Living conditions in the homes for the ageing persons.
- Factors inhibiting the ageing persons from availing the help/facilities of the homes for the ageing persons.

- Survey of existing services provided by the homes and day centres for the ageing persons on nation wide basis.
- Care of ageing persons by the family members/society in the areas such as social, psycho-logical, physical, financial and recreational.
- Legal provision for the care and support of ageing persons and its extent of implementation.
- Methodological research for studies on ageing persons with specific reference to low socio-economic status.

BIBLIOGRAPHY

1. Bhanumati, K., Rajkumar, E. and Richard, J., Family Type and the Aged, *Journal of Family Welfare*, 20(4), 1985.
2. Bobrov, Lev., Problems of the Aged-work Therapy for the Aged, *Social Welfare*, 33(3), June, 1986: 15-16.
3. Bose, Ashish, Aspects of Aging in India. *Social Action*, 31(1), 1982: 1-19.
4. Chaudhury, D.P., Problems of the Aged and the Infirm, *Kurukshetra*, 22, 1974: 7-9.
5. Chopra, R.M., Aging in India: Need of a Developmental Approach, *Social Welfare* 36(5), Aug. 1989: 31-32.
6. Dave, P. and Vaswani, T., A Teaching Module on "Aging Women", Presented at International Workshop—Women and Development: A Critical Appraisal of Household Level Research Methodologies, Baroda, Gujarat, India, July, 5-14, 1989: 1-24.
7. Ghosal, B.C., Care of the Aged, *Yojana*, 26 (10, 1982: 10.
8. Girimaji, P.R., Aged Women and the Law, *Vikasini*, 6 (11), Jan-March, 1991: 8-9.
9. Hayslip Bert, Jr. and Panek Paul, E., Adult Development and Aging, New York, Harper and Row, Publishers, 1989.
10. Jain, Madhu and Menon, R., The Graying of India. *India Today*, Delhi, 30 Sept., 1991: 46-55.
11. Joshi, C.K., Medical Problems of Old Age, *Indian Journal of Gerontology*, 84(3), 1971: 64-68.
12. Joshi, Uma, Aging Population—Implications for Home Scientists, Baroda, India, 1989: 27-29 p. Mimeographed. Paper read at the Biennial Conference of the Asian Regional Association for Home Economics, Singapore, July, 1989.

13. Kubitchek, J., Depression Among Old People is a Major Medical Problem, *Social Welfare*, April 1990: 35.
14. Luthra, Pran Nath, "Do not Segregate the Aged from the Main Stream", Aging and Welfare of the Elderly in India. *Social Welfare*, 38(3) June 1991: 35-36.
15. Maeda, D., Family Care in Japan, The Gerontologist, 23, 579-583 in *Adult Development and Aging* by Hayslip B. Panek P. Harper and Row Publishers, New York, 1989.
16. Nair, G.R., Problems of the Aged in India. *Yojana*, 26(1), 1982: 4-6.
17. INDIA, Report of the Seminar on.Programmes and Services for the Aged, New Delhi, National Institute of Public Co. and Child Development.
18. Pagdi, Gayatri, 'So, Who Needs a Walking Stick?' *Sunday Review, The Times of India*, 29th September, 1991: 1.
19. Sinha, J.N., Problems of Aging, New Delhi, Classical Pub. Co., 1989.
20. Ziemba, Judes; P.oop, Kathleen and Wittenberg, Sally, "A Magic Mix", from Children Today, Published by the Office of Human Development Services, U.S. Department of Health and Human Services, Span, May, 1991: 20-21.

11

PROBLEMS OF ELDERLY WIDOWS OF BARODA– GUJARAT

Rameshwari Pandya &
Priti Shah

Introduction

In India, a married Hindu woman is most commonly blessed with the words, "Sada Suhagin Raho" meaning may you never be snatched off your wifehood. These words reflect the general attitude of society towards the widow versus the married woman, whose husband is still living. The problems of Indian Elderly Widows are not confined to Vrindavan, Mathura, Tirupati and the other holy towns where widows have traditionally congregated. In every fourth household in India there is a widow. Only a very small minority of widows could claim to be comfortable, secure and well looked after (Sachdev 2000). The dictionary meaning of the term widow is,

> *"A woman whose husband is dead and she has not married again".*

In India, elderly widows have to cope up with profound changes and tackle the stormy inner debates. Conflicting pressures are put from all sides and actions are demanded in all kinds of ways. A widow has to bear much pain and humiliation as long as she lives. On the death of her husband, a widow is first shocked by the reality that she may have to face the world on her own, perhaps for the first time in her life. This is particularly the case with Indian women who have spent most of their married lives depending on their husbands for support, decisions and protection. They are therefore unprepared to face the situation on their own.

Hindu society is a patriarchal society and has patriarchal attitude to women's role and values in society. The status of women shows that Hindu society is a male dominated society and bias, discriminatory attitude and inhuman practices prevails towards women. An andocentric society followed Manu's codes and did not allow women to develop a sense of autonomy or personal freedom. In India, women are rarely educated; married early; not encouraged taking up employment and their public participation is limited. Moreover, they were neither expected nor encouraged to develop a sense of autonomy or have control over their lives. The status of elderly women cannot be studied in isolation but has to be seen in the light of social, economic and political development of the nation.

In the Indian context, widowhood also means a loss of self-esteem, dignity, social position and rights. Widows are the unfortunate victims of nature and for centuries they have been ill-treated. India has the highest prevalence of widowhood in the world. From all over the developing world there are evidences that millions of elderly widows and their children live in conditions of acute insecurity, deprivation and even violence. This is a matter of great regret and disappointment.

Those left behind by the dead die a thousand deaths. Nothing could be closer to this truth for the widows and their families. Widowhood is a critical and a very hard period in a woman's life. Widowhood brings sudden and unhappy change in the life of a woman. What ruins the enjoyment of widow life? Death of a husband means not merely a loss of financial and emotional support but creates a big void in a woman's life. The problems of widowhood are manifold.

Psychological Problems

Each decade of human life span has its own emotional problems and the moments of uncertainty. Widowhood brings in its fold, a number of problems for the widow, and she lives a life of isolation, dependency, anxiety, depression and mental morbidity, which are some of the psycho-social problems associated with widowhood. Emotionally she suffers the most and she has to make many compromises with her life. A large number of widows feel anxious about their future.

The elderly widows are pitied or shoved aside because of the structure of society, which makes them feel more useless and insecure. It is a trap of a piece of bad luck for which they are unprepared; feel uncertain, sensitive and self-conscious.

Widowhood implies a shift in position from that of secured to an unsecured woman. Widowhood compels the woman to reassess her own worth and ability in the light of changed position. The self evaluation of new position and roles depend not only on her own characteristics like age, educational level, economic status, nature of obligations, family support, but also on the evaluation of others including her in-laws, neighbours, peers and others. As a widow, she feels insecure, isolated, depressed and has an unwanted feeling. She also faces difficulty in dealing with day-to-day activities. In such a situation, widows expect help from the group of people around her, which may be her parents, in-laws, children, friends and relatives with whom she can share her views and feelings, who will listen to her patiently and try to understand her.

For the widow the death of husband means the loss of love and security, increase in household work especially in the handling of children and redistribution of household work especially home related responsibilities. It takes a long time and lot of courage for a widow to pick up the threads of her life, to get over the loneliness, emptiness and to start living a normal life.

Social Problems

India is a land of diverse geography and culture - it's natural that social problems will also be diverse. A sensitive person can experience the different anomalies that beset ones local environment. Women suffer a lot due to this heterogeneous nature of the Indian society with its structure based on social and economic inequalities. These inequalities are inherent in the traditional Indian social structure.

In the traditional Hindu culture, a woman's life had meaning only in relation to other men such as husband or son. In childhood, a female must be subjected to her father, in youth to her husband, when her lord is dead to her sons: a woman must never be independent.

In a traditional society like ours, a woman derives her social status from her husband. Thus, there is a drastic change in a woman's life after the death of her husband. Widowhood not only disrupts her social environment but also brings change in her life style and it affects her dress, food, make-up participation in various social and religious functions. She feels out of place in her in-laws as well as parent's house. Added to this she is not trained or accustomed from the beginning to lead an independent life. In fact widowhood pervades almost all the spheres of widow's life. She has to shun all ostentation in life. They remain subjugated and their self-esteem gets injured. Widowhood brings in its fold number of socio- economic problems not only for the widows but also for the young children and other dependants in the family.

Widowhood may be perceived as a new position involving major changes in a woman's role, both in the family and society. They are expected to confirm to an enormous burden of restrictive customs like:

- Wearing white saris.
- Foregoing all decorations and cosmetics.
- Foregoing pickle, spices and eating only bland food.
- Never singing and dancing.
- Remaining in seclusion and avoiding social gatherings such as weddings, puja, etc.
- Never looking at any man outside the immediate family.

And if a widow is caught not following any of these customs, she is criticised. Punishment ranges from psychological abuse, fines, social boycotts, dis-inheritance, ex-communication and even death. Widows have deleterious effects not only because of the sudden loss of the spouse but also because the community feels obliged to feel sorry for them which arouse an unconscious hostility. Socio-economic conditions aggravate this social problem.

Financial Problems

In India husbands are the main bread-winner, therefore, their death brings in fold a number of socio-economic problems, not only for the widow but for the young children and other dependants in the family also The sudden demise of husband reduces the family income drastically and puts the whole family into financial bankruptcy.

The problem of financial stringency gets more aggravated where the late husband leaves no savings or assets. In such circumstances, the family looks forward to financial help from parents, in-laws, relatives, friends, etc. The widows, generally gets such help for the mourning period, which varies normally from 6 months to 1 year. The widow has no alternative but to become self-dependent but this becomes difficult for those who have little or no education or vocational training before widowhood.

A widow is called apathetic if she stays at home and does not earn for supporting her family. On the other hand she is also blamed if she goes to work. A widow in either case is suspected of infidelity and cursed for indulging in immoral acts. But still a widow has to continue with her job until her children mature or she gets regular support from somewhere else. The death of a husband becomes catastrophic for widows in economic terms, living arrangements and access to property.

Few problems in contemporary society are receiving lot of attention and care, like many people are concerned about issues of child labour, problems of adolescent and violence against women. But not many people have expressed their concern about the status of elderly widows in India.

The present study aims at finding out "Problems of elderly widows residing in Vadodara in the year 2001-2002.

Selection of the Sample

The sample for the study comprised of 125 widows residing in Vadodara during the year 2001- 2002.

Sampling Technique

"Purposive and Snowball Sampling Method" was used for selecting the sample for the study. Final sample for the study belonged to Tarsali, Harni, Karelibaug, Gorwa, Alkapuri, Dandia Baazar, Raopura, Fatehgunj areas of Vadodara city.

Construction of the Tool

An interview cum structured questionnaire schedule was constructed to collect the data from the respondents. The final questionnaire was divided into 3 sections as follows:

Table 1
Construction of the Tool and the Response System

	Sections	*Aspects*	*Response System*
I	Background Information	• Age • *Socio-economic status	Checklist
		• Employment Status	2 point scale
		• *Personality Dimension	2 point scale
		• Number of children	Open ended
II	• Problems	• Psychological • Social • Financial	3 point scale
	• Government widow pension scheme	• Awareness and extent of Availing	2 point scale
	• Coping up strategies	• Psychological problems • Social problems • Financial problems	2 point scale
	• Positive attributes	—	2 point scale
III	Suggestions	—	2 point scale Open ended

* For socio-economic status, K.G. Desai's standardised scale (Adapted).
* For Personality Dimension, V.S. Shantamani and A. Hafeez's standardised scale.

Collection of the Data

Data collection was done in December-January, 2001-2002. The investigator personally interviewed all the widows and before starting the interview, rapport was established with them.

Findings and Discussion

The problems faced by widows in India are mainly: Psychological, Social and Financial. All these problem areas are interdependent. In simple words, any minor problem could have repercussions on the psycho-social and financial problems. Steps should be initiated to improve the status of widows by concentrating on alternatives and the coping up strategies to be adopted to overcome the problems like living arrangements, accomplishing and fulfilling responsibilities, utilisation of leisure time, spiritual well being, training programmes and so on.

Background Information of the Widows

Table 2
Percentage Distribution of The Respondents Showing Their Background Information

(N = 125)

Sl. No.	*Variables*	*Frequency (f)*	*Percentage %*
(a)	Age group:		
	(i) Below 50 years	45	36.0
	(ii) Above 50 years	80	64.0
(b)	Socio-economic Status:		
	(i) Low	50	40.0
	(ii) Middle	50	40.0
	(iii) High	25	20.0
(c)	Number of children:		
	(i) 1 child	18	14.4
	(ii) 2 children	48	38.4
	(iii) 3 children	29	23.2
	(iv) 4 and above	30	24.0
(d)	Employment Status:		
	(i) Employed	72	57.6
	(ii) Unemployed	53	42.4
(e)	Personality Dimension:		
	(i) Introvert	18	14.4
	(ii) Extrovert	107	85.6

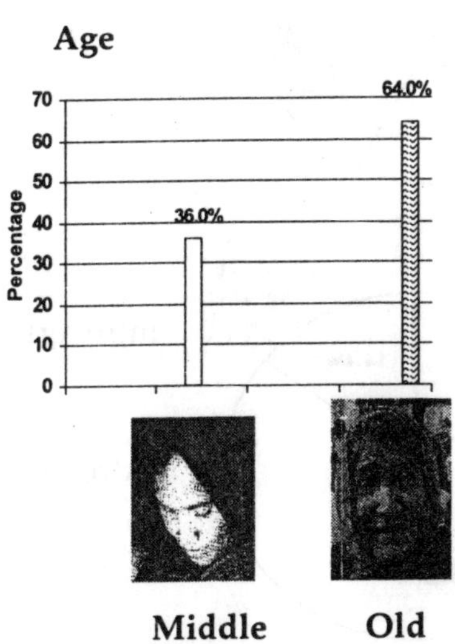

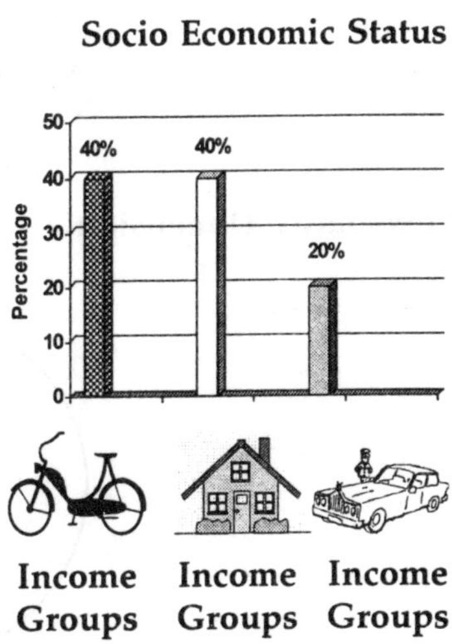

Number of Children

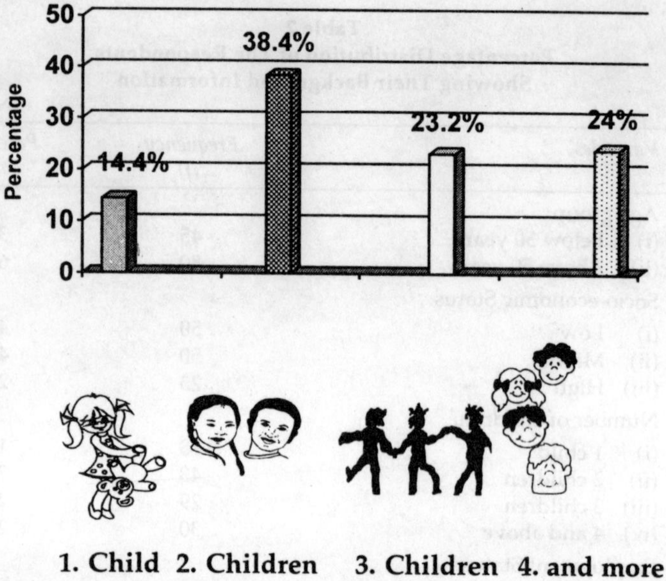

Employment Status

Personality Dimension

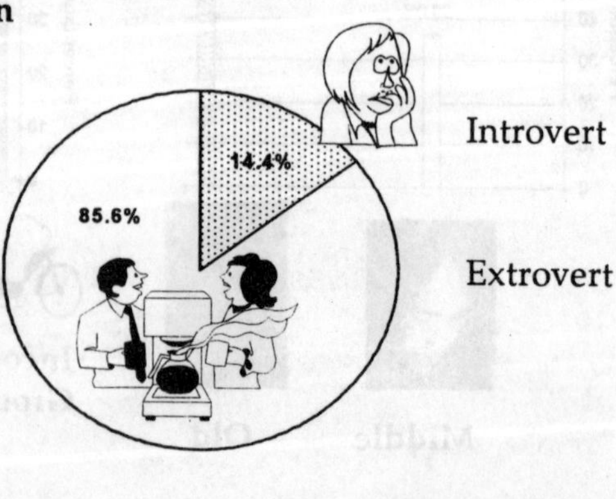

Table 2 reveals that 64.0 percent of the respondents belonged to the age group of 50 years and above. Further it is seen that equal number (40%) of the respondents belonged to both low and middle socio-economic status, whereas only 20 percent of the respondents belonged to the high socio-economic status.

The table also indicates that 38.4 percent of the respondents had 2 children, whereas 24 percent of the respondents had 4 and more children. Further, it was found that 23.2 percent of the respondents had 3 children and in comparison 14.4 percent of the respondents had only 1 child.

It is further seen that little more than half (57.6%) of the respondents belonged to the employed group, whereas 42.4 percent of the respondents were not gainfully employed.

Table 2 also indicates that majority (85.6%) of the respondents were found to be extrovert in comparison to only 14.4 percent who were introverts.

Considerable evidences in the literature and researches of Home science education and sociology indicated that the widows face multiple and conflicting social exploitations. Widows would like to be on their own and mould their own life. But, traditionally they face subjugation in one form or the other. They are made responsible for their husband's death. Life for them means continuous adjustment and it includes process of fitting one's self into the given circumstances. These pre-conceived attributes have loaded our social life styles with a thinking, which envisages the unwritten law that the weaker sex needs to be protected, pampered and given privileges by the stronger and dominating sex of the society. Thus personality of an individual respondent motivates them to behave and adjust accordingly and hence it acts as a driving force in a widow's life to set up their new life with new aims and expectations.

Table 3 indicates that majority (75.2%) of the respondents belonged to nuclear families, whereas, 24.8 percent of the respondents belonged to joint families. Further, it is seen that little less than three-fourth (70.4%) of the respondents were staying with their children, whereas, 11.2 percent were staying alone. Few (8% and 7.2%) stayed with their in-laws and parents respectively and very few (3.2%) stayed with relatives other than in-laws.

Table 3 also indicates that little less than half (48.0%), married at an age less than 18 years, 45.6 percent of the respondents got married between 18-25 years and very few (6.4%) got married at more than 25 years of age.

Table 3
Percentage Distribution Showing Other Characteristics Related To Background Information Of The Respondents

(N = 125)

Sl. No.	*Other Characteristics*	*Frequency (f)*	*Percentage %*
(a)	Type of family:		
	(i) Joint	31	24.8
	(ii) Nuclear	94	75.2
(b)	Staying at present:		
	(i) Alone	14	11.2
	(ii) Parents	9	7.2
	(iii) In-laws	10	8.0
	(iv) Children	88	70.4
	(v) Relatives (other than in-laws)	4	3.2
(c)	Age at marriage:		
	(i) < 18 years	60	48.0
	(ii) 18 - 25 years	57	45.6
	(iii) ≥ 25 years	8	6.4
(d)	Age of widows when their husband expired:		
	(i) < 20 years	–	–
	(ii) 20-30 years	33	26.4
	(iii) 31-40 years	46	36.8
	(iv) 41-50 years	22	17.6
	(v) > 51 years	24	19.2
(e)	Cause of husband's death:		
	(i) Accident	36	28.8
	(ii) Long term illness	58	46.4
	(iii) Natural calamity	4	3.2
	(iv) Any other (Riots/heart attack)	27	21.6
(f)	Span of married life:		
	(i) < 15 years	48	38.4
	(ii) 15-30 years	48	38.4
	(iii) > 30 years	29	23.2

It is further seen that 36.8 percent of the respondents became widows between the age of 31-40 years, 26.4 percent between 20-30 years whereas; none of the respondents became widow at age less than 20 years.

Table also reveals that the main cause of death of husband was long term illness (46.4%) like asthma, high blood pressure, cancer, paralysis, breathing problem and other such illnesses, whereas, little more than one-fourth (28.8%) of the respondents husband expired because of accident and very few (3.2%) died due to natural calamity.

Social consequences for widows are many and varied and have been discussed in the sociological literature. According to 1991 census of India, there are over 33 million widows in this country. This is 8 percent of the total female population or one out of every 13 women. Widows have been viewed as objects of pity, unfortunate, destined to suffer the rest of their lives and face such other problems. Problems include difficulties experienced by widows in their day-to-day life. The extent of problems faced would differ from widow to widow. It is of course possible that certain problems may be overwhelming for them if it continues for a longer period. In such situations, widows may not be able to cope up with them and may need help from others. Thus a better insight into some aspects would help communities to make widows, a satisfied, happy and productive group. Our society needs to change their attitude and help widows stand on their feet with dignity and pride.

At present, the situation is that widows have to strive for their own living. Indian society follows a trend of alienation for women from parental home after marriage and limited support from in-laws after her husband's death. At times, widows due to lack of education have lack of direction and is completely disheartened. Moreover, when she lacks inheritance rights from her deceased husband, she is only sometimes, protected by her father, brother or other natal family members. Women's faces challenges, compromises and adjustment after widowhood. She continues living on the basis of her children and past memories of her deceased husband.

Thus, ways of coping up depends on cause of husband's death, the age when she became a widow, her span of married life, with whom she is staying at present.

Problems Reported by Widows

Table 4, reveals that little less than half (49.6%) of the respondents reported moderate psychological problems, whereas, little more than one-fourth (27.2%) of the respondents had high psychological problems and little less than one-fourth (23.2%) of them reported low psychological problems.

Table 4
Percentage Distribution of the Respondents According to the Psychological Problems Reported By Widows

(N = 125)

Psychological Problems	*Frequency (f)*	*Percentage (%)*
Low	29	23.3
Moderate	62	49.6
High	34	27.2

Some of the psychological problems, which widows experience, are isolation, feeling of loneliness, helplessness, alienation, lack of support and lack of encouragement. Deprivation of love is harmful to the personality and result in emotional starvation. Loneliness and depression may lead to mental disorder and suicidal tendencies. Widows have higher incidence of mental disorder and higher suicidal rate because of greater isolation and feelings of insecurity and uselessness.

Table 5
Item Wise Distribution of the Respondents According to the Psychological Problems Reported By Widows

(N = 125)

Sr. No.	*Items*	*(I. I.) Intensity Indices*
1.	Psychological problems faced after your husband's death:	
	(a) Lonely	1.26
	(b) Frequent mood fluctuations	1.26
	(c) Easily hurt	1.16
	(d) Irritable	1.14
	(e) Unwanted	0.39
	(f) Completely burdensome on others	0.24
	(g) Disgusted	0.20
2.	Troubled with the thought of remarrying	0.01
3.	Face problem in satisfying sex urge	0.03
4.	Face problems dealing with the following males:	
	(a) Electrician	0.20
	(b) Plumber	0.16
	(c) Shopkeeper	0.09
	(d) Postman	0.03

Table 5 contd.

Sr. No.	Items	(I. I.) Intensity Indices
5.	Neglected in major decision making	0.25
6.	With time, psychological problems:	
	(a) Needs compromise	0.87
	(b) Worse	0.11
7.	Change in Children's behaviour after husband's death:	
	(a) Do not follow your suggestions	0.40
	(b) Do not listen to you	0.38
	(c) Criticise you	0.16
	(d) Unsympathetic towards you.	0.15
8.	Change in family members behaviour after your husband's death:	
	(a) Do not follow your suggestions	1.13
	(b) Do not listen to you	1.07
	(c) Criticise you	0.94
	(d) Dominate you	0.94
9.	There is no one in whom you can confide	0.99
10.	People do not approve your friendship with opposite sex	0.45
11.	Feel like committing suicide	0.04

Table 5 indicates that respondents face psychological problems after their husband's death. Sometimes, they felt lonely, had frequent mood fluctuations, felt easily hurt and irritable. They also felt that with time, psychological problems needed compromise, as they had no one in whom they could confide. They also felt that family members did not follow their suggestions, listen to them, criticised and dominated them.

Very few times, respondents felt unwanted, completely burdensome on others and disgusted. They were troubled with the thought of remarriage and faced problems in satisfying their sex urge. They also faced problems while interacting with males like electrician, plumber, shopkeeper and postman. They felt that with time, psychological problems became worse and that they were neglected in major decision- making. Children did not follow their suggestions, criticised them, did not listen to them and were unsympathetic towards them. Society did not approve of their friendship with the opposite sex and respondents also felt like committing suicide.

Table 6, indicates that little more than half (54.4%) of the respondents reported low social problems, whereas, 34.4 percent of them reported moderate social problems and just 11.2 percent had high social problems.

Table 6
Percentage Distribution of the Respondents According to the Social Problems Reported by Widows

(N = 125)

Social Problems	Frequency (f)	Percentage (%)
Low	68	54.4
Moderate	43	34.4
High	14	11.2

Table 7
Item Wise Distribution of the Respondents According to the Social Problems Reported by Widows

(N = 125)

Sr. No.	*Items*	*I. I.*
1.	Face problems in following social customs after widowhood like —	
	(a) Wearing white saris only	0.31
	(b) Stop wearing ornaments	0.30
	(c) Foregoing food with pickle and spices	0.12
2.	Face problems in performing religious rites because you are a widow	0.29
3.	Face criticism when attending social functions from :	
	(a) Relative	0.40
	(b) Neighbours	0.31
	(c) Children	0.02
4.	Society's impression about you at present	
	(a) Criticise you	0.21
	(b) Avoid you	0.19
5.	Society keeps a watch on your every action	0.54
6.	Society does not accept your family as a complete family	0.39
7.	Face problems in interacting with people	
	(a) Cannot maintain relationship with new people for a long time	0.53
	(b) Cannot talk to new people easily	0.46
8.	Face problems in expressing your difficulties and feelings to the family members	0.32
9.	Accused of creating conflicts in life of married couples	0.15
10.	Comparing yourself with a married women, find problems in terms of	
	(a) Low status	0.91
	(b) Personal freedom	0.78
	(c) Instability	0.22

Widows want to remain fully integrated in society, but it is society that segregates them and creates frustration and unhappiness in their lives. Widowhood acts as an invitation to worries, sorrows, problems, misfortunes, instability, dependency, fear, struggle, in all a combination of problems. In our patriarchal society, where women right from birth is over protected and when she suddenly finds herself widowed is completely directionless due to lack of education and proper knowledge.

Table 7 reveals that sometimes respondents felt that their status and personal freedom had reduced when compared to married women. Very few times, respondents faced problems in following social customs like, wearing white saris, ornaments and foregoing food with pickle and spices. They also did not face major problems in performing religious rites. The few times that they faced criticism were from relatives and neighbours. Very few times children and society criticised and tried to avoid them. Moreover, very few times, society kept a constant watch on their every action and did not accept their family as complete family and accused of creating conflicts in the life of married couples. They also did not face any major problems while interacting and expressing their feelings in front of people.

Table 8 reveals, that more than half of the respondents (51.6%) reported low financial problems, whereas 35.2 percent of them had moderate financial problems. Very few (7.2%) of the respondents reported high financial problems.

Table 8
Percentage Distribution of the Respondents According to the Financial Problems Reported By Widows

(N = 125)

Financial Problems	*Frequency (f)*	*Percentage (%)*
Low	72	57.6
Moderate	44	35.2
High	9	7.2

Widows have to fight on all fronts. She is the one who has to plan things according to priority. Her priorities begin with her children's demands and ends with compromises of her own feelings and necessities. She tries to give the best to her children but she is not successful at all times in fulfilling their demands, as she has limited flow of income and she has hardly any income to plan for her savings, investments, shares and policies and thus she has no experience in dealing with such matters. Moreover, in her earlier life, she had never been involved in the economic decisions.

Table 8 (a)
Item Wise Distribution of the Respondents According to the Financial Problems Reported By Widows

(N = 125)

Sr. No.	*Items*	*I. I.*
1.	Face problems in dealing with following financial matters:	
	(a) Shortage of money	1.00
	(b) Unable to manage with people like tax consultant and share broker	0.36
2.	Face financial inadequacy for:	
	(a) Buying clothes, jewellery etc. for yourself	0.66
	(b) Fulfilling children's needs and demands	0.62
	(c) Spending on recreational activities	0.19
3.	Injustice was done to you when receiving your property share	0.16
4.	Face difficulty when you approach people for getting money	0.13
5.	Savings for future purposes like:	
	(a) Any likely emergency	1.12
	(b) For buying assets	0.25
6.	Incurred debts and face stress because of that	0.42
7.	Do not have a steady and sure monthly income	0.11

Table 8(a) indicates that sometimes respondents faced shortage of money for buying clothes, jewellery for themselves and fulfilling children's needs and demands. Sometimes they planned for savings for likely emergency.

Table 9
Percentage Distribution of the Respondents According to the Overall Differences in Problems Reported by Widows

(N = 125)

Problems	*Percentage (%)*			*I.I.*
	Low	*Moderate*	*High*	
Psychological	23.2	49.6	27.2	1.56
Social	54.4	34.4	11.2	1.02
Financial	57.6	35.2	7.2	0.62

Table 9 reveals differences in problems according to intensity indices that majority of the respondents reported psychological problems as their major problem followed by social problems and least was the financial problems.

It is a known fact that the widows have to live in pitiable conditions. They are deprived of various social, economic and religious rights and facilities. In general the position of elderly widows is very low in India. They are exposed to humiliation and are treated in several inhuman ways. Various crude and unjust practices are followed in India. Widowhood is a critical and hard period in a woman's life. Widowhood may have deleterious effects not only because of the sudden loss of the spouse but also because of the lack of well- defined cultural expectations regarding the role of the widow.

It is worse in India because of the sex-segregated character of society, the conditions of poverty and the traditional value system. Widows are the most vulnerable section of the society and their position becomes more precarious because of the set boundaries.

Thus it can be seen that widows' lives are always surrounded with problems and some or the other worries. All the problems and botheration in a way are interrelated to each other. But still the trend and the data indicate that widows have more psychological problems, then social problems and followed by financial problems.

(A) Psychological Problems

When data were analysed to test null hypothesis that there will be no significant difference in psychological problems faced by widows according to the socio-economic status, the data reveals as per Table 10 that the t-cal. value of 2.19 when compared to t-tab value was found to be significant at 0.05 level of confidence with df=98. This indicates that a significant difference existed in psychological problems faced by widows according to socio-economic status.

Table 10
t-values Showing Differences in Psychological Problems Reported by Widows According to Socio Economic Status

(N=125)

SES	$\overline{X}$	*SD*	*Low*	*Middle*	*High*
Low	48.78	13.21		2.19*	1.87 NS
Middle	43.56	10.46			0.13 NS
High	43.24	9.48			

* Significant at 0.05 level with df=98, t-tab=1.98.

Thus the data led to conclude that socio-economic status of the respondent plays an important role in increasing or decreasing their psychological problems. Most of the time, low socio-economic status respondents were occupied with activities, which included interaction with many people and satisfying the basic needs of her family members and in this routine had no time for herself. This held true with the Middle class respondents also as they faced psychological stress. But in contrast, the respondents with higher socio-economic status lived a luxurious life and spent their time in parties, clubs involving in recreational activities. They did not have to worry about financial adjustments and thus comparatively needed to make less compromise. They had sufficient time and money to spend in the activities of their interests.

Widowhood and ageing confers a peculiar struggle in a woman's life. They face enormous burden in their new life and at the same time they often end up as the sole source of material and emotional support. These constraints make it exceedingly difficult for women to effectively play the dual role of breadwinner and the head of the house. Thus in the light of the above findings it was found that, psychological problems faced by widows varied according to the socio-economic status.

Table 11
t-values Showing Differences in Psychological Problems Reported by Widows According to Personality Dimension

(N=125)

Personality Dimension	$\overline{X}$	*SD*	*Introvert*	*Extrovert*
Introvert	53.61	11.97		3.27*
Extrovert	44.23	11.13		

* Significant at 0.05 level with df = 123, t-tab = 1.98.

When data were analysed to test null hypothesis that there will be no significant difference in psychological problems faced by widows according to personality dimension, the data reveals as per the table 11 that the t-cal. value of 3.27 when compared to t-tab value was found to be significant at 0.05 level of confidence with df=123. This indicates that a significant difference existed in the Psychological problems faced by widows according to Personality dimension. Table revealed that introverts faced more psychological problems than extroverts. Hence the null hypothesis was not accepted.

Old widows maintain emotional attachment with their deceased husband regardless of the length of time widowed. The widows were found to relate their grief to their deceased husband on a more symbolic and abstract level. Grief and attachment were positively related to widows for the first ten years, then it slowly declined with the passage of time but it was not completely ever removed.

When extrovert and introvert personalities are compared, there is more chance of an extrovert widow readjusting and resettling in her life quickly. This is because an extrovert knows how to let out her emotions and feelings through words and actions. Her motto in life is to remain happy in all circumstances and she can adjust easily with people from all age groups and tries to forget her sorrows. On the contrary, an introvert old widow never expresses her feelings and emotions and therefore, others are not aware of her likes and dislikes. She lives in her own world and never participates in any social activities be it discussion, debate or social functions.

(B) Social Problems

When data were analysed to test the null hypothesis that there will be no significant difference in the social problems according to Age, the data reveals as per the Table 12 that the t-Cal. values when compared to the t-tab value were found to be significant at 0.05 level of confidence. This indicates that a significant difference existed in the social problems faced by widows according to age. The table revealed that young and middle age group respondents faced more social problems than upper middle and old age group respondents. Hence the null hypothesis was not accepted.

When women are suddenly widowed, they find themselves to be very vulnerable and are unable to adjust to the new situation. In majority of the cases, widow's role changes to one of the 'responsible person' in the family. But the loss of status in the family and the society and the sudden loneliness that they face, lead them to think that they are unproductive members in the family and society and that they are no longer wanted by other people. The development of this feeling makes adjustment, doubly hard to accomplish. The main crux of the problem is that our society does not accord positive value and status to widows.

Table 12
t-values Showing Differences in Social Problems Reported by Widows According to Age

(N=125)

Age	$\overline{X}$	*SD*	*Young*	*Middle*	*Upper Middle*	*Old*
Young	29.53	10.10		2.32*	5.91*	7.03*
Middle	22.15	9.48			3.58*	4.89*
Upper Middle	15.31	6.41				1.51^{NS}
Old	13.16	6.29				

* Significant at 0.05 level with df = 43, t-tab = 2.02, with df = 49, t-tab = 2.01, with df = 53, t-tab = 2.01, with df = 68, t-tab = 2.00, with df = 72, t-tab = 2.00.

Table 13
t-values Showing Differences in Social Problems Reported by Old Widows According to Employment Status

(N=125)

Employment Status	$\overline{X}$	*SD*	*Employed*	*Unemployed*
Employed	20.40	9.32		3.81*
Unemployed	14.32	8.08		

* Significant at 0.05 level with df=123, t-tab=1.98.

When data were further analysed to test null hypothesis that there will be no significant difference in social problems faced by widows according to the Employment Status, the data reveals as per the table 13, that the t-cal. value of 3.81 when compared to t-tab value was found to be significant at 0.05 level of confidence with df=123. This indicates that a significant difference existed in the social problems faced by widows according to employment status of the respondent. Table revealed that respondents who were employed faced more social problems than respondents who were unemployed. Hence the null hypothesis was not accepted.

Employment acts as a way of life for widows. It is a bond with reality, her contact with the human community and forms participation in the business of purposeful existence. It gives meaning and significance to her life. Through employment, society incorporates values, which teaches us to cherish most highly, self-reliance work, achievement contribution to family and to the society.

Employment status to some extent changes a woman from her submissive behaviour to assertive behaviour with a broader perspective in life. If a respondent is employed then family income increases which raises the standard of living in areas of food, clothing, education, entertainment and facilities of modern amenities at home. But at the same time, employment of women increases her physical labour as she has to manage two fronts, the home and her job. On the other hand, not gainfully employed lady has less sources of income as she is dependent on others for her survival. Compared to employed respondent, she lives more of isolated life and period of forced mourning is quite prolonged for them. She as such contributes in different household activities, but it remains unaccounted in economic terms.

(C) Financial Problems

When data were analysed to test null hypothesis that there will be no significant difference in financial problems faced by widows according to Age, data reveals as per the table 14 that the t-cal. values when compared to t-tab values were found to be significant at 0.05 level of confidence. This indicates that a significant difference existed in financial problems faced by widows according to Age. The table revealed that young and middle age group respondents faced more financial problems than upper middle and old age group respondents. Hence the null hypothesis was not accepted.

Table 14
t-values Showing Differences in Financial Problems Reported by Widows According To Age

(N=125)

Age	$\overline{X}$	*SD*	*Young*	*Middle*	*Upper Middle*	*Old*
Young	21.38	11.96		1.59 NS	4.31*	5.82*
Middle	16.43	8.33			3.51*	5.42*
Upper Middle	10.36	6.12				1.96 NS
Old	7.88	5.20				

* Significant at 0.05 level with df = 49, t-tab = 2.01, with df = 53, t-tab = 2.01with df = 68, t-tab = 2.00, with df = 72, t-tab = 2.00.

At all stages of life, widows have to face financial problems in some or the other form. The financial situation of widows irrespective of their age group is far from satisfactory. Most of them do not have much of savings. On the other hand, they continue to have financial liabilities such as completing education of their children, arranging marriages of their daughters and so on. Inflation has made their financial condition even more miserable. The financial problem of widows belonging to upper middle and old age is comparatively less, as they have already accomplished their goals and finished all their major responsibilities. But at times, they too face financial problems as grown up children prefer to stay away from them. Many widows seem to squander the provident fund amount and experience serious difficulties in their later life. Some of them invest their money in dubious schemes and lose everything. A few do not know where to invest and get regular income out of it.

So, according to the set trend of our society, more a person is financially stable, more support or attention a person gets from the society, in comparison to people who are less financially sound. Moreover, people belonging to the old or upper middle age group have less financial responsibility than that from the young age group. Thus according to the age group of the respondents, the financial problems vary.

When data were analysed to test null hypothesis that there will be no significant difference in financial problems faced by widows according to Employment Status, the data reveals as per the table 33 that the t-cal. value of 2.55 when compared to t-tab value was found to be significant at 0.05 level of confidence with df=123. This indicates that a significant difference existed in financial problems faced by widows according to Employment status. Table revealed that respondents who were employed faced more financial problems than respondents who were unemployed. Hence the null hypothesis was not accepted.

Table 15
T-values Showing Differences In Financial Problems Reported by Widows According To Employment Status

(N=125)

Employment Status	$\overline{X}$	*SD*	*Employed*	*Unemployed*
Employed	13.86	8.01		2.55*
Unemployed	10.01	8.70		

* Significant at 0.05 level with df = 123, t-tab = 1.98.

This could be due to the fact that an employed widow can well plan for the future and can even have savings as they had a definite source of income. The main sources of income for the respondent whether employed or not gainfully employed could be family pension, financial support from children or other family members.

Unfavourable attitude towards widows is becoming fairly universal nowadays. Family members, due to lack of money forced to resent widows, as they become an added financial responsibility. As such family members face difficulty in fulfilling their first family's basic needs and in such conditions, they have to spend additional money for the non-contributing member, which puts the head of the family or earning member in difficulty. Financial insecurity, dependency, loss of spouse may lead to loss of home and prestige. When independence is lost, it leads to frustration and conflict. This becomes a barren and unproductive period in the life of widows.

Once an individual is aware of the different financial schemes, rules and regulations of financial organisations and has some assets, one can have a much improved standard of living A person being an extrovert or introvert does not contribute in solving the financial problems in any way, as necessity was the main criteria, which made her financially independent. Thus the fact that the respondents being an extrovert or introvert made no difference in the financial problems that she faced.

Awareness Among Widows Regarding Government Widow Pension Scheme

Table 16, reveals that majority (84%) of the respondents had low awareness regarding government widow pension schemes, whereas 15.2 percent of the respondents had moderate awareness and respondents with high awareness were almost negligible (0.8%).

This could be mainly due to the lack of publicity regarding government widow pension schemes. Another reason could be that in India, from the day a girl is born, she has no true identity for herself. She is always known in reference to another male. A woman's identity is limited to being a good daughter, sister, wife and mother. She does not have any opportunity to conquer new realms and face the intellectual world.

Table 16
Percentage Distribution of the Respondents According to the Awareness Among Widows Regarding Government Widow Pension Scheme

(N = 125)

Awareness of Pension scheme	*Frequency (f)*	*Percentage (%)*
Low	105	84.0
Moderate	19	15.2
High	1	0.8

Another reason for low awareness regarding government widow pension scheme, could be the fact that widowhood increases with an increase in age - 50 percent in the age group of 50 years, 64 percent in the age group of 60 years and 80 percent in the age group of 70 years and above (Sachdev, 2000). With an increase in age, their responsibilities were less as their children were settled and therefore she did not require financial help for her primary needs. These could be the reasons for low awareness about any scheme. This holds true for government widow pension schemes also.

Schemes are not much publicised through mass media, and widows are also not much exposed to media and therefore, are not aware of things around them for their betterment. If a widow is working, she is very busy with her dual responsibilities of home and job and thus does not have time to concentrate on other activities. Contrary to this, widowed women who are at home are less educated and therefore, ignorant about the different schemes or policies meant for them. They are totally dependent on others for emotional, social and financial support.

Due to various social problems that widows' face, majority of them prefer not to expose themselves to the outside world and therefore, they are not able to get information about the benefits available to them. Government has set up the government widow pension scheme from several years for financial help to widows, but old widows are ignorant about this scheme as government does not take the initiative of publicising this scheme, so the beneficiaries are unaware of this scheme.

Table 17, reveals that respondents gathered information about the government widow pension scheme from friends, government officials, family members and shared it with other friends during social gatherings.

Table 17
Itemwise Distribution of the Respondents According to the Awareness Among Widows Regarding Government Widow Pension Scheme (N = 125)

Sl. No.	*Items*	*Intensity Indices*
1.	Source of information about the government widow pension scheme:	
	(a) Friends	0.38
	(b) Government officials	0.36
	(c) Family members	0.05
	(d) Television	0.02
	(e) Social workers	0.02
	(f) Radio	0.01
	(g) Newspaper	0.01
2.	Discussed government widow pension scheme with friends	0.34
3.	By which means government widow pension scheme was discussed:	
	(a) Interacting during social gatherings	0.33
	(b) Through letters	0.02

Moreover, old widows had few sources of income like salary, support from family, few assets other than liquid assets, which declined the need for government widow pension scheme. Therefore, widows never tried to gather more and more awareness regarding the government widow pension scheme.

After data collection, it was found that out of total respondents, very few of them were availing of the government widow pension scheme. This was due to the rules and regulations of the State government and Social Welfare Department for financial resettlement of widows.

- Son's age should not be more than 21 years
- Age of widow should be between 18-60 years
- Annual income of family should not be more than Rs.3600/-
- Personal annual income should not be more than Rs.1200/-
- Resident of Gujarat State.

Majority of the widows did not qualify in all the criteria's mentioned above and thus were unable to avail of the widow pension scheme.

Table 18
Summary of Anova Showing Differences in Financial Problems Reported by Widows According to Personality Dimension

(N = 125)

Source	*Df*	*Sum of squares*	*Mean squares*	*F -Cal.*	*F-Prob.*	
Between group	1	102.93	102.93			
Within group	123	8849.34	71.94	1.43	0.23	NS
Total	124	8952.27				

NS - Not significant at 0.05 level with df = 1, F-tab = 3.92.

When data were analysed to test null hypothesis that there will be no significant difference in financial problems faced by widows according to Personality dimension, data reveals as per the table 18 that the F-Cal. value of 1.43 when compared to F-tab value was found to be not significant at 0.05 level of confidence at 1 df. This indicates that no significant difference existed in financial problems faced by elderly widows according to Personality dimension. Hence the null hypothesis was accepted.

There are political, social and economical forces, which help a woman to get her status in the society. The impact of western education has brought in Indian women, slowly but potently a new conception of themselves and a new concern about the conditions that surrounded them.

Coping Up Strategies Followed by Old Widows

It is seen from the table 19, that most of the time, respondents had close contacts with children and respondents confided in them only if they had a problem. Further it was observed that sometimes respondents had contacts with parents, in-laws and she confided in her parents and friends for sharing her feelings.

Table 19 also reveals that widows had close contacts with her brother, relatives, sister and she confided in her in-laws, colleagues, relatives, ex-colleagues, but this happened very few times only.

Widowhood is characterised by certain physical and psychological changes. However, it is seen that this leads to poor adjustment rather than to better adjustment and to unhappiness, rather than to happiness. Effect of widowhood differs from individual to individual due to different heredity socio-economic background, education and living pattern. Those living with their near and dear ones are better adjusted and happier than those living alone.

Table 19

Itemwise Distribution of the Respondents According to the Coping up Strategies Related to Psychological Problems Followed by Widows

(N = 125)

Sl. No.	*Items*	*I. I.*
1.	Close contacts with the following:	
	(a) Children	1.84
	(b) Parents	1.00
	(c) In-laws	0.78
	(d) Brother	0.53
	(e) Relatives (other than in-laws)	0.52
	(f) Sister	0.49
2.	Confide in the following persons:	
	(a) Children	1.66
	(b) Friends	0.70
	(c) Parents	0.65
	(d) In-laws	0.42
	(e) Colleagues	0.36
	(f) Relatives (other than in-laws)	0.30
	(g) Ex-colleagues	0.08
3.	Persons in whom you confide and they help you when you have a problem	1.62

Old widows preferred to stay in nuclear families with children as both of them are living for each other and therefore their bonds were strong. They shared everything and confided in each other. On the other hand, widows staying in joint families or if parents and in-laws resided nearby, she had contacts with them and sometimes confided in them also. Working women confided in her colleagues, who were of her age, or her brother or sister to ease her grief.

The self-determination of the widows gave them an extra courage to fight against obstacles. They began with doing their choice of work and started living life as she wanted to, as it would provide her with satisfaction on all fronts. By doing this, she could become an ideal role model for other widows too.

Thus, to conclude it was found that widows had different coping up strategies to overcome their psychological problems.

Table 20
Itemwise Distribution According to the Coping up Strategies Related to Social Problems Followed by Widows

(N = 125)

Sl. No.	*Items*	*I. I.*
1.	Leisure time activities:	
	(a) Watching television	1.34
	(b) Religious activities	1.19
	(c) Shopping	0.48
	(d) Reading	0.40
	(e) Morning walk	0.39
	(f) Evening walk	0.28
	(g) Listening to radio	0.23
	(h) Playing games	0.14
	(i) Watching movies	0.11
2.	Visit friends and relatives:	
	(a) Daily	1.07
	(b) Once a month	0.67
	(c) Once a week	0.07
	(d) Twice a week	0.07
3.	Reasons for visit to friends and relatives:	
	(a) Change of mood	1.38
	(b) Attending ceremonies	0.90
	(c) During illness	0.85
	(d) Religious functions	0.71
	(e) Whenever you need help	0.26
	(f) Birthdays	0.09
4.	Encouraged to participate in following:	
	(a) Discussion on current news	0.50
	(b) Various activities and competitions organised at community level	0.41
	(c) Organise functions	0.34
	(d) To take up leadership roles	0.28
5.	Associated with any welfare organisations	0.06

Table 20 indicates that the respondents coping up strategies were related to social problems. Sometimes respondents watched television, participate in religious activities during leisure time. Some of the respondents daily or once a month visited friends and relatives; it was mainly for change of mood, attending ceremonies, during illness or religious functions and ceremonies.

Respondents spent leisure time in shopping, reading, morning walk, playing games, listening to radio, watching movies and visiting friends and relatives once a month or twice a week. Very few times respondents were associated with welfare organisations or were encouraged to participate in activities, competitions, organise functions, discuss on current news and take up leadership roles.

Old widows face a lot of social problems and therefore have to use coping up strategies to overcome it. It was felt that widows associations could be formed in different localities and these associations could start some intellectual, social and recreational activities. These associations can also take up some socially useful activities and try to indicate to others, that they are still useful members of the society. Involvement in religious activities can also be considered as it gives solace to many. Reading of scriptures, discussions on different themes could be encouraged.

Widows should be encouraged to remain active, engage in social activities, get more and more involved in the society as long as one can. A few hours of useful social activity will help them in getting companionship outside their homes. Widows will be in a better frame of mind to accommodate to their new form of life. Members of the family will also be eased of considerable tension of trying to find ways of keeping the widows occupied fruitfully and thus give her necessary change. So, widows now have both the alternatives, whether to involve in active life or withdraw into own shell of loneliness. They must choose from these alternatives depending on one's own inclinations.

Thus the respondents were encouraged to regularly participate in social gatherings, functions and activities, which kept them busy as well as active all the time. It acted as coping up strategy to overcome their social problems.

Table 21, indicates that sometimes respondents asked for help from family members during financial crisis and as assets they mainly possessed house. Very few of them asked for help during financial crisis from son, friends, relatives or used their savings or asked for credit. In the form of assets they possessed ornaments, land, vehicle or had own business.

Widowhood leads to worries, sorrows, problems, misfortunes, instability, dependency, fear, struggle and courage in all a combination of various problems. In our patriarchal society where women right from birth are over protected. When they suddenly find themselves widowed they are completely directionless due to lack of education, proper knowledge and are unaware about the realities of life. Many of them are such that they had never thought of becoming independent or doing a job. Once they are widowed, financial crisis was a major problem as the breadwinner was no longer with them. They are bound to take up jobs and take care of people dependent on them. At times in spite of earning widows face financial crisis and thus they seek help from family members, son, friends, and relatives. Thus, according to priorities widows plan, whether they should give importance to their children's education, their marriage or buy assets for a secure future. Thus, with lot of hardships, widows resets to the sudden new changes in their life.

Table 21
Itemwise Distribution of the Coping up Strategies Related to Financial Problems Followed by Widows

(N = 125)

Sl. No.	*Items*	*Intensity Indices*
1.	Take financial help at the time of money crisis from:	
	(a) Family members	0.55
	(b) Son	0.30
	(c) Friends	0.30
	(d) Savings	0.26
	(e) Relatives	0.25
	(f) Asking for credit	0.18
	(g) Daughter	0.06
2.	Assets other than liquid assets:	
	(a) House	1.12
	(b) Ornaments	0.45
	(c) Land	0.30
	(d) Vehicle	0.30
	(e) Any other	0.06

Positive Attributes Reported by Widows

In majority of the cases ,widows lacked basic needs including money, proper food, domiciliary services and recreation. They are regarded as burden on the society. They are maltreated on one pretext or the other. With the disappearance of the joint family system, there are no community pressures on the recalcitrant members, and widows become the worst sufferers of this trend. At times, if widows are compelled to stay with family members, they are ill-treated. Issue of remarriage is not encouraged in our society and is considered as a taboo for them. Widows themselves do not prefer to remarry as proposals are mainly from widowers, divorcees who also have children and widows feel that in such situations, proper care cannot be given to own children, new husband and his children can be more demanding.

All these circumstances act as a challenge which widows need to overcome. Their aim is to overcome all the barriers for which they develop qualities like hard work, regaining confidence in themselves, being optimistic and much more. At times, widows feel they are useful to the society and her experiences and knowledge of life are valuable. They are also remembered in the days of celebrations and festivities. Some of the widow's full life is spent in religious activities and thus they are encouraged by the society.

Table 22
Itemwise Distribution of the Respondents According to the Positive Attributes Reported by Widows

(N = 125)

Sl. No.	*Items*	*I. I.*
1.	Mental attitude towards life after husband's death:	
	(a) Hard working	1.82
	(b) Relaxed	1.79
	(c) Open minded	1.79
	(d) Optimistic	1.73
	(e) Confident	1.70
	(f) Emotionally strong	1.70
	(g) Assertive	1.66
	(h) Relieved	1.41
	(i) Ambitious	1.36
	(j) Competitive	0.80
2.	Received remarriage proposals from:	
	(a) Widowers	0.06
	(b) Divorcees	0.05
	(c) Unmarried men	0.05
3.	Attitude of family members on arrival of friends and relatives:	
	(a) You are informed when they come	1.90
	(b) You are included as part of the conversation	1.76
	(c) You get privacy when talking to them	1.59
4.	Society's impression:	
	(a) Support and help you	1.43
	(b) Appreciate you	1.10
	(c) Sympathetic with you	1.03

Table 22 reveals that most of the time, it was reported by the widows that, after their husband's death they became hard working, relaxed, open minded, optimistic, confident, emotionally strong, assertive and said that family members informed and included them in conversations with friends and relatives.

Further the table indicates that widows sometimes felt relieved, ambitious, felt competitive and got privacy while talking to friends and relatives. It was also found that sometimes society supported and helped them, appreciated them and sympathised with them.

Thus in the Indian social set-up, widows have to shun all ostentation in life. With time, they have adopted and adjusted to the sudden change in their lives and found alternative ways to live. Widows realised that with time, they had to learn new skills for improving their standard of living. They started working hard and became more ambitious and competitive to make a career and thus increase their status. With time, they also felt relaxed and relieved, which they may not have felt, if they had an unhappy married life. Now they could take their own decisions and thus became emotionally strong and confident in whatever they did. These situations also made them optimistic in their behaviour, as she realised her potentialities and hidden talents which helped in giving them a new meaning in life.

Suggestions Obtained from Widows

Table 23, indicates that the respondents suggested awareness regarding government widow pension scheme by viewing television. Further, it was suggested to increase the amount of pension money by the respondents, so that widows could get better benefits.

Table further reveals that respondents felt that society should support and help them and suggested that regular interaction with friends is one of the ways of improving one's life. It was also observed that Government and NGO's could also extend help to widows by associating with social groups and organisations.

The table also depicts that more of the respondents felt the need for counselling and guidance services for improving their life, whereas, majority of the respondents wanted to increase their income by taking vocational training. Above all majority of the respondents wanted organisations to provide them with their husband's job, so that the total amount of monthly income and facilities provided to widows do not vary and the situation remains the same as before widowhood.

Table 23
Item Wise Distribution of the Respondants According to the Suggestions Obtained From Widows For Improving their General Condition

(N = 125)

Sl. No.	*Items*	*Intensity Indices*
1.	Ways to develop awareness:	
	(a) Television	0.88
	(b) Posters, leaflets, pamphlets, newspapers	0.54
	(c) Radio	0.08
2.	Ways of improving government widow pension scheme:	
	(a) Increase the amount of money	0.87
	(b) Short procedures	0.54
	(c) Efficient administration	0.40
	(d) Regular distribution of pension amount	0.10
3.	Social participation that could change widow's life:	
	(a) Regularly interacting with friends	0.79
	(b) Passing leisure time in doing hobby work	0.77
	(c) Participating in social gatherings	0.53
	(d) Accompanying family members for picnics, movies	0.27
	(e) Participating in major decision making	0.13
4.	Institutions recommended for widows:	
	(a) Guidance and counselling services	0.74
	(b) Employment placement services	0.56
	(c) Recreational institutions	0.32
	(d) Special institutions	0.14
5.	Vocational training to increase their income	0.91
6.	Society's attitude should change towards widows:	
	(a) Support and help them	0.82
	(b) Give equal importance to them	0.77
7.	NGO's and Government organisations can help in improving life of widows:	
	(a) Associating widows with social groups, organisations.	0.71
	(b) Starting widow clubs	0.61
	(c) Encouraging widow remarriages	0.49
	(d) Organising conferences and seminars	0.22
	(e) Opposing wearing of white sari	0.18
	(f) Opposing practice of shaving head	0.10
8.	Support from organisations:	
	(a) Helping widows to get husband's job	0.94
	(b) Getting husband's financial assets	0.93
	(c) Understanding legal and property rights	0.30

Contd....

Sl. No.	Items	Intensity Indices
9.	Financial actions to help widows:	
	(a) Opening joint accounts	0.86
	(b) Having joint property	0.26
	(c) Proper knowledge about shares	0.22
	(d) Having joint business	0.05

Very few widows suggested that awareness regarding the government widow pension scheme can be developed through posters, leaflets, pamphlets, newspapers, radio and suggested improvement in administrative procedures so that did not face too many problems in attaining the benefits due to them. Moreover, they recommended regular distribution of pension amount. They wanted more recreational institutions and wanted encouragement towards remarriages and opposed wearing of white saris, shaving of head and want conferences and seminars organised so that they could understand their legal rights and have better knowledge about financial aspects. They also suggested social gatherings, accompanying family for picnics, movies and participating in major decisions to change and improve their life.

With time widows wanted to improve their life. On the basis of the responses given to the open-ended question, the following suggestions were given:

- Self respect is the biggest thing, so do not involve in matters where people do not respect you, but behave in a way that you expect others to behave with you.
- Do not expect anything from anyone; instead make yourself independent as there is no alternate to hard work and by being optimistic, having faith in God, clear heart, mind and living for others becomes the key to success in life.
- Do not trust everyone and everything. Make yourself strong and confident so that society's comments and abuse do not bother you and do not feel guilty if you cannot find time for children as you are working for their betterment.
- Further, it was suggested that if by wearing coloured saris, sticking bindi and wearing black thread you are

saved from mis-happenings and comments, then you should go ahead and do it as feelings for your husband will not decline by doing so. Many supported increasing girls' education and supported widow remarriages and wanted more social relations as one never knows when help may be needed. Moreover, it was felt that one should keep oneself busy, so that a pessimistic feeling does not arise. Widows also recommended financial help for setting up small-scale business units so that they could become independent. They wanted more and more information of financial schemes, policies and shares and wanted to plan finances according to priorities, so that they could avoid borrowing of money as far as possible.

An overview of the predicaments faced by elderly widows, are limited freedom to remarry, insecure property rights, social restrictions on living arrangements, restricted employment opportunities and lack of social support. There have been variety of arrangements made by different groups in India to deal with the panic that ensues, when in the eyes of patriarchal authority, a woman becomes a widow and therefore, becomes a potential bearer of independent status. It may be deduced that the precarious situation most of the widows face would be greatly eliminated if they managed to establish independent land and property rights. It is striking that, having failed to implement a protective regime for a widow's basic survival rights, the state has also failed to provide adequate welfare coverage for them, although a number of mostly token social security schemes have been designed towards that end. A plethora or reasons why social security plans fail. The amounts granted in the pension schemes might allow widows to barely support themselves, but cannot be stretched far enough to provide for additional dependants. And given the rather rigid criteria under which widows can qualify for various welfare plans, it is no surprise that many millions end up living as destitute.

The anthology urges researchers to examine widowhood as a "cause of deprivation" and asks activists to help organise widows, address their grievances, and ensure they have access to entitlements like jobs, land, education, financial and social support. Widows primarily are portrayed as victims, which is a challenge for future research on this subject. Widows in India should be cohesive, well-organised and informative, articulating the struggles of women to attain basic respect and basic rights, and suggests the first steps for taking innovative approaches to incorporating widows' own demands for a better quality of life, in a programme of social improvement.

BIBLIOGRAPHY

1. Agarwal, B., Widows versus Daughters or Widows as Daughters? Property, Land and Economic Security in Rural India. *Sociological Abstract*, February 1999, p. 219.
2. Baarsen, V., Berna, S., Johannes, H., Snijders, Tom, A.B., And Knipscheer, Kees, P.M., Do Personal Conditions and Circumstances Surrounding Partner Loss Explain Loneliness in Newly Bereaved Older Adults? *Sociological Abstract*, February 2000, p. 350.
3. Bordavekar, K.S., Retirement and its Social Implications, Dissertation (M.Sc.), M.S. University, Baroda, 1973.
4. Bothra, Payal., Widows: Socio Economic Aspects, Dissertation (M.Sc.), M.S. University, Baroda, 2000.
5. Byles, Julie, E., Feldman, Susan And Mishra, G., For Richer for Poorer in Sickness and in Health: Older Widowed Women's Health, Relationship and Financial Security. *Sociological Abstract*, April 2000, p. 1025.
6. Chawla, Geet, The Elderly Role as Recipients and Providers of Socio-emotional Care Within Three Generational Families, Dissertation (M.Sc.), M.S. University, Baroda, 1994.
7. Chen, M.A., Widows in India, Sage Publications, New Delhi 1998, p. 450.
8. Chen, M.A. and Dreze, J., Widows and Health in Rural North India, *Economic and Political Weekly*, Vol. 27, October 1992, pp. 24-31.
9. Cherubini, C., Widows in Post-tridentate Rome, *Dissertation Abstract International*, Vol. 59(10), April 1999, p. 3930A.
10. Chiu, L., Chuan, F., The Adjustment Process of Elderly Widows, *Dissertation Abstract International*, Vol. 60(12), June 2000, p.4604 A.
11. Danforth and Mc Call, M., Listen to My Words Give Meaning to My Sorrow: A Study in Perspective Transformation in Middle Aged Women Who Experience Loss of Spouse. *Dissertation Abstract International*, Vol. 60(9), March 2000, p. 3233 A.
12. Dave, Tejal, Life Style of Single Women, Dissertation (M.Sc.), M.S. University, Baroda, 1998.

13. Deborah, D., Grief and Attachment in Young Widowhood, *Dissertation, Abstract International,* Vol. 60 (7), January 2000, p. 2383A.

14. Deoras, Adjustment in Old Age: An Introductory Survey, *Indian Journal of Applied Psychology,* Vol. 16 (1), March 1990, pp. 44-47.

15. Desai, K.G., The Preparation and Standardisation of a Socio-economic Status Scale in *Gujarati Journal of Educational and Pscyhology,* 44(4), January 1987.

16. Fooken, I., Old and Female: Psychosocial Concomitants of the Aging Process in a Group of Older Women. In Munnichs, M.A. Joep and others (Eds), Life Span and Change in a Gerantological Perspective Orlando: Academic Press, 1985.

17. Ganguly, Critical Issues on the Status of Women. An Advisory Committee on Women's Studies, ICSSR, 1977.

18. George, Thangam, Life Style of Elderly Couple Staying Independently,Dissertation (M.Sc.), M.S. University, Baroda, 1995.

12

ELDERLY ABUSE IN THE FAMILY

K. Rethi Devi

Introduction

The ageing of population is a world wide but recent phenomenon. The advancement in physical and medical sciences, economic development, and rapid expansion of public health services along with social welfare and social security measures have resulted in increase of life expectancy. It has brought about a demographic transition leading to sharp increase in the population of the aged, which according to 1981 census forms 4.8 crores.

India is passing through a phase of rapid socio-economic transformation. As a result, the joint-family system is gradually breaking down giving way to nuclear family. Forces of modernisation, technological changes and mobility have introduced changes in the life-style and values of the people that have adversely affected traditional respects as well as attitude of empathy and care for the aged. Migration of the younger people from rural areas to the cities and towns worsens the situation of the old who either stay behind, leading a life of isolation or moving along with sons and daughters to towns or lead their life in cramped situation. Even increasing literacy amongst women accompanied by their employment outside the home in offices and in factories also leaves no time for those women to take care of the old at home. Besides, there is now greater investment by the family on education and upbringing of children. The high cost of living and changing priorities affect the intra-family distribution of income in favour of the younger generation. The old people have been at the receiving end of these socio-economic changes.

As a result, in modern societies the social position of the older is much more insecure than was the case in many earlier cultures, where old age often brought prestige, wealth and power. Not only did older people usually have a secure position in the community but also they retained important duties within the family. Much of this has disappeared in modern societies to day.

In the past the old were never a burden to the family. An old man continued to work in the farm or home till late in his life. The old women nursed their grand children and provided native medicine to the sick in the family. The wisdom and experience of the old was an asset to the community. It compensated the lack of literacy, training and the devices of storing and retrieving of knowledge. The young learnt trade and skill by imitating the old and the experienced. Naturally, therefore, age received its due recognition and honour.

But then things have changed from bad to worse in the recent past as far as the aged is concerned. Nowadays, the elderly are not given the same respect as they used to get before. They are not shown adequate care and attention by their family members partly due to the limited resources and partly due to growth of individualism in modern industrial life. All these aspects lead to greater alienation and isolation of the aged from the rest of his/ her family and society at large. It is of course true that the aged in India is not as handicapped as the aged in some parts of the Western world. However, it is beyond doubt that the aged in India now have a feeling of being neglected, if not being led down or despise.

As the population of the aged increases and due to the socio-economic transformations which India passes through resulted in a number of problems for the aged. Among the most prominent problem faced by the elderly is the abuse by the family members and also by the people of the society. This elderly abuse in the family is a kind of domestic violence, which has been taken for granted by the Researchers. But the abuse of elders is a serious issue which has to be tackled otherwise it will damage the physical, mental and emotional condition of the elders. Hence this study has been attempted with a focus to find out the abuse of elders in the family.

METHODOLOGY

Objectives

1. To identify the type of abuse directed towards the elders.
2. To analyse the relationship between sex, occupation and income of the elders and their abuse.
3. To identify the chief abuser.

The universe of the present study is the aged population (60+) in the Kannankurichi Village, Salem District. The total samples comprising 50 aged both male (25) and female (25) is selected following the random method. Particular village has been selected purely based on convenience. The random selection of respondents has been made from the electoral lists available at the Panchayat Office. Using interview schedule the data has been collected which was analysed in terms of frequencies and percentages.

Result and Discussions

The present sociological study focused on 50 elderly persons who falls within the purview of the middle income indicates that the average age of aged males and females are 66 years and 65 years respectively. The age distribution analysis indicates that the males live longer than females as comparatively high proportions of male represent age groups beyond 65 years. As regards the educational background of the aged it is surprising to note that irrespective of sex not even a single aged is illiterate. On a closer look at the data it is found that comparatively the aged males show better educational achievement than the females. It is even surprising to note that two women possess professional qualification. The occupation of the aged prior to their retirement has significant bearing on their social life as well as on health and psychological needs. With this intention the occupation of the aged was analysed and it is noted that the sample of male aged comprised of 60 percent government servants (clerks, cashier, peons, professor, superintendent, etc.) 24 per cent private employers (clerks, cashier, accountant etc.) and 16 per cent public sector employers. As regards the female aged 32 per cent of them are housewives. But among the employed only five (29%) of them are government employed who worked as teacher, typist and clerk. Even two women worked as social worker and it is interested to note that even at the age of 65 they continue to serve the society by continuing the work.

The status of the aged in the family depends upon their contribution to family and also how they engage themselves after retirement. The economic crisis has forced many of the aged to reduce/adjust their needs eventually leading to psychological depression among the aged. As members of society they too have to fulfil certain social obligations like attending marriages, deaths of kins or friends, making gifts to their daughters and grand children at the time of their visits and so on. To meet such obligations some of the aged are found to be at work, and few others think that their economic dependency certainly and gradually gives rise to conflict in the family and to avoid this they ought to go for small works. 40 per cent of the men who are of this view are engaged in occupation as accountant, watchman, clerk etc. These are the people who still have certain commitments in the family and all of them are not entitled to get the pension benefits since they are not government servants. On the contrary majority of the women respondent have feeling that retirement marks the period of rest for them. Hence these women are not productively engaged. On the other hand, only eight per cent of the women are employed and they think that they should contribute to the family and to the society as long as they can and these women are continuing their work as social worker. Those who live independently on their own income are found over-confident and develop the ethic 'Work till death'. When the income of the aged was analysed it is noted that nearly sixty eight per cent of the male aged are getting income of more than Rs.600/- per month and most of the government employees come under this category. On the other hand, only twenty per cent of the aged women fall under this category. Though only eight respondents were house-wives, when it come to the income, which shows that those (9 women) respondents who were once employed do not come under the category of government servants to get the pension benefits and even those who got a lump sum on their retirement did not invest the money for their future since they have family obligations to fulfil.

In the present study, three types of families have been identified in which the aged are living, viz., Joint families (i.e.) either living with son or daughter, post-parental families (couples living alone after the children have left home) and extended families, where the aged are living with their close kin. Both the aged who are living in post-parental families and those who are living with kin are found to have the grown up and economically independent children. But number of reasons such as social migration of their children, higher education, conflict in the family, growing individualism, and so on has forced the aged to live in post-paternal families or with close kin. Only 24 per cent of the male and female are living together as couples without sons and daughter, when asked for the reasons for staying alone many of the couples are of the view that they do not want to migrate to other places along with either their sons or daughters since they think that they will have a strain relationship if being together and they do not want to sacrifice their independence, privacy and freedom. Those living with sons and daughters constitute 60 per cent (12% daughters and 48% sons) and 72 per cent (56% sons 16% daughters) among the males and females respectively.

With the traditional joint family system loosing its control over resources and there by denies authoritarian role to the aged and hence they do not have a major role in decision making with regard to important matters in the family. A large proportion of household is now headed by sons (and others of younger age) where the aged do not receive the same deference and care as in the olden days, and very often they are not consulted at all. This is true in the present study where only 32 per cent respondents (20% males and 12% females) accepted that due importance is given to their decision at family level and comparatively views and suggestions of the males are honoured in decision making relating to financial, social, and religious matters than the views of aged females. In the same way irrespective of sex those who are below 66 years are given more importance in decision-making and almost all the males in this category is continued to work even after retirement. A few aged male and female even said that they are not even bothered if they have not been given important role in decision making but they are hurt more when their wards have finalised the marriage of their grant children without even informing them. The next important issue is whether the elderly are having a good quality of life or not. Now the question arises what is meant by a good quality of life? It means whether the aged is reasonably satisfied with his day to day living within the circumstances of his life, in terms of food, shelter and general mental and physical health. Many of the aged are not satisfied about their quality of life marked by emotional insecurity, lack of care etc.

The aged persons living alone and with relatives are found feeling most frustrated as they are uncared in the community and thus develop a sense of isolation. Although 32 per cent of aged living with daughters expressed their dissatisfaction over present condition of living, more than 25 per cent are happy and satisfied. Many complaints, that their houses are very much cramped, with poor ventilation, dust and lack of basic facilities such as toilets, water and sanitation. When asked about the type of care and medical treatment available 26 per cent of them living with sons, six per cent staying with relatives, eight per cent living with daughters and four per cent staying alone reported non-availability of adequate care during illness. A great majority of them over 7-percent felt that adequate diet and medicine were denied to them during illness. The caretaker shows lack of interest to prepare a separate food for them even during illness. These respondents are longing to have their traditional food pattern not only during illness but also other times. But they are given chunk food, which they considered are not good for their health. Whenever their health problem is taken to the notice of the care taker, they keep a deaf ear to their complaints saying that these are the signs of old age and hence they have to bear every thing. But they are least bothered to consult a doctor and give medicines to cure it. This sort of complaint is more among those who live with their sons and they blame their daughter-in-law for this. Majority of the older couples who live together, separate from any kith and kin accepted that most of their health problems are dealt within the home through mutual care and only on rare occasion they go to nursing home or hospital. These elderly people do not want the help they receive to take the form of living with their children while they are still able to care for themselves. They like to keep their own home, their own friends, their independence and privacy.

Almost all the respondents accepted that some form of abuse had been directed towards them at one time or other and the most common form of abuse experienced by the aged are neglect, lack of attention, denial of freedom, lack of health care, food etc. Sex wise analysis of abuse experienced by the elders revealed that among the female neglect is followed by denial of freedom and lack of attention. On the other hand for male denial of freedom is followed by neglect and lack of attention. It is a well-known fact that men lose their freedom after their retirement and it is worse when they do not contribute anything to the family. On the other hand females have a feeling that the family members do not properly care them. This results in neglect. On the whole though variation is seen a closer examination revealed that females tend to be victims of abuse more frequently than men. Lack of freedom is the common form of abuse experienced by all the age group and as the age increases they have complaint such as denial of food and health care. These aged have a feeling that the tastes of the food is not according to their desire and the food which is more liked by them are not given to them even occasionally. The caretakers try to satisfy only the needs and taste of the younger generation specially their children. Those who have complained that they have not been given the freedom accepted that they are not free to buy things for themselves, free to say anything and freedom to take decision on their own. Those who are above 70 years are more worried since their movements are curtailed. They are strictly instructed not to come in front of gathering like friends, when they visit their houses and they are also warned not to open their mouth unnecessarily in front of others. They said that they have been given a separate room with all facilities so that they can engage themselves full time in watching Television. This results in passive neglect, where the elderly person is left alone, isolated and forgotten.

Employment status of the respondents after retirement has an important bearing on the extent of abuse shown towards the aged. The degrees of different forms of abuse experienced by the employed aged are comparatively less than the unemployed. Though the abuse extended towards the aged are greater for the unemployed, further analysis revealed that pensioners are less affected by the abuse. To quote from a great Philosopher Sankaracharya, "Yoúr family is attached to you so long as you earn, with frail body no income, no one in the house even the wife care for you".

After identifying the major forms of abuse experienced by the elders, it is decided to identify the chief abusers. In the present study it is identified that females are the major abusers who constitutes 70 per cent. Among the females, daughter in law dominate than daughter in abusing the elders. This is in accordance with the views expressed by Black and Sonnet, 1977; Lau Kosberg 1979; who said that females are more likely to be the abusers than males. It is possible that woman are more likely to be offenders, may be because they are more likely to be responsible for the care of the elder or because society has higher expectation for woman when it comes to the care of both the very young and the very old dependants, thus acts such as failure to provide care are considered abusive if committed by a woman, but are not necessarily considered abusive if committed by a man. Usually, the family as well as the society expects the oldest child, the most responsible child, a single child or the child who seems closest to the parent becomes the caregiver. If the child fitting any of the above characteristics is a male, his wife (the daughter-in-law) may become the actual caregiver. In this situation the family may just have assumed that the daughter-in-law would serve as caregiver, but she do not want the responsibility. Her feelings about this may be expressed either verbally or non-verbally to other members, especially the aged for whom she is to care. This may also be another reason why the daughter-in-law is considered to be the main abuser.

Conclusion

It may be concluded from this study that almost all the aged in the study experienced one form of abuse in the family. The most common forms of abuse experienced by them are neglect, lack of attention, denial of freedom, food and health care. Sex and employment status has got relationship with abuse. The male aged and the pensioners are less subjected to abuse. It is also found that females are the chief abusers viz., daughter-in-law and daughter.

Though the traditional family bonds and solidarity are changing, any improvement in the general well being of the aged must begin within the context of the family. There is a great need to consolidate the family bonds in the society where these have been snapped and where the process of loosening of these bonds has already started. There is a need of proper social intervention so that these bonds get consolidated and strengthened.

The national policy has to be framed in such a manner that it includes all social security measures of the aged so that they need not depend on their children to look after them in old age. A large family was always considered as insurance against neglect of the old parents. The limiting family size in India could be effective only when there is a comprehensive social security scheme applicable to the senior citizens in our country.

Let me conclude by quoting a Columbian psycho geriatrician, Dulcey-Ruiz, statement that there is a need to change the idea of age being passive, useless, dependent and isolated into one that is active autonomous and socially participative". Then ageing will cease to be a problem. All they want is not comforts but feeling needed. An average family size of four children over the generations gives an individual many more close relations than a family size of two, which is more common today. And in other cases there is only one child to take the full responsibility. So far society as a whole there is an increasing problem of the elderly.

BIBLIOGRAPHY

1. Anita Joshua, Abandoned in their Twilight Years, *Hindu*, May14th 1998.
2. Block, M.R., and Sinnott, J.D., The Battered Older Syndrome: An Exploratory Study, Final report to the United States Administration on Aging, The University of Maryland, Center on Aging, 1979.
3. Ebersole Priscilla and Hess Patricia, Towards Healthy Aging, The C.V. Mosby Company, Toronto, 1985.
4. Jogan Shankar, Social Problems and Welfare in India, Ashish Publishing House, New Delhi, 1992.
5. Lau, E & Kosberg, J., Abuse of the Elderly by Informal Care Providers, Aging 5: 10-15, 1979.
6. Richard, J. Gelles, & Claire Pedrick Cornell, Intimate Violence in Families, Sage Publications, New Delhi, 1985.
7. Robert, T.Sigler, Domestic Violence in Context, Lexington Book, Toronto, 1989.
8. Sandhya Baliga, Social Security for the Aged, Govt. Action Research Development Journal, Vol: 2, No.2, February 1996.
9. Swaminathan, Integration of the Aged into the Development Process of India, in Aged in India by R.N. Patti & B. Jena, Ashish Publishing House, New Delhi, 1989.
10. Vijayakumar, S and M. Surya Narayana, Problems of the Aged in Rural Sector, op.cit.

PART–III

REHABILITATION

13

DEPRESSION: A MAJOR HAZARD IN WORK PARTICIPATION OF SENIOR CITIZENS

Chandra Paul Singh

Introduction

Old age is a normal period of life span with its own characteristics. It is known as a period of decline in which the physical, mental and social capacities are restricted. Our society has always valued people according to their output and contribution. As a result people have developed certain myths about old people such as they are senile, elder people resist change; they have more psychiatric problems, etc. Many other stereotypes about old age also prevalent in the society are, that the old people are rigid in thought and manner, quarrelsome and outdated in terms of morality and skills. Elizabeth Ferguson (1975) describes some of the myths and stereotypes about the elderly:

"Stereotyped notions about ageing and the elderly exist in all segments of the population. Many of them are myths, but they are held tenaciously, and sound data to rebut them scarce. The ageing are generally thought to be less intelligent, less able to learn, more rigid, riskier as employees, less ambitious, and therefore more easily satisfied, less able to adapt and cope..."

These myths and stereotypes about old age indicate that society is prejudiced toward the elderly who had been productive and useful members of this social system and contributed a lot in the development of our society. These prejudices seem to be developed because of the present socio-economic changes and individualistic concerns. These myths and stereotypes are so negative that the word 'old' is not accepted in good sense, therefore the people advanced in years are called in different names such as "golden agers", "senior citizens". "elderly persons", "persons in harvest years", in the "twilight years" etc.

Ageing of the population is a universal phenomenon. The number of aged individuals in out population is growing because of improved health standards, better living conditions, priority to the subject of health in public policy, better health care and growing awareness among people regarding health and diseases. Therefore the life expectancy is increased, which was only 47 years in 1950 is 62 years presently and expected to be 70 years in the year 2025. Total population is expected to be treble within this period but United Nations predicts a five-fold increase in the population aged over 60 years and the aged over 80 years will increase seven times their present number. It means that one person in every seven will be over sixty years of the age in 2025 in comparison to just one in every twelve in 1950.

The population of aged in India has been continuously growing. The increase in the absolute number and the proportion of grey population in India is clearly evident in the following table:

Table 1
Trends in Absolute number and Proportion of Elderly (60 years and above) in India

Year	*Absolute Number*	*Proportion*
1961	2,46,99,125	5.63
1971	3,26,80,995	5.93
1981	4,15,37,602	6.28
1991	5,56,05,593	6.58
2001	7,16,97,634	7.08

Source: S.I. Rajan. U.S. Misra and P.S. Sarma, India's Elderly, Sage Publications India, New Delhi 1999, p.p. 46 and 48.

Moreover the growth rate of elderly has been higher as compared to overall growth rate in India except in the decade of 1971-1981. Trends in overall growth rate of the total population and growth rate of elderly persons are being revealed in Table 2:

Table 2
Total Population and Growth Rate of the Elderly in India

Year	*Overall Growth Rate*	*Growth Rate of the Elderly*
1961-71	2.17	3.23
1971-81	2.83	2.71
1981-91	2.55	3.39
1991-2001	2.02	2.89

Source: S.I. Rajan. U.S. Misra and P.S. Sharma, India's elderly, Sage Publications India, New Delhi 1999, p. 56.

As pointed out by United Nations, "As a consequence of social development and achievements of twentieth century, long life has become a reality for hundreds of millions of people throughout the world. In the coming decades it will become a reality for millions more. In the past only a few people attained old age. In the future only a few will not reach it." In the light of this important statement, which indicate towards the changes in demographic map we must think about bringing change in our thinking, attitude, prevailing myths and stereotypes about old age mentioned in the beginning of this paper. Need not to mention that these stigmatic attitudes about elderly are very much responsible for the present position and status of our senior citizens. They are considered as 'Depreciated Human Capital'. All this leads to more and more deterioration in physical health, mental capacities and psycho-social condition of elderly people.

Change in Perception

Let us look into our old traditions and customs. The old people not only enjoy respect and status but they contribute also in many ways, as head of the family and experienced member of the community. It is generally said that disappearance of joint family system is responsible for the deterioration in the traditional respect and status of the old people. But the contraction of joint family alone is not responsible for the marginalisation of the elderly. Complex factors like urbanisation, migration of youngsters to cities and abroad, the crunch of space, inflation, assertion of individualism is also responsible for this. It has been observed that when old people were given proper status in family, accepted as important members of the community, given enough time to chat with their friends and younger family members they remain physically fit and mentally sounder. It is note worthy that presently the lack of time because of changing socio-economic compulsions changed our values and the elderly are the victim of this.

It is the natural reality that physiologically ageing is characterised by diminishing of body functions, which also affect the psychological health of the aged. The facts about changes in capacity of elderly persons are explained in detail by Cohen (1985). He explained that recent studies on psychological aspects of ageing reveal that:

1. Changes caused by the ageing process are compounded with associated changes in physical health, in life style, in motivation and personality.
2. Poor performance may be the product of sensory deficits, anxiety, and lack of interest rather than mental deterioration.
3. Intelligence tests, which measure vocabulary, verbal ability and factual knowledge, show little age effects.
4. Tests measuring ability to manipulate or transform information (such as backward digit span, or digit symbol substitution and some tests of spatial reasoning) generally reveal a decline.
5. Common factors such as diminished rate of information processing and a diminished capacity of working memory are seen to underlie performance decrements on many tasks.
6. In the realm of perception, learning and memory tests have revealed, that the process of retrieval (memory) is relatively more effected by aging than encoding or storage, that capacity of working memory ('holding store') is the vulnerable component and that attentions] processes are more likely to be age-impaired.

As the age increases there is a gradual loss in capacity to perform physically but it is also true that old people constitute an invaluable and vast reservoir of knowledge and experienced human resource. Undoubtedly the prevailing myths, stereotypes and social situations resulted out of socio-economic changes effect the physical health and psychological condition of elderly people. Should we allow these myths, stigmatised attitude and stereotypes to destroy this important reservoir? All such myths, stereotypes and social situations forces our senior citizens to under estimate their capacities and usefulness to the society and they unknowingly become the victim of psychological problem known as depression.

What is Depression?

Changes of mood are normal phenomena in our daily life. In a normal course the reaction to success and achievement is elation and to failure, loss and inability the reaction is depression. These reactions are short-lived though the duration may vary according to the intensity of the cause, situation and circumstances of the affected person. Depressive reactions are mood disorders in which tension and anxiety are expressed in the form of dejection and self-depreciation, somatic disturbances and repetitive complaints of feeling inferior, hopeless and worthless (Norman Cameron, 1963). Depression becomes abnormal if the state continues indefinitely. The person remains morose and talks little. His thoughts are pessimistic and full of despair. The subtypes and symptoms of depression in old age are largely similar to those for younger persons, but difference exists with somatic concerns in the elderly. In old age depression is characterised by very often delusions of disease or dysfunction of body organs. It generates a feeling of distress and insecurity.

In advanced age when body function start diminishing, regular source of income disappear or insufficient, family and social relations start shrinking, a sense of uselessness start overpowering the person. He may start losing interest or pleasure in normal activities, and remain preoccupied with worries for his future life. In such situation the elderly people start suffering from Nihilistic delusions. *Nihilistic delusions* are especially common in elderly and they are inclined to feel that some terrible catastrophe hangs over them that a desolate loneliness is coming which will lead to end every thing. It is true that physical changes do occur with ageing and that these changes are mostly in the direction of deterioration. In old age the person has been worrying about his health though the illness may not be serious. Chronic and unrelieved pains, or some disease, which limits the person's mobility, are some common symptoms. Infections, alcohol, metabolic disturbances or its treatment are known to cause mental symptoms, which include depression.

Frequency and Etiology

The study and understanding of depression in old age is linked in its relationship to the brain change and the life events that accompany the ageing process. The changes in the brain because of ageing process are biological by nature. However, life events are also related to the occurrence and precipitation of depression among elderly. The cluster of depressive disorders of all types major depression, dysthymia, atypical depression and dysphorias are found within the range of 13 percent to I5 percent of the general elderly population. The major depression is found from one to two percent (Johan A. Talbott et al., 1988). Most depression episodes in old age are noted to be preceded by a negative life event, generally bereavement or physical illness and disability. The absence of a confidant predisposes to depression in the face of a severe adverse life event. These facts seem in accordance with the widely hold view that in old age depression is frequent and is a consequence of the isolation and loss of close persons, health, material resources and status that characterise this phase of life.

Precipitating Factors

The people who are especially vulnerable to psychotic episodes are hypersensitive to certain general situations. These situations are:

1. The loss or threatened loss of a major source of gratification;
2. the loss or threatened loss of one's basic security;
3. an upsurge of erotic or hostile impulses;
4. a sudden increase in guilt — conscious, preconscious or unconscious; and
5. reduced general effectiveness of ego adaptation or defence. In old age when the person is subject to many changes in life such as loss of spouse or a close friend or a loved one, a sudden financial crisis, abrupt shift in the place of residence etc. is more vulnerable to depression. In spite of the rich experiences of life maturity, he starts feeling himself dependent upon others and seeks help to maintain his equilibrium. Loses and failures or even the mere threat of loss or failure may prove dangerously disturbing.

We can say that depression may be precipitated by certain situations such as (i) loss of love, (ii) loss of personal security and (iii) loss of self-esteem.

Mr. Das retired as a government school teacher in 1992. Joined in a private school where he was very much appreciated by students and school management, for his hard work, dedication and good teaching. After two years, sudden sickness of his wife and her death disturbed him a lot and now he left his job restricted himself to his house. Do not interact with any body. When I contacted him, first he avoided talking anything but after some time he narrated his situation. He said that now he has lost the taste in everything, *'Kucch bhi karne ka man nahin hai. Sub kucch bemaine ho gaya hai.'* and start remembering the hay days of his life, how his wife co-operated with him in the days of difficulties, in educating his children who are well settled now, how she managed his house with limited resources and tried to satisfy the needs of all members of family.

I contacted his neighbours and his co-teachers in the private school where he joined after retirement. They explained that he was very healthy and active when he was working but now he has lost his health as well as interest in work. Mr. Das himself agreed that day by day he is losing his health as well as interest in work, while, when he was working he feel himself fit. Now he looks stunned by grief. His back looks slightly bent, his eyes are mostly fixed on the ground and his brow is furrowed. He now looks to be a person who has lost everything in life.

There are many cases like Mr. Das who are suffering from the problem of depression, which is one of the various reasons responsible for under-utilized or unutilized or wasting of capacities, talent, knowledge and experience of the senior citizens. This is not merely an individual or a family loss but a national loss and a serious problem. In the interest of society at large and for aged particularly their capacities, talents, knowledge need to be harnessed properly.

WHAT TO DO?

Treatment

The patient should be examined by a physician and suitably investigated to find out removable causes, if any. The removal or the treatment of the causes may result in a sudden and marked improvement in the mental state and depression. In patients, who are on any long-term therapy for some chronic disorder and have become depressed, the identification and removal of the offending drug by the physician are important; the result may be quick and satisfactory. All other patients need psychiatric care, and a specialist should be consulted for the purpose. Very useful drugs are available to alleviate depression. In a few patients in whom depression cannot be lifted with drugs, ECT (Electro Convulsive Therapy) may become necessary, and is usually effective.

The family must give psychological support to the patient. Love, care and understanding from the family and friends in times of crisis are invaluable sources of succour. The techniques of reassurance, appreciation, encouragement and approval from others can prove effective.

Prevention

This is the most important factor in dealing with depression in the aged. The greatest problem of old age is loneliness. Old people want to talk, but there may be few who would sit down and talk to them. In such situation the following steps are needed:

- It would be proper that the younger generation regularly spend some time with the elderly at home.
- The senior citizens should be encouraged to continue to have an active interest in life.
- The elderly must be involved in decision making for the family on important occasions and important matters.
- They should regularly attend social functions like weddings, engagement ceremonies and birthday parties, etc. and thus keep their interest in the family and the community alive.
- Those who by nature are not very social, should be encouraged to pursue hobbies like music, playing cards, chess, etc., in which much physical effort is not involved. Reading, writing or even looking after grandchildren, and generally making oneself useful to the family and the community ward off depression.
- A common mistake that many people make is lack of planning on what to do after retirement. How to use their

time and consider alternate plans are some disturbing questions for them. Government should make arrangements at District Employment Offices to help the needy senior citizens in planning their future.

- In every hospital at district level there should be proper arrangement of counselling and consultation for elderly people.

By this we can better equip our senior citizens to with stand the ups and downs of life in old age and ensure the best possible use of their capacities, talent, knowledge and experience. Senior citizens need to maintain a high degree of independence and self-mastery resulting in self-respect and dignity. Utmost care should be taken to keep their self-respect and dignity maintained and provides opportunity to their power of judgement, knowledge and skills to contribute to society and to live a satisfying life.

REFERENCES

Elizabeth Ferguson: *Social Work: An Introduction*, 3rd Ed. Philadelphia: J.B. Lippincott, 1975, p. 238.

Gibson, R.W. et al.: *On the Dynamics of many Manic-depressive Personality*, Amer. J. Psychiat, 1959.115, 1101-1107.

Johan A. Talbott, R.E. Hales, S.C. Yudofsky: *Text book of Psychiatry*, Jaypee Brothers, New Delhi, P. 1128 - 1133.

Norman Cameron: *Personality Development and Psychopathology — A Dynamic Approach*; Houghton Mifflin Company Boston, 1963. p. 413, 522.

Pati, R.N, Jena, B.: *Aged in India* (1989), Ashish Publishing House, New Delhi.

Poonam Goel: *Wrinkled Existence*, The Hindustan Times, October 18, 1998.

Rajan, S.I., Mishra, U.S., Sarma, P.S.: *India's Elderly-Burden or Challenge?* (1999), Sage Publications, New Delhi.

Reenu Narula: *The Nowhere People*, The Tribune September 12, 1998.

The Economic Times, May 23, 1982.

Upadhyay, R.K.: *A study of the Problems of the Aged and Need for Social Intervention in the State of Haryana and Himachal Pradesh*, Project Sponsored by Ministry of Welfare, Govt. of India, New Delhi, 1992.

Zastrow, *Charles: Introduction to Social Welfare Institutions*; Chapter 15, Problems Experienced by the Elderly: Gerontological Services, (1978), The Dorsey Press, Ontario.

14

OLDER PERSONS AND SOCIAL WORK TREATMENT

Damodaran Sivakumar

Introduction

The United Nations, the Inter-Governmental Organizations, the Non-Governmental Organizations, the National and State Governments and territories have been studying the population problems, especially the tempo of people getting old and chalking out Plans of Action to better their conditions of life and time management. Population projections of the Population Division of the United Nations shows that the population ageing will be a problem to all the populations of the world

The various professionals and academics started reviewing the ageing situation. The Sociologists, Journalists, Historians, Psychologists, Doctors, Scientists, Technologists, politicians, Administrators, the General Public, the Professional Social Workers and the Literacy men have started deliberating the ageing issues and problems.

Here the author attempts to provide the bird's eye view of the population characteristics of Older Persons and methods and techniques of social work treatment.

The following three tables provide a picture of population characteristics of Older Persons in the world and in the more developed countries, less developed countries, least developed countries, Asia and India.

Table 1 show that the percentage of the world population above the age of 60 will raise from 10 percent in 2000 to 21.1 percent in 2050. The rate of increase in more developed countries is from 19.

Table 1
Older Persons in the World

Regions	*Age*	*2000*			*2025*			*2050*		
		Total	*Males*	*Females*	*Total*	*Males*	*Females*	*Total*	*Males*	*Females*
World	60+	10.9	8.9	11.1	15.0	13.6	16.3	21.1	19.4	22.7
	65+	6.9	5.9	7.9	10.4	9.2	11.6	15.6	14.0	17.3
	80+	1.1	0.8	1.5	1.9	1.4	2.5	4.1	3.0	5.0
More Developed Regions	60+	19.4	16.5	22.2	28.2	25.2	31.0	33.5	30.2	36.5
	65+	14.3	11.6	16.8	21.3	18.4	24.1	26.8	23.5	29.9
	80+	3.1	2.0	4.2	5.4	3.8	7.0	9.6	7.0	12.0
Less Developed Regions	60+	7.7	7.1	8.3	12.6	11.6	13.5	19.3	17.9	20.7
	65+	5.1	4.6	5.6	8.4	7.6	9.3	14.0	12.6	15.4
	80+	0.7	0.5	0.8	1.3	1.0	1.6	3.3	2.5	4.0
Least Developed Regions	60+	4.9	4.5	5.3	5.9	5.5	6.4	9.5	9.0	10.0
	65+	3.1	2.9	3.4	3.8	3.4	4.2	6.3	5.9	6.7
	80+	0.4	0.3	0.4	0.5	0.4	0.6	1.0	0.8	1.1
Asia	60+	8.8	8.1	9.5	14.7	13.6	15.8	22.6	20.9	24.3
	65+	5.9	5.3	6.5	10.0	9.0	11.0	16.7	15.0	18.4
	80+	0.8	0.6	1.0	1.7	1.3	2.1	4.2	3.2	5.2

World Population Ageing 1950-2050, United Nations
Department of Economics and Social Affairs, Population Division, New York, 2002.

4% in 2000 to 33.5% in 2050. The rate of increase of aged population in Asia is 8.8% in 2000 to 22.6% in 2050. The percentage of women in the aged population is more than men in all regions and increasing year after year. This is because of the fact that the average life expectancy of women is more than men.

Table 2
Sex Ratio of the Aged Population

	Sex Ratio (per 100 women)	*2000*	*2025*	*2050*
60+	World	81.2	84.4	85.0
	More Developed Countries	70.7	77.0	78.2
	Less Developed Countries	88.4	87.6	86.8
	Least Developed Countries	86.7	87.2	90.6
	Asia	88.8	88.5	86.8
65+	World	76.2	79.9	80.6
	More Developed Countries	65.4	72.4	74.2
	Less Developed Countries	84.5	83.6	82.4
	Least Developed Countries	75.9	71.6	73.4
	Asia	84.3	84.2	82.3
80+	World	53.1	57.7	60.7
	More Developed Countries	44.2	51.3	55.7
	Less Developed Countries	64.9	63.0	63.0
	Least Developed Countries	75.9	71.6	73.4
	Asia	61.2	60.9	62.2

The sex ratio is given as the number of men for every hundred women. Sex ratio of 60+ population of the world increases from 81.2 in 2000 to 85.0 in 2050. In Asia it is 88.8 in 2000 and 90.6 in 2050.

For the 65+ population, the sex ratio of the world increase from 76.2 in 2000 to 80.6 in 2050 and for 80+ populations, the sex ratio increases from 53.1 in 2000 to 60.7 in 2050.

The sex ratio of the least developed countries is higher than other countries. The sex ratio in Asia, among the aged population is higher than the world average.

The percentage of older population in India as per estimates of the Population Divisions of United Nations increases from 7.6% in 2000 to 20.6% in 2050. The sex ratio among the aged population is higher in India when considering world average as well as the average sex ratio of Asia. As a larger population of people is becoming old it is essential to improve their living and working conditions.

Table 3
Population Ageing in India

Older Persons	2000			2025			2050		
	Total	*Male*	*Female*	*Total*	*Male*	*Female*	*Total*	*Male*	*Female*
60+	7.6	7.1	8.2	12.5	11.7	13.2	20.6	19.5	21.8
65+	5.0	4.6	5.4	8.3	7.6	9.0	14.8	13.7	15.9
80+	0.6	0.5	0.7	1.3	1.0	1.5	3.1	2.6	3.6
Sex Ratio									
60+		91.8			92.5			90.9	
65+		90.2			88.5			87.6	
80+		81.8			71.4			73.7	

Studies conducted by the author in Kerala show that social work treatment can effect enormous changes in the personality of older persons conducive to sustainable social development and improvement of their living and working conditions.

Social Work treatment comprises of scientific application of social work principles, methods, techniques and skills in the socio-psychological, economic, cultural and informational development of every older persons his/her family, group and community.

Social work is a helping, enabling and problem solving processes. It provides life long experiences, growth opportunities, alternatives and choices for better living. It improves the quality of life. It enhances the social functioning of individuals, groups, families and communities. It brings down morbidity. It promotes disease-free, disability-free and accident-free life expectancy. It promotes peace and social harmony. It sustains interest in real and true life. It prevents and corrects social deviance and it promotes de addiction. It provides living, social work, employment and educational skills. It promotes desirable demographic transition. It promotes better physical, mental, social and spiritual health. It promotes dignity of labour, collaboration, co-ordination, linkage, social expression and public relations. It promotes pushpayurveda and horticulture. It balances the environment. It provides healthy and happy housing and habitats, transport, sport, vocation and creative and entertaining leisure time.

The methods of social work include social casework, social group work, community organization, social action, behaviour modification, social work journalism, social politics, social economics etc. The techniques of social work include social work administration, social work research, social diagnosis, social work treatment, social work indicators, creative literature in social work, creative media in social work etc. Its strategies include collaboration and co-ordination with Sociology, Journalism, Social Sciences, Behaviour Sciences, Health, Sciences, Engineering, Technology, Arts and Literature. It provides leadership to professions and disciplines in all walks of life.

Hence it may be noted that social work treatment is an important technique of professional social work. It has an important role to play in the betterment of older persons. The various fields of social work like Medical Social Work, Psychiatric Social Work, Gerontological Social Work, Family Social Work and Developmental Social Work have direct applications in Social Work Treatment.

Social Work Treatment

1. As far as social work treatment with older persons are concerned, it is essential to have in depth interviews with older persons at various sessions to sum up psycho analytical case histories of every older person.It may help to understand the physical, social and psychological health and illness at any given period of time. Individual and group counselling and individual and group therapy can be applied to solve illness, boredom, fatigue, monotony etc. Here teamwork with doctor and other professionals, and collateral interviews with others are essential.
2. History of social work and emotional relationship, history of participation in social programmes, etc. have to be assessed in case of every older person to understand social and emotional handicaps and required social case work and social group work treatment.
3. History of informational deficiencies of every older person has to be ascertained to provide fuller information to heal his/her unmet informational needs. Felt needs have to be met for adjustment and enhancement of social functioning. Social work treatment should also consider suitable living arrangement for individual older persons, groups of older persons, families of older persons, neighbourhood of older persons, suitable family re-union etc.

4. Skill training is essential to improve older person's personality. Skill training can be undertaken at an individual basis or in-group process. The following are the skills to be trained for each older person to become a civilised individual.

(a) Programme Planning and Policy Analysis

An apt example would be the participation of the older person in the campaign for people's planning under the auspices of the State Planning Board at the Grama Sabha and ward committee. Social work skill training to the aged is essential for it.

(b) Independent Decision Making

In the day to day work and life every older person has to decide independently his participation in familial, group, household or community events. He should be helped to make independent decisions by consulting or collaboration, or through communication with others. Social work skill training is essential for enabling him to make independent decisions.

(c) Enlisting Peoples' Participation

This is the third important social work skill. In a strategy for social transformation the older person has to get participation from the maximum number of persons in preparing plans of actions, behaviour modification and plan implementation. An example would be the work of older person working as a volunteer under pulse polio immunisation. The older persons can be given social work training to understand the above skill.

(d) Learning Actual Social Life in Different Socio-Cultural Milieus

An older person working as a communicator for development programmes need training in this social work skill to work in different socio-cultural milieus.

(e) Appreciating Welfare and Development Programmes for the Rural and Urban Poor

Social work skill training enables the older person to familiarise and to appreciate welfare programmes to work as a volunteer among urban/rural poor.

(f) Establishing Linkages and Co-ordination

It enables the older person to link and co-ordinate health, hygiene, waste management etc. to promote civic responsibilities

(g) Self evaluation and Guided Group Interaction

The older person always has to perform self-evaluation for future well being. Group activities of the older persons have to be guided by a professional social worker so as to provide better opportunities and growth experience.

(h) Self-expression and Public Relations

This is essential for the older person for successful group and community activity. It increases transparency and socialisation of individual and group behaviour. Deficiencies can be found out and rectified.

(i) Fund Raising

Training in social work skill of Fund raising enable the older person to work for human development programme, which need to raise fund. Transparency and current and comprehensive reporting and social audit are essential.

(j) Appreciating and Working for Social Justice

Social work skill training on social justice is very essential for an older person to enhance his personality.

(k) Appreciating Dignity of Labour

The older persons with experience, knowledge, expertise and training can teach the youth on the above social work skill under professional guidance of social worker.

(L) Advocacy

The older person can provide leadership for advocacy in the community against casteism, dowry, corruption etc. The social worker can guide the older persons for such programmes.

(M) Counselling

It has a healing effect. It provides growth opportunities, alternatives and choices for self esteem. The social worker can help the older persons through counselling whenever there is a personal, family, group or social problem.

(n) Social Management of Community Facilities

There are a large number of community facilities in the society like toilets, street lights, waiting sheds, reading rooms, market, health centres, etc. The older persons under guidance of the social worker can effectively manage these community facilities.

(o) Leadership

The older person with his life long knowledge, experience and skills could lead social, cultural occupational, political and economic groups for sustainable development. The social worker can guide the older persons to take up leadership for social progress.

(p) Leisure Time Management

Proper leisure time management is used for the social, cultural, physical ,psychological and spiritual health of the older persons. It is essential to train the older persons on the above social work skill.

(q) Peace, Harmony and Development

Peace, harmony and development, improvement of the quality of life, happy housing, happy neighbourhoods and social work based sports should be trained under social work treatment for better life of the older persons.

After a discussion of 17 important skills for social work training of older person now let us have a discussion of other important factors of social work treatment.

5. The health of the older person is determined even at the time of conception. The couple should be physically, socially, psychologically, emotionally and intellectually healthy at the time of conception of the child. The couple should be uniformly healthy during the period of child bearing and the birth of the newly born. As this has an important effect on the new born as he/she passes through every age until old age.
6. Every physical, psychological, intellectual, emotional and social experience of the newly born, which through various stages of the life cycle, culminates in his health and skills in

the old age. So the above experiences have to be planned at every stage that they culminates in the physical and psycho-social well being to attain happiness and peace for every older person.

7. The physical, social and cultural environment also plays a very important role in social work treatment of individuals, groups and families at the various stages of the life cycle.
8. Synoptic, intermediate and ultimate causes of illness of every older person have to be ascertained to apply immediate, intermediate and ultimate treatment models based on living and working conditions.
9. Every individual, group, family and community has to visualise the life at old age and programmes for the better utilisation of the life in old age.
10. There should be thorough awareness in the family and community that healing is possible through spouse communication and agreement, sibling communications, inter-generational communication, socio-psychological and cultural awareness and cross cultural counselling.
11. Every older person has to be given awareness on social economics and social politics to solve his own or his/her family's own social, political and economic problems.
12. The scientists should come forward to help the social worker and the older persons to help them to help themselves to transfer and utilise technologies for the betterment of the older persons. Integration of social work and journalism strategies are also essential for technology transfer and technology utilisation. An important point in social work treatment is socio-psychological and informational preparedness.
13. Social work treatment should also deal with self-care and proper daily routine of the older person. Provision of individual, group and community experiences and growth opportunities are also important.
14. Collaboration, co-ordination and linkage with other professions like nutrition, sociology, psychology, psychiatry, medicine, and nursing, pharmacology and community participation are also essential.

15. Another important point in social work treatment is policy analysis and co- operation with public and civic administration and full development of clients and peer's personality.
16. It is also important that fighting social maladies like superstition, human abuse, substance abuse, cheating, crime, delinquency and squalor and preventing social deviance, suicides, conflict, violence and terrorism should become part of social work treatment. Provisions of information under Development Support Communication (DSC), Therapeutic Communication (TC), Journals of Social Work, Family Welfare Communication (FWC), Reproductive Health Communication (RHC), Human Service Information Technology Applications (HUSITA) etc. increase the efficiency of professional social work treatment. Promotion of health, welfare and social work literacy campaigns for enhancement of social functioning are also essential.

When enquired the older persons of Kerala they answered several questions, which are of importance to social work treatment. It provides youthfulness to the old when they participate in meetings of socio cultural complexes, older persons committees/pension committees etc. It also provides opportunities for them in the preparation of tea, sharing of love and promotion of friendship and fraternity.

Even though they may have several problems, they forget it when they go for prayer fraternity, the minds are open up and mind becomes full of happiness. It helps to see more people and to share the valuable experiences. The older persons have to give more love to children and youth and pardon the wrong things they may have done. Do not see the children and youth below their status. If the older persons give more love they can reach more love. When they become old forgetfulness, laziness and sleeplessness will be more: they have to realise this situation. An understanding of this will help them for better life. Human rights and social work and personal justice should be shown to older persons. Banks should help them economically. An older person can see Television, read books, write letters or books can look after business and care for small kids to utilise their time.

Life of older persons should he based on truth and dignity and have to discharge their duties and responsibilities correctly.

For this they need training even in older age in the field of exercises, nature cure, social work, etc. Government/local bodies should take the responsibility for provision of tour facilities to the aged .They should be given subsidised health facilities for general health and specialist health services. Presently a large number of old persons could not offer for proper health care. So they live in a morbid condition

Older persons with knowledge and skills should have the facilities to offer consultancy services in the field of their special interest, experience and expertise. They should be helped to get a minimum earning. The aged have to consider their belongings, their people as their own, to satisfy themselves and their remembrances have to be used to evaluate their present to become happy.

Pensioner should be given awareness and social work treatment along with financial benefits. The aged persons' participation in social progress will lead to sustainable social development. They can very well attend programmes of home management. They should be given training to adjust with the thought, feelings and aspirations of the young generation for social progress.

They should be given reservation and subsidy in buses and trains. Special courts are essential for older persons in the model of family courts so as to speed up legal processes wherein the aged person is a party.

Old age homes should not be considered as business concern, social commitment should be there. Old age homes should become part of low self-governments. There should be training and consultancy services, exclusively for the aged under social work programme of each Local self-government. Social work sector should be broadened and trained aged persons should be given more responsibilities under the local bodies' level. There should be enough community participation in such programmes from people of all ages. Older persons with tension should get benefits of counselling and social work treatment. The good activities of the older persons should be appreciated at the familial, group and community level. Programmes should promote social security. The older person can work for health and hygiene Training programmes should motivate the older persons to work in social institutions, libraries, consumer associations. Traffic training programmes, health'clubs, kudumbashree, decentralised planning, temple arts, traditional arts etc. The pensioners should realise their responsibilities to government and public. There should be enough training and awareness programmes to prevent the aged from alcoholism, substance abuse, smoking, pan and tobacco chewing, etc.

The programmes should be there to prevent alienation of aged from the youth. The aged should not become a burden on the youth. The aged can prepare pictorial albums. They can do social service and engage themselves in social development programmes. The progress and problems of the local areas can be diagnosed by these older persons to do the needful for the economic development, environmental protection and model citizenship development. They can promote urbanization by providing urban facilities to the rural areas without loosing the charm, beauty, tranquillity and serenity of the rural areas. They can also work for medicinal plant nurseries and green belting in the appropriate places of the habitat system. The responsibilities of the older persons are much greater as time moves on. In turn, the children and the youth should realise their essential responsibilities to older persons for well being, social work treatment and happier and healthier life.

REFERENCES

Sivakumar, Damodaran (2001), "Integration of Strategies for the Care of Older Persons — A Cross Cultural Study". *Indian Journal of Gerontology*. Vol. 15 Nos. 3 & 4, 2001, Jaipur, India Page 278 – 286.

Sivakumar, Damodaran (2002), "Role of Peoples Participation in Empowering Families for Care of the Elderly", in *Ageing Indian Perspective*, ed. L. Thare Bhai, Decent Books, New Delhi, pp. 91-97.

Sivakumar, Damodaran (1996), *"Social Work Based Health Care for the Middle Aged and Elderly — A State Plan of Action"*, Aiswarya, Sarala Mandiram, Mythanam, Varkala — 695 141, Kerala State, India (Paper presented at health education seminars at the District level under Government of Kerala).

Sivakumar, Damodaran (1998), United Nations International Year of Older Persons — 1999, *Loyola College of Social Sciences Alumni Bulletin*, Thiruvananthapuram, December 1998.

Sivakumar, Damodaran (1992), "Progress and Problems of Social Development with Special Reference to Kerala". *Ph.D. Thesis in Social Work*, Kerala University.

Sivakumar, Damodaran (1989), *"Social work Treatment, Family Health Counselling and Therapeutic Communication"*, Aiswarya, Sarala Mandiram, Mythanani, Varkala — 695 to 141, Kerala State, India.

Sivakumar, Damodaran (1980), *"Social Development Administration at the District Level"*, Family Welfare Communication Action Research Centre, University of Kerala, Kariavattom, Thiruvananthapuram — 695 to 581, India.

United Nations, (2002), *"World Population Ageing 1950-2050"*. Department of Economic and Social Affairs, Population Division, U.N. New York.

15

INSTITUTIONALIZED ELDERLY IN PUNJAB—A SOCIOLOGICAL STUDY OF AN OLD AGE HOME

Jasmeet Sandhu and Tripti Arora

Introduction

Human population is ageing and so are the concerns about the aged. Ageing is a natural, universal and irreversible process. It is a multidimensional process, having biological, psychological and sociological dimensions. Terms like elderly, aged and senior citizens are used to refer to that section of the human population who have reached a certain chronological age (usually 60 yrs.), have undergone degenerative anatomical and physiological changes, decline of mental abilities and loss of active role in the society.

Old age constitutes one of the major challenges confronted by the societies in the present century. Demographic transition coupled with increasing life expectancy is adding elderly to the world's population. Increase in the proportion of the aged was first experienced by the developed countries and now developing countries are also witnessing the same.

According to U.N. forecasts (Kumar 1995) elderly population is going to increase more rapidly in Latin America and South East Asia. India the second most populous country in the world is also foreseeing this increase. The proportion of elderly in India's population has risen from 5.63 per cent in 1961 to 6.58 per cent in 1991 and is expected to be 7.08 in per cent 2001and 9.87 percent in 2021 (Irudaya Rajan, Mishra and Sarma 1999.23). Sharma and

Xenos (1992) have analysed aging in India on the basis of census data and the results have broadly indicated that the states of Kerala, Tamil Nadu and Punjab are likely to experience rapid increase in their old age population in the coming decades. Singh (2001) studied the aging trends in Punjab and found that the rate of growth of the 60+ population (2.81 per cent) in the state is higher than that for the general population (2.10 per cent). The increasing numbers of elderly in India in general and in Punjab in particular is a matter of serious concern and social planning.

Elderly constitute one of the most vulnerable sections of the society. They are not only physically weak but, are also lacking in economic resources, self esteem and social status. Elderly in India have enjoyed high status, respect and authority in the past. Moreover due to high mortality rate and low life expectancy few attained old age. Family used to be the only system of total support and care of the elderly. Family in India has been mostly patrilineal, patriarchal, patrilocal multigenerational group. Under the changing socio-economic and demographic conditions family is unable to provide total support and care to the elderly. Besides, due to changes in the occupational structure and decline in the family size sons do not always stay with their parents, as used to be the case in India. In the event of all these changes living arrangements of the elderly has emerged as an important area of research.

After analyzing the census data Shah (1999) concludes that more elderly are now living in joint households, with one or more married sons and some other relatives than about fifty years ago; they are also living in single member or husband wife households. Some elderly are living at Pilgrim centers and some in old age homes. Shah further argues that although old age homes at the moment cater to a very small fraction of elderly but the way institutional support is coming up and the manner in which their number is increasing is an indication of recognition of need for institutional support.

Institutional support for the elderly in the form of old age homes is a western concept. Living in old age homes is not approved in the Indian culture (Dandekar 1996). Irudaya Rajan and Kumar (2003) analysed the National Family Health Survey (1992-93) data and found that a large majority of the elderly in India are living with their kin (88 per cent), 6 per cent of them are living with their spouses alone due to displacement or migration of their children and only 6 percent of the elderly are living alone. They conclude that family is still taking care of the elderly in a big way.

Although institutional care for the destitute has always existed in India but for the elderly especially as an alternative living arrangement is a recent concept. A countrywide survey (Ara 1995) reveals that there are 356 old age homes in India and the state of Kerala has the maximum number of old age homes. These old age homes (OAHs) are of different type. Some offer free stay facility, other offer pay and stay facility. Some are meant only for the sick, some, only for women and some for a particular community only. In Punjab there are four old age homes for the elderly and five are for the handicapped and destitute (Irudaya Rajan, Mishra and Sarma 1999, 237).

There are about 12.75 million elderly in India who are without family background and they constitute about 30 per cent of the total population of the elderly (Ara 1995). The old age homes in India cater to only one per cent of the needy elderly (ibid). According to Dandekar(1996) about 300,000 elderly lived in old age homes in India because no where in India elderly prefer living in old age homes and because of lower proportion of elderly in India little has been done by the government or non-government agencies.

There are very few studies on the institutionalized elderly in India. Dandekar (1996) did a survey of old age homes in Maharashatra and gathered data from the inmates on various aspects such as their family background, reasons for stay at the old age home etc. In another study Irudaya Rajan , Mishra and Sarma (1999) surveyed 126 elderly living in 7 old age homes in Tamil Nadu and Kerala focusing on their demographic profile, feelings about living arrangement, experience in old age home and means of subsistence. Both these studies are pioneering attempts at understanding the institutionalized elderly in India.

The present study is an exploratory study of an Old Age Home in a town in Amritsar District in Punjab. The study has been conducted with the following objectives;

1. To study the institutional arrangement and the facilities being provided by the old age home.

2. To study the socio-economic background and personal characteristics of the inmates.
3. To study the family and family relationships of the inmates.
4. To study the reasons for shifting to the old age home.
5. To study their response to institutionalization.

The data were collected through interviews with the staff and the inmates. At the time of survey there were 88 inmates. Inmates of 40 odd numbers rooms were interviewed with the help of an interview schedule. In total 45 inmates were interviewed.

Singh Old Age Home*

Singh old age home was set up in 1959 by Chief Khalsa Diwan, a Sikh religious institution. It was opened at *Khalsa Parchark vidyala* (School imparting religious education), which already had some residential rooms, a gurudwara, a dining hall, a hospital, a tube well for water supply and lot of open space. There were just 3 inmates for 3 years. Then grants were procured from Social Welfare Department, Social Welfare Board and individual donations. The HelpAge India also gave some grant. A local Committee was set up in 1967 to look after the affairs of the OAH. This committee meets once a month and is the decision making body.

The old age home is spread over two acres of land and has two residential blocks, the old and the new. There are 80 rooms with attached bathrooms, a Community Hall, a Library, a First aid room and a Hospital. Each room has one bed, two chairs, one small table, one small wire mesh cupboard for food etc., one dustbin, one bucket and 1 mug. The inmates are provided one bedding, comprising of one mattress, one quilt, two blankets, one pillow with cover, and two bed sheets and 2 sets of seasonal clothing. There is a ceiling fan in each room. There is a *gurdwara* where the elderly go for their morning and evening prayers and there is park, which has a few benches and a few chairs. The inmates are given things of personal use such as Soap, oil etc in the first week of every month. In the winters the inmates get hot water for bath and also given room heaters.

The staff includes four cooks, two attendants, one male and one female attendant, one washerwoman, three sweepers, two gardeners, one peon, one gatekeeper, one compounder and one nurse. They get funds from the 'Chief Khalsa Diwan, interests of the Bank deposits, individual donations and the payments made by some of the inmates. According records during 1999-2000 the old age home had income of Rs. 1.48 million and an expenditure of Rs. 1.11 millions.

The admission to the old age home is regulated by the local committee on the basis of availability of accommodation. It is open to the men and women who are more than 60 yrs of age, irrespective of their caste or religion but the applicant must be free from any infectious or contagious disease and should be fit to take care of his daily routine.

The old age home provides all the necessary facilities to the inmates. Besides boarding and lodging the inmates have library facility, medical facility, and open lawns. There is a T.V. set, a radio set, a record player and a tape recorder for the use of the inmates. Loudspeakers are also fitted in the *verandahs* to relay the *Kirtan,* news and other programmes. Occasionally the inmates are also taken out by a special transport to other religious places and places of interest. So the institution provides the inmates with all the facilities to lead a peaceful and dignified life.

Daily Routine

The inmates get their bed tea at 6 AM and then they go through their morning chores. They go to the *Gurudwara* to listen to the holy kirtan from 7 AM to 9:30 AM. They are served breakfast from 9:30 AM to 10:00AM. They visit the library between 10 AM and 12.30 PM. Lunch is served from 12.30 to 1.30 PM. They take rest till 4 PM and then they are served with tea. They again visit the gurudwara from 5 PM to 6:30 PM and then they have their dinner. Every inmate gets ½ kg milk and some fruit every day in addition to the nutritious food. Thus, their daily routine keeps them occupied throughout the day.

CHARACTERISTICS OF THE INMATES

(a) Socio-Economic Characteristics

Table 1 reveals that out of 45 inmates studied hailed from both rural as well as urban areas and were from within Punjab, Haryana, Jammu and Kashmir, Rajasthan and Delhi.23 of them were males and 22 females, majority of them were Sikhs (33), were from upper castes and (31) were educated (37). The inmates were almost evenly by distributed in the five age categories i.e. 60-64 years, 65-69 years, 70-74 years, 75-79 years and 80 years or more. Majority of them (30) were widowed. In their active adult life eleven of them were in jobs, nine were in business, nine were farmers, nine were labourers or venders and twelve of them were housewives. About half of them had some property or economic assets which had been snatched by their children but, thirteen of them still have some property or assets in the form of bank balance, cash, pension etc. Twenty-three of them pay between Rs.150/- to Rs.600/- per month to the old age home for their expenses. So, we can conclude that the inmates of this old age home are both male and female, mainly from the Sikh religion and upper castes, majority are educated and widowed and that they come from varied socio economic groups. About half of them also pay some moderate amount for their expenses. On the other hand Irudaya Rajan, Mishra and Sarma (1999) found that in old age homes in Kerala and Tamil Nadu majority of the inmates were females, below 70 years of age, and currently married.

Table 1

A Synoptic View of the Characteristics of the Inmates

Sex	*Sex categories*	*Number*	*Percentage*
	Male	23	51.11
	Female	22	48.89
	Total	45	100.00
Religion	*Religions category*	*Number*	*Percentage*
	Hindu	12	26.67
	Sikh	33	73.33
	Total	45	100.00
Caste	*Caste Category*	*Numbers*	*Percentage*
	Upper	31	68.89
	Middle	14	31.11
	Total	45	100.00
Age in years	*Age Group*	*Numbers*	*Percentage*
	60-64	10	22.22
	65-69	8	17.78
	70-74	9	20.00
	75-79	10	22.22
	80 or more	8	17.78
	Total	45	100.00

Contd.

Literacy	Category	Number	Percentage
	Illiterate	8	17.78
	Up to Matric	31	68.89
	Up to graduation	6	13.33
	Total	45	100.00
Marital Status	*Category*	*Number*	*Percentage*
	Never-married	4	8.89
	Married	9	20.00
	Widowed	30	66.67
	Divorced/Separated	2	4.44
	Total	45	10.00
Occupation in Adult Life	*Category*	*Number*	*Percentage*
	Housewife	12	26.67
	Labour/Vender	9	20.00
	Farming	4	8.89
	Business	9	20.00
	Job	11	24.44
	Total	45	100.00
Property or Other Assets	*Category*	*Number*	*Percentage*
	Have it	13	28.89
	Had but Snatched by Children	22	48.89
	No	10	22.22
	Total	45	100.00

(b) Family Relationships of the Inmates

Study of family of the inmates would help us understand their institutionalization in a better way. Table 2 shows that nine inmates did not have any child, another nine had only sons, five had only daughters and 18 had both sons and daughters. In terms of the sex and number of children, 27 inmates had one or more sons, 14 had none (Table 3). Similarly 21 had one or more daughters and 20 had none. So majority of the inmates had children, both sons and daughters.

As far as relations with the family are concerned, 18 had estranged relations with their children, 11 had good relations, 3 had estranged relations with sons but good relations with daughters and 13 of them had no one in their family (Table 4). So majority had estranged relations with their children.

Table 2
Children of the Inmates

Children	*Number*	*Percentage*
No Child	9	20.00
Only sons	9	20.00
Only daughter	5	11.11
Both sons & daughters	18	40.00
Not applicable	4	8.89
Total	45	100.00

Table 3
Number of Sons and Daughters of the Inmates

Number of Sons/Daughters	*Sons*		*Daughters*	
	No.	*Percentage*	*No.*	*Percentage*
None	14	31.11	20	44.44
One	12	26.67	6	13.33
Two	10	22.22	11	24.45
Three or More	5	11.11	4	8.89
Not Applicable	4	8.89	4	8.89
Total	45	100.00	45	100.00

Table 4
Relations Of Inmates With Their Family Members

Relations	*Number*	*Percentage*
Estranged	18	40.00
Good	11	24.44
Estranged with sons but good with daughters	3	6.67
Not applicable	13	28.89
Total	45	100.00

(c) Stay at the Old Age Home

As already mentioned, out of 45, only 9 inmates were married and out of these 5 were living with their spouses in the old age home while spouses for 4 inmates were living separately.

Table 5 shows that majority of the inmates have been living here for 25 yrs, while some have been living here for 6-10 yrs and some for 11 years or more. Before shifting to the OAH, majority of the respondents (26) were living with their children (22 with their sons and 4 with their daughters), 8 with their relatives, 3 with their friends and 8 inmates were living alone (Table 6). It shows that before shifting to the old age home, majority of the inmates was living with their families.

Table 5
Duration of the Stay in the Old Age Home

Category	*Number*	*Percentage*
Up to 1 year	6	13.33
2 – 5 years	26	57.78
6 – 10 years	8	17.78
11 or more years	5	11.11
Total	45	100.00

Table 6
With Whom was the In mate Living Earlier?

Category	*Number*	*Percentage*
With Sons	22	48.89
With Daughters	4	8.89
With Relatives	8	17.78
With Friends	3	6.66
Alone	8	17.78
Total	45	100.00

Table 7
Reasons For Shifting to the Old Age Home

Response Category	*Number*	*Percentage*
Have no sons and did not want to live with married daughters	4	8.89
Conflicting relations with sons or their wives	20	44.44
Wanted independent peaceful life	8	17.78
Loneliness	7	15.56
No body to look after	6	13.33
Total	45	100.00

Reasons for shifting to the old age home are presented in table 7. The most common reason stated by the inmates was conflicting relations with their sons and son's wives. 20 inmates reported that their sons and daughters in law would insult them and would make their lives miserable. 8 inmates who belonged to the well to do section of the society stated that they came to the old age home because they wanted to lead an independent and peaceful life without any interference from any one. 7 inmates came because they were living alone and would feel lonely, 6 had no body to take care of them and 4 inmates joined the old age home because they did not have sons and they did not want to stay with their married daughters. The reasons stated by the inmates of Singh old age home are different from the reasons found by Dandekar (1990) in her study of old age homes in Maharashatra. In her study majority of the inmates moved to the OAHs because they had no body to care and had no money (44.7 percent). Eighteen percent moved because of disagreement with sons and 9.8 per cent because they wanted to be independent. But in the present study, disagreement with sons is the major reason and desire to be independent is an important reason to move to the old age home. So, majority of the inmates came to the institutionalized care because of their differences with their son's but some others came here to have a corporate, independent and peaceful life. This is particularly important because this shows that attitude towards institutionalized care is changing and elderly are considering it as an alternative to family living.

Five inmates were living in the old age home along with their spouses. All the inmates expressed satisfaction with the institutional care. Some of them remarked that the inmates of old age home were their family, which shows that despite differences and disagreement with family, it still continues to be an important grouping for them. All of them stated that they have good friendly relations with the other inmates and they help each other in case of need. All, except one, stated to be having good relations with the staff and were happy and satisfied with their life. 20 inmates out of 45 had some health problems such as; joint pain, backache, Diabetes, High Blood Pressure., Paralysis etc. Others had good health. The inmates with health problems stated that the old age home is taking good care them, they have regular check up and get medicines etc. but sometimes they also have to get their own medicines. On the whole they were satisfied.

The inmates, despite having been driven out of their families either out of compulsion or out of choice were enjoying their institutional life. They spent their leisure time by chatting, gossiping, watching T.V., and reading and by having discussions among themselves. They did not feel bad about institutionalization. Rather, they expressed their opinion that more old age homes are needed and society should make arrangements for the institutionalization of elderly. Ara (1995) considered old age homes as the last resort and staying there as equivalent to being thrown in a dust bin. But, that was not the case with the inmates of this old age home. They were not ashamed of their stay rather; they were enjoying their corporate living. As a result of institutional living they were able to construct their own community in which gender, class, caste and religious differences have no significance. Foreseeing the future the government and voluntary agencies in Punjab and in India must make arrangements for institutional support and care for the elderly.

Note: This is the revised version of the Paper Presented in the XVth World Congress of ISA, held at Brisbane, Australia, July 2002.

REFERENCES

Ara Shabeen, "Old Age Homes—The Last Resort", *Research and Development Journal,* Help age India, Vol. 2, No.1 Oct. 1995, pp. 3-10.

Dandekar K., *The Elderly in India,* Sage Publications, New Delhi, 1996.

Kumar, Vijaya, "Aging in India—An Anthropological Outlook", *Research and Development Journal*, HelpAge India, Vol. 2, No. 1, Oct. 1995, pp. 41-45.

Irudaya S. U.S. Mishra and P.S. Sarma, *India's Elderly — Burden or Challenge,* Sage Publications, New Delhi, 1999.

Irudaya Rajan, S. and S. Kumar, "Living Arrangeménts Among the Indian Elderly Evidence from National Family Health Survey", *Economic and Political Weekly,* XXXVIII, No. 1, Jan 4-10, 2003, pp.75-80.

Shah, A.M.: "Change in the Family and The Elderly", *Economic and Political Weekly,* Vol. XXXIV, No.20, May 15-21, 1999, pp.1179-1182.

Sharma. S.P. and Xenos P., "Aging in India; Demographic Background and Analysis Based on Census Materials", *Occasional Paper No. 2,* Registrar General and Census Commissioner of India, New Delhi, 1992.

Singh K.P., "Aging Trends in an Agrarian State — A case study of Punjab", *Guru Nanak Journal of Sociology,* Vol.22, No.1, April 2001, pp.15-28.

16

VOLUNTARY AGENCIES AND CARE OF AGED

(A Study Based on the Institutions for Aged Persons in Varanasi)

Umesh Kumar Singh

Introduction

The city of Varanasi, popularly known as Kashi, stands high in the Hindu psyche with all its glory of antiquity, religious symbol and sacred spaces. With its rich religio-cultural ethos, this city has a unique and important meaning for devout Hindus. Presence of the holy river Ganga and variety of gods enshrined in thousands of temples furthermore makes this city holiest in Hindu belief system. Every religious ritual and activity provides more beneficial results if conducted in Kashi. It is believed that nothing dies in Kashi. Even when people die in this city, they do not die but get salvation from the cycle of birth and death (Justice, 1997; Parry, 1994). It is in this sense Kashi is described in ancient Hindu scriptures as *mukti dayani* or *moksha dayani* (Eck, 1983, 1985; Lannoy, 2002; Saraswati, 1975). Those who are living outside Kashi keenly desire to die in Kashi, if not, at least cremation in Kashi or immersion of the ash in the river Ganga at Kashi. Not only dying, cremation and other after death rituals, but simply living in this city helps liberation of the soul from its bondage and for accumulation of *punya* (Justice, 1997). In this context age old association of Kashi with old age becomes clear. Since time immemorial people in old age use to come to this place finding it a fitting abode in post-*grihasthashrama* days and to get religious bliss and salvation by living in this city observing religious activities till death, if luck permits. All this makes Varanasi a unique place for studying old age. In the city one may find not only the variety of older persons but a range of alternative institution and charitable organization for the aged.

The present study is an exploration of the role of voluntary agencies in the care of aged persons in the religio-cultural context of the city of Varanasi. The basic assumption of the study is that in Varanasi the nature and functions of the voluntary agencies involved in the care of aged persons reflect the religio-cultural ethos of the city. Though, these organizations provide different types of services to the aged persons yet their major thrust is to provide overall psychic gratification to the older ones within the broader frame of reference of Hindu belief system and value structures.

The study attempts to understand the types of religio-cultural organizations available for aged persons in Varanasi. It tries to know the facilities provided by these organizations and the activities performed by them. The study further explores the kinds of inmates availing the services of these organizations. It seeks to understand the life situation of the old aged persons living in these organizations, what life-values they hold and whether they are satisfied in the institutional setting available to them.

For the purpose of the study four major voluntary organizations of the city have been selected. Data for the study have been gathered through formal interviews with the inmates and functionaries of these voluntary organizations. Informal talks with inmates and close observation of their daily routines have also been done for a comprehensive understanding of the life-situation and life-values of the inmates of these organizations.

Major Care Agencies for Aged Persons in Kashi

Most of the formal institutional apparatuses available for old aged persons in Varanasi share the cultural and religious ethos of the sacred city. No doubt, it is the welfare orientation which has created old age homes, but in Kashi the religious orientation is much more dominant. These organizations have been established by philanthropic and charitable institutions to provide old aged persons a shelter to live in and facility to conduct religious rituals.

The present study has covered following voluntary organizations of the city –

1. ***Ramakrishna Mission Home of Service: Home for the Aged, Luxa, Varanasi***

Ramakrishna Mission Home of Service started its service in Varanasi in 1900. This religious charitable organization is situated in the heart of the city and is very close to the holy river Ganga. Over the year's number of institutional complex have developed within the beautiful green campus. A 230-bedded hospital is the nodal institution that provides medical and health services to the poor, destitute, and patients suffering from a variety of diseases. The campus has got a Saadhu Niwas as residence for the dedicated band of medical professionals and social workers who serve the organization in variety of capacities. It has got a place of worship and religious congregation as well as a book shop/publication centre to promote Mission's literature and messages. But the old age home situated within the campus both for the man and woman is the unique organization of its kind in North India. This aged home is adjacent to the general hospital, which can provide adequate medical help to the old person in need. Moreover the proximity of river Ganges and holy temples nearby provide additional attraction to the aged persons who want to remain in close touch with the religious symbol and sacred spaces. The Home has 40 rooms for men and women in separate buildings.

This institution is a branch center of the Ramakrishna Mission, Belur Math, West Bengal, and have branches in India and abroad. Its Home for the Aged has pay and free facility as well. It provides medical, food and laundry facilities to the inmates and sometimes attendants are also provided. Those inmates who are not very old or sick are given opportunity to render their services to the social and charitable activities of the organization. Admission of those inmates is mostly preferred who have been associated with the Ramakrishna Mission, otherwise the person's history may be considered as criteria. Widows, unmarried, and persons not having any family support are preferred. Seventy percent of the accommodation is free of any charge whereas for the paid facility no rate is fixed, charges are made as per the person's wish and/or capacity. Paid facility also has provision for monthly installment. This institution is more popular among the Bengali community.

2. *Kashi Labh Mukti Bhawan, Misir Pokhra, Varanasi*

Kashi Labh Mukti Bhawan, established in 1958, is run by Dalmia Charitable Trust. It caters mostly to the lower middle class and lower class aged persons belonging mostly to the eastern parts of Uttar Pradesh and Bihar. In this institution aged people are brought at the very fag end of their life to attain the religious benefits of dying in Kashi. These aged persons are either have terminal illness or very old with no hope to survive any longer. They are brought by their family, and the family waits for the death and cremation.

This institution has 12 rooms. A small amount of two rupees is charged per day from the inmates' family members for electricity charges, whereas food and other services are provided free. On death, funeral arrangements are also made available by the organization. Religious programmes of *bhajan* and *akhand kirtan* are performed everyday for the benefits to the inmates.

3. *Kashi Mumukshu Bhawan, Assi, Varanasi*

Kashi Mumukshu Bhawan started its services in 1920. This organization is run by a charitable trust named Kashi Mumukshu Bhawan Sabha. This organization provides accommodation to two categories of people. Firstly to those aged persons who are outsiders but want to spend their last days in Kashi. These people on account of their religious intentions are called *kashivasis* though they are not native of the city. In the secondly to those religious personage are included who are *sadhus, sanyasis* and mendicants and have a desire to pass their last days in Kashi remaining attached to their ascetic life and observing religious activities in the holy city. There are around 40-50 rooms meant for the aged *kashivasis*. The institution is situated in the southern part of the city near the confluence of river Assi and Ganga. It offers residential facility to those aged persons who have cleared their family obligations and want to practice the value of *vanaprasthashrama* with a desire to take benefits of *kashi labh* as well. Pilgrims are also provided residential facilities but only for few days. Rooms are allotted to the aged persons on lifelong basis on payment of the charges prescribed by the Trust.

This institution usually prefers those aged persons who are spending a retired life and are not less than 65 years of age. Husband and wife both are allowed to live together if they wish so. But in all these cases they must have some or other family/ relative contact that could be called during their illness or at the time of death. The organization also has strong reservations against religion and caste of its inmates. Only those aged persons are permitted to avail the facilities that are Hindu and belong to upper castes namely Brahmin, Kshatriya and Vaishya. The organization arranges regular *pravachan* and *katha* to the benefits of its inmates. Daily *pooja* and *arati* are also performed in the temple situated inside the campus.

4. *Missionaries of Charity's Nirmal Hriday: Home for the Poor and Destitute, Shivala, Varanasi*

A missionary of Charity's Nirmal Hriday at Varanasi is a branch centre of the mother organization established by Mother Teresa in Calcutta. Away from the hustle and bustle of the city life, this institution is situated in a narrow lane at riverside. This organization is working in Varanasi for the last 25 years or so and is not typically meant for the aged persons only. Rather it caters to the poor and destitute persons of all age groups and does not make any discrimination on basis of religion, cast and gender. This institution run on the funds and guidelines of its main centre at Calcutta and is looked after by the nuns recruited by the central organization. It is also aided by the donation and charity of the common people.

Nirmal Hriday serves those people who are destitute, seriously ill, or very poor. These people are brought by the persons of the Missionaries or by social workers. The inmates include those who have no one to look after them and are not in a mental and physical state to look after themselves. They are housed in dormitories and provided food and medical facilities by the nuns who are trained paramedics as well. No charge is rendered for the facilities and services provided to the inmates. Moreover the institution provides a two-hour daily tuition to the non-school going local children free of cost.

This organization has capacity to accommodate approximately 86 persons, which is usually full all the time. Nearly fifty percent of the inmates belong to the older categories whereas remaining includes assorted categories of other age groups. The institution does not take children as they are sent to its sister organization situated in the other part of the city. In case of female, the young women are rarely admitted howsoever their condition may be precarious. The organization follows Christian spirit of service and honours its inmates' religion. Even on death, the inmates are given funeral according to their religious belief.

The Inmates of Old Age Homes

Kinds of inmates availing the organizations under the study have varied socio-economic background and personal history, and they also have different reasons for availing the services of these institutions. Institution wise every institution seems to cater the needs of a specific set of old aged persons and this makes every institution unique in their own way. Yet, in most of the cases, there is a shared feeling of religiosity and awareness of the cultural ethos of the city that binds the inmates and the organization in an organic unity.

In Ramakrishna Mission's Home for the Aged one may find inmates having different life's travails, yet at one point all these diversified parts seem to end up creating a common present, that is their landing up in the institutional settings and having an altogether new life pattern. Most of the inmates of this institution have opted this institution with considerable pre-planning and forethought. Broadly the inmates of this institution may be classified into three groups. First group of aged persons are those who have no dependable familial and kinship networks to take care of their problems and predicaments of old age, or else they were so harassed by their immediate family and relatives because of their property or because of their precarious status of widowhood, divorcee status or remaining single throughout the life that they opted to take solace in the institution. In all these cases the religious symbol of Kashi and quality of facilities available in the Mission's Home seem to be background factors behind their choice for this particular organization. The second group of inmates have entirely different motivating factor for availing the old age home facility. These aged persons too have opted on their own to shift to old age home to distance themselves from their family simply to avail an independent life and involving themselves in religious activities on the holy soil of Kashi. They may be dissatisfied with the care and respect available back home or they are simply just driven by the strong feeling of renunciation and get involved in religious activities to find psychic bliss and satisfaction in old age. The third group of the inmates is of those aged persons who do not have choices of their own. There are some who had been compelled to move to institutional care because of their acute poverty and destitution, whereas other part of this group constitutes those aged persons who have been brought by their family for better care and management to which the family found difficult to provide.

Major chunk of the inmates of the Ramakrishna Mission's Home for the Aged comes from the first two groups. Moreover in this organization it is the higher caste and upper middle class aged persons who are in greater proportion than low caste and low-income group people. Majority of the inmates of this institution belong to the Bengali community who have joined the institution also because of availability of Bengali cultural ethos.

The inmates of Kashi Labh Mukti Bhawan are those who are on the verge of death because of their sickness or simply because of becoming very old. These inmates usually are in state of senility and are not in position to air their wishes and desires. These aged people are brought by their family and close relative so that the dying person could get some religious benefits through passing days in Kashi, could have a peaceful death and salvation thereafter. These persons mostly belong to the nearby areas of eastern parts Uttar Pradesh and Bihar. Sometimes residents of the city who are not housed in the *kashi khanda* also avail the facilities of Kashi Labh Mukti Bhawan. These people are mostly from rural background and usually belong to upper caste and lower middle class or low economic stratum. Stay of the inmates in the organization varies depending upon the period till when they are alive. Thus the duration of stay might be from few days to weeks or even months. Sometimes it also happens that the aged person recovers from illness and senility and is taken back to home by the family members.

Older persons availing the services of Kashi Mumukshu Bhawan are entirely different from the inmates of the other organizations covered under the study. Inmates of the Kashi Mumukshu Bhawan are financially well off and possess freedom in choosing their own destiny. Sometimes it is their family situation that drives them to take shelter in the institution but still they seem to have some sort of social support networks as the organization's rule requires contact people who could come over if the inmate gets seriously ill or dies.

Most of the inmates of this institution are retired people belonging to the age group of 65 years and more. All of them are Hindu and belong to upper cast. They come from almost every states of India. Though their earlier occupational career were of diverse nature yet a sizable proportion of them were businessmen.

These older persons usually have strong passion for Kashi and follow the belief associated with the city regarding the benefits of living and dying in this city. But this is not the only reason that has brought them to this institution. They have different stories to tell regarding the emerging new equations in their family where adjustment and harmony between them and the younger members are failing, forcing them to avail some residential alternatives in form of present Home.

Though the number of male inmates is more but there are also those who live along with their spouse. In some cases family members and relatives come to visit them, sometimes they themselves go to visit their kith and kin. There are also those inmates, though few in number, who stay here only few months a year especially during auspicious months and remaining time they live with their family.

The aged inmates of the Missionaries of Charity's Nirmal Hriday may belong to different religion, caste and health status, but what one may find common among them is their poverty and destitution. Some of these cannot even recall their religion, caste or past life and have serious physical and mental ailments which is being taken care of at the institution by its nuns and co-inmates who became volunteers. These people are brought from railway station, roadside, or other public places. They do not have any family at all or they are just abandoned by their family because of their poor health and/or old age. Some of these aged persons are mentally retarded and demented and seem not to respond to their immediate surroundings – with their blank faces they just stare at everything that they find worth staring, be it the curious visitor or ceiling of their room.

A comprehensive picture of the kinds of inmates belonging to all four institutions under the study presents a canvas of changing hues, thus revealing heterogeneous categories of inmates where each inmate can be viewed as an isolated and unique entity, however, sharing the same destiny. In Ramakrishna Mission's Home for the Aged and Kashi Mumukshu Bhawan, the inmates are more in terms with their choice and independence thus making the individual supreme in these organizations. As against this, the interaction of organization is more with the family members of the inmate in case of Kashi Labh Mukti Bhawan, as the sick and dying person has no choice of his own and it is his family which is in direct interaction with the organization for the ultimate help and solace of the dying old person. The organization seems to hold supreme in the instance of Nirmal Hriday which though follow humanitarian charitable cause and provide excellent services to its inmates along with an atmosphere of relative comfort and peace through religious activities, but still more close to a typical institutional settings adhering to the rules and regulations of the organization.

The Life-Situation and the Life-Values of the Inmates

Day-to-day life-situation of the inmates and their routine activities in the organization varies depending on the institution they are living in. Not only this, they also hold different life-values that depict their belief pattern and mind set.

The life-situation and life-values of the inmates of the old age homes included in the present survey depict some common strands and considerable variation too. In the case of Kashi Labh Mukti Bhawan the physical facilities available to the dying old person in the room are minimum and his daily course consists of administration of medicines by the family members/helpers, small quantity of food intake and if the inmate have capacity to recognize and talk, then exchange of information about the physical condition of the inmate and the well-being of the family members. In this terminal stage, the inmate has lost every control and authority over his personal and familial matters and it is the close relatives attending him who give directions and control over the dying person. As regards the life-values of the inmates of this Bhawan, it may be said that most of the time he or she has lost the vision and *sanskaras* of the days gone by. It is the attendants who often remind them of remembering the names of gods and goddesses or helping them in performing some basic rituals connected with the life cycle of the person who is about to die.

Similarly in the case of destitute of Nirmal Hriday the daily course is governed by the rules and regulation of the Home and it is the nuns and volunteers who help the inmates in the process of personal hygiene, meals, medicines, etc. Those who are extremely old, physically infirm and mentally imbecile, they have very little to have freedom of operation in arranging and performing their daily routines. Their utter helplessness is sublimated by the adequate intervention of the organization. The inmates of this organization have little to define their own life-values. Awfully dependent and remaining confined to norms and rules of the organization, they are rather unconscious of the familial and social ostracism they have faced in their earlier life and are also unaware of the symbolism of the deep humanitarian help meted out to them in the organization. The Christian sense of compassion and service to humanity, irrespective of caste, creed and status, provide a new canvas to their life and the destitution, helplessness and abject poverty of their life get blurred in the overall humanitarian approach of this organization.

As against the foregoing institutions the life-situation and life-values of the inmates of other two organizations are entirely different. Both in Ramakrishna Mission and in Mumukshu Bhawan the aged person stands as an atomistic individual who has a free will and individual decision to start his entry into these old aged homes. The inmates of these organizations are self-conscious persons who with meticulous care and future programming have decided to spend the rest of their life in these old aged homes. In Ramakrishna Mission, both in the male and female sections of the old aged home, the daily course of life is very well checked out with ample room for pursuing individual hobbies, interests, or other self-directed activities. They are allowed to social service activities of their choice or else to indulge into the religious activities. The life-situation of this organization provides a wide variety of activities and freedom of judgement to the inmates. Most of these inmates are educated persons with middle class background therefore their life-values persist to a very large extent while residing here. Music, book reading, gardening are pursued till these inmates become very old. Even the entertainment facility within the building in the form of TV room keeps them abreast of latest developments in the world outside and also provides them entertainment through the various programmes available to them. However, the religiosity of the old age gradually becomes the dominant theme and as they advance in age, more devotional and religious activities are pursued.

In Mumukshu Bhawan the story is slightly different. The inmates in spite of the fact that they are very individualistic in their approach towards life, yet it is the obsession with religion which govern the life-situation and life-values of the inmates once they become the inmates of this organization. Most of the daily activities revolve around religion. Bathing in the river Ganga, visit to nearby temples, listening *katha/pravachan*, observing religious rites and having discourses and informal talks with knowledgeable religious personage, *vedanti, karmakandi, jyotishacharya, tantric*, are the very satisfying activities of the inmates. The pleasure of life in Mumukshu Bhawan is the knowledge and bliss to be attained in realms of spiritualism and metaphysics and not in the ordinary comforts of the material life. The life-values of the inmates of the Mumukshu Bhawan is though selected quite early in life, yet its crystallization becomes a reality in the spiritual atmosphere of Mumukshu Bhawan and the holy city of Kashi. The agonies of the earlier life and the material comfort which one have had in the younger days are quite forgotten and it is the heavenly ecstasy that becomes ultimate goal towards the end of the life. Mumukshu Bhawan performs the role of a facilitator in the long process of attainment of spiritual bliss.

Concluding Remarks

Our survey of the old aged homes run by different charitable organizations in the holy city of Kashi makes it very clear that culture, especially religion, can provide a very valuable 'context' to the life-situation and life-values of the aged persons. In spite of the fact that in contemporary society the primary bonds and the basic social institutions have changed considerably and are failing in their support mechanism and care of older people, yet the dominant religiosity ingrained in the Hindu culture has yet not lost its influence on the society so far as the care of the old aged person is concerned. The general tenor of the modernizing society may be towards individualism, formalism, and goal-directed and self-centered activities, yet in the case of old aged homes in Kashi, the compassion, the charity and the societal help to the helpless are still the dominant norms. The aged persons in the charitable and religious organizations for old aged are allowed to pursue the traditional religious and cultural goals, and their life in the old aged homes instead of becoming alienated, fragmented and splintered, becomes an organic unity through the pursuance of the religious goals and a keen desire to attain *moksha* in Kashi. This socio-cultural integrative role of the old aged homes in Kashi is what we miss elsewhere in the formal old aged homes being developed in modern times.

BIBLIOGRAPHY

1. Eck, D.L. (1983), *Banaras: City of Light*. London: Routledge and Kegan Paul.
2. Eck, D.L. (1985), Banaras: Cosmos and Paradise in the Hindu Imagination. *Contributions to Indian Sociology*, 19 (1), 41-55.
3. Justice, C. (1997), *Dying the Good Death: the Pilgrimage to Die in India's Holy City*. Delhi: Sri Satguru Publications.
4. Lannoy, R. (2002), *Benaras: a World Within a World*. Varanasi: Indica Books.
5. Parry, J.P. (1994), *Death in Banaras*. Cambridge: Cambridge University Press.
6. Saraswati, B. (1975), *Kashi: Myth and Reality of a Classical Tradition*. Shimla: Indian Institute of Advance Study.